David Nelson Camp

Camp's Higher Geography

David Nelson Camp

Camp's Higher Geography

ISBN/EAN: 9783337389215

Printed in Europe, USA, Canada, Australia, Japan

Cover: Foto ©Paul-Georg Meister /pixelio.de

More available books at **www.hansebooks.com**

CAMP'S
HIGHER GEOGRAPHY,

PREPARED TO ACCOMPANY

MITCHELL'S SERIES OF OUTLINE MAPS,

AND DESIGNED FOR

GRAMMAR AND HIGH SCHOOLS,

AND FOR THE

HIGHER CLASSES OF DISTRICT SCHOOLS.

BY

DAVID N. CAMP,

PRINCIPAL OF THE CONN. STATE NORMAL SCHOOL AND STATE SUPERINTENDENT OF COMMON SCHOOLS.

Entered according to Act of Congress, in the year 1862, by

O. D. CASE & CO.,

In the Clerk's Office of the District Court of the United States, for the District of Connecticut.

CASE, LOCKWOOD & CO.,
ELECTROTYPERS AND PRINTERS,
HARTFORD, CONN.

PREFACE.

The following work has been prepared for use in High Schools and Academies, and for the higher classes in District Schools. The lessons are arranged to accompany Mitchell's Series of Outline Maps, but can be used independently, as the book is complete in itself. The maps are exact transcripts of the Outline Maps reduced in size, and the key to the maps in the book is also a key to the larger maps.

The map questions are prepared to test the pupil's knowledge of the most important things in map studies, after he has carefully studied the map with the key.

The geographical definitions, it is believed, are exact, and sufficiently comprehensive; and the lessons in descriptive geography include the more important facts relative to countries and cities, and are so arranged as to facilitate the comparison of different countries, and assist in generalization and classification.

The cuts have been specially prepared for this work, and the subjects have been selected, not only as illustrations of the text, but as worthy of extended study by the pupil.

The Outline Maps have been revised and improved so as to present to the eye, in a clear and distinct manner, the divisions of the earth's surface with the natural features of each.

HINTS TO TEACHERS.

In introducing the study of Geography to a class of young pupils, their attention should first be directed to the school yard, or a portion of the road, or fields; prominent objects should be pointed out, and their relative position and distance noted. The whole should then be represented on the blackboard, by the teacher. Thus would be conveyed to the child the idea of a map. This map should be copied on a slate, by each member of the class, and recited from as a lesson. Additions of surrounding fields, roads and prominent objects, should be made at successive lessons, till a map of the district, village, town, or city, is completed.

Various natural features should be described when located, such as brooks, ponds, hills and islands; the points of the compass indicated; the boundaries, peculiarities, and general features of the whole taught orally, and by actual view of the same if possible.

By similar and successive steps, the geography of the county and state should be taught, while an outline of the same is made upon the board and copied by the class.

In the use of this book let the mathematical terms employed in geography be carefully explained with a globe or other apparatus, and the definitions be well learned and fully illustrated.

In the study of the maps, the pupil should be taught to remember the various natural objects from their form and position, and not alone from the numbers which mark them.

In using the Outline Maps, the map should, if convenient, be suspended on the north side of the room. In recitation, the pupils can name the objects as pointed out by the teacher, or can point them out as called by the teacher, or some member of the class. Commencing with the upper left hand corner of each map, let the countries and natural bodies of land and water be learned and recited in their order, classified as follows:

1. Countries.
2. Oceans, Seas, Gulfs and Bays.
3. Straits, Channels and Sounds.
4. Islands.
5. Capes, Peninsulas and Isthmuses.
6. Mountains and Deserts.
7. Lakes and Rivers.
8. Cities and Towns, (not recited on Map No. 1.)

The pupil should become so familiar with each map, the natural features represented, the political divisions and the locality of places, as to recognize them at once without numbers or names.

This attainment can be secured by a careful study of the map with the key in the geography, and by drawing the map on the slate or paper, putting down the parallels and meridians, and accurately filling up the outline with the natural and political divisions. The objects given in Roman letters should be learned first.

HINTS TO TEACHERS.

In the location and description of countries or other bodies of land, and bodies of water, it is well for the teacher to give a model to be followed by each member of the class. Thus in describing

A COUNTRY OR STATE.—Locate and bound.

AN OCEAN, SEA, GULF OR BAY.—Give its direction from the nearest coast, and tell with what bodies of water it is connected.

A STRAIT, CHANNEL OR SOUND.—State between what countries or islands it lies, and what bodies of water it connects.

AN ISLAND.—Give its direction from some country or larger island, and what water surrounds it.

A CAPE.—Tell from what country or coast, and into what body of water it projects.

A PENINSULA.—Mention the body of land with which it is connected, and the bodies of water nearly surrounding it.

AN ISTHMUS.—Mention the countries it connects and the bodies of water it lies between.

A MOUNTAIN.—Tell in what part of what country it is situated; if a range of mountains, give the direction in which it extends.

A LAKE.—Tell in what part of what country it is, and give its outlet if any is named.

A RIVER.—Tell its source, direction, and into what body of water it flows.

A CITY OR TOWN.—Locate and tell whether a seaport or not.

Each map is to be reviewed by promiscuous questions. A few of these have been given. But the teacher should multiply and vary them, as circumstances require.

The questions on the maps are followed by a brief description of the countries represented. The more important facts are given on each country. But a full description could not be given, without increasing the size and price of the book far beyond the wants of our schools. This can much better be obtained from gazetteers, geographical dictionaries and cyclopedias, than from any text-book.

For classes of advanced scholars, topical instruction will often be found the most beneficial.

For this purpose, let a country be selected and a topic given to each member of the class. Each pupil should then consult reference books, such as cyclopedias and books of travel, and from all available sources obtain the information desired, and be prepared to stand by the map, before the class, and give a connected, intelligent account of the facts he has obtained, without questions or suggestions.

The following list of topics is given to be varied to suit the size and capacities of the class.

LIST OF TOPICS FOR ADVANCED CLASS.

1 Name of Country, Situation, Extent and Boundaries.
2 Coast, (indentations and projections.)
3 Rivers and Lakes, (water-sheds.)
4 Surface, (mountains, plains, plateaus, &c.)
5 Soil and Climate, (how varied and affected.)

CONTENTS.

6 Productions, (animal, vegetable and mineral.)
7 Manufactures.
8 Commerce, (exports and imports.)
9 Cities and Towns, (capitals, seaports and manufacturing towns.)
10 Traveling Facilities.
11 Inhabitants,. (population, manners and customs.)
12 Government.
13 Education and Religion.
14 History, (Colonial Possessions.)
15 Miscellaneous. (Natural curiosities, places and objects of interest, distinguished persons, &c.)

CONTENTS.

	Page.		Page.
Preface,	3	No. 7, Asia,	126
Hints to Teachers,	4	No. 8, Africa,	142
Mathematical Definitions,	7	No. 9, Oceanica,	156
Geographical Definitions.		No. 10, The Physical World,	164
The Earth,	8	**Descriptive Geography.**	
Natural Divisions, Land,	8	North America,	29
Natural Divisions, Water,	9	British Provinces,	35
Description of Maps,	10	United States and Mexico,	49
Hemispheres,	10	South America,	86
Size, Motions and Circles of Earth,	11	Europe,	103
Latitude,	11	Asia,	131
Longitude,	12	Africa,	146
Zones,	12	Oceanica,	160
Maps, with Key and Questions.		**Physical Geography,**	167
No. 1, The World,	14	Land,	167
No. 2, North America,	24	Water,	172
No. 3, British Provinces,	32	The Atmosphere,	175
No. 4, United States and Mexico,	40	Geographical Distribution of Plants,	177
No. 5, South America,	82	Geographical Distribution of Animals,	178
No. 6, Europe,	96	**Vocabulary and Tables,**	180

HIGHER GEOGRAPHY.

DEFINITIONS OF MATHEMATICAL TERMS USED IN GEOGRAPHY.*

Q. What is a sphere?

A solid bounded by a surface every point of which is equally distant from a point within, called the center.

Q. What is the diameter of a sphere?

The distance from one side to the other through its center.

Q. What is the circumference of a sphere?

The distance round it.

Q. What is the axis of a sphere?

The straight line about which it revolves.

Q. What are the poles?

The ends of the axis. A hemisphere is half a sphere.

Q. What is a circle?

A portion of a plane bounded by a curved line every point of which is equally distant from a point within, called the center. The bounding line is called the circumference.

NOTE. In Geography, the term circle is sometimes applied to the circumference.

Q. What are great circles of a sphere?

Those which pass through its center. All which do not pass through the center are small circles.

Q. What is an arc?

A portion of the circumference of a circle.

Q. How are arcs measured?

Every circle is divided into 360 degrees, every degree into 60 minutes, every minute into 60 seconds, and these are used for the measurement of arcs.

* This lesson should be illustrated by a sphere or by figures on a blackboard.

GEOGRAPHICAL DEFINITIONS.

1. THE EARTH.

Q. What is Geography?
A description of the surface of the Earth.
Q. What do we understand by "the Earth?"
The globe or world on which we live.
Q. What is its form?
It is round or spherical, like a ball.
Q. Of what does the surface of the earth consist?
Of land and water.

2. LAND.

Q. What portion of the earth is land?
About one-fourth part—the other three parts are water.
Q. What are the principal divisions of land?
Continents and Islands.
Q. What is a continent?
A very large extent of land, surrounded by water, as the Eastern Continent and Western Continent.

NOTE. Divisions are sometimes called continents, as Asia, Africa.

Q. What is an island?
A portion of land less than a continent, entirely surrounded by water, as Australia.
Q. What other natural divisions of land?
Peninsulas, Isthmuses, Capes and Promontories.

NOTE. These divisions are parts of continents or islands.

Q. What is a peninsula?
A portion of land almost surrounded by water. Africa is a peninsula.
Q. What is an isthmus?
A narrow neck of land connecting two large divisions of land, as the Isthmus of Darien.

Q. What is a cape?
A point of land extending into the sea, as the Cape of Good Hope.
Q. What is a promontory?
A high point of land extending into the sea.
Q. How is the earth diversified?
By Mountains, Hills, Plains and Valleys.
Q. What is a mountain?
A high elevation of land. A continuous elevation, or a number of mountains connected together, is called a chain or range of mountains, as the Andes.

NOTE. The tops of the highest mountains are covered with ice and snow, even in the warmest regions of the earth.

Q. What is a volcano?
It is a mountain sending forth fire and smoke, also lava or melted stones, from an opening at the top, called a crater.

NOTE. Some volcanoes are constantly burning, while others are intermittent in their eruptions.

Q. What is a hill?
An elevation of land not so high as a mountain.
Q. What is a plain?
A level tract of land.

NOTE. High and extended tracts of land are called Table Lands, or Plateaus.

Q. What is a valley?
A portion of land situated between mountains or hills.
Q. What is a desert?
A sandy, barren tract of land.

NOTE. A fertile spot in a desert is called an oasis.

Q. What is a shore, or coast?
A portion of land bordering on the water; as the Atlantic coast—Long Island shore.

GEOGRAPHICAL DEFINITIONS.

MOUNTAINS, HILLS, PLAINS AND VALLEYS.

3. WATER.

Q. How is the water divided?

Into Oceans, Seas, Archipelagoes, Gulfs, Bays, Sounds, Channels, Straits, Lakes, and Rivers.

Q. What is an ocean?

It is the largest extent of water,—as the Pacific ocean.

Q. How many oceans are there?

Five.—The Northern, Southern, Pacific, Atlantic and Indian. They are all connected and form one vast body of salt water.

Q. What is a sea?

A collection of salt water smaller than an ocean, and nearly surrounded by land.

Q. What is an Archipelago?

It is a sea containing many islands.

NOTE. The term archipelago is also applied to groups of islands.

Q. What are gulfs and bays?

Portions of the sea or ocean, extending into the land.

Q. What is a strait?

A narrow passage connecting two large bodies of water.

Q. What is a channel?

A wide strait.

Q. What is a sound?

A strait or channel that may be measured with lead and line.

Q. What is a lake?

A body of water surrounded by land, except where it receives or discharges its waters.

NOTE. The water of most lakes is fresh. Salt Lakes are generally called seas,—as the Caspian.

Q. What is a river?

A large stream of water, flowing from its source into larger streams or other bodies of water.

NOTE 1. Small streams are called creeks, rivulets, brooks or rills.

NOTE 2. The banks of a river are the land bordering on its sides. The right bank is that on the right hand side as you descend the stream, and the left bank is on the opposite side.

GEOGRAPHICAL DEFINITIONS.

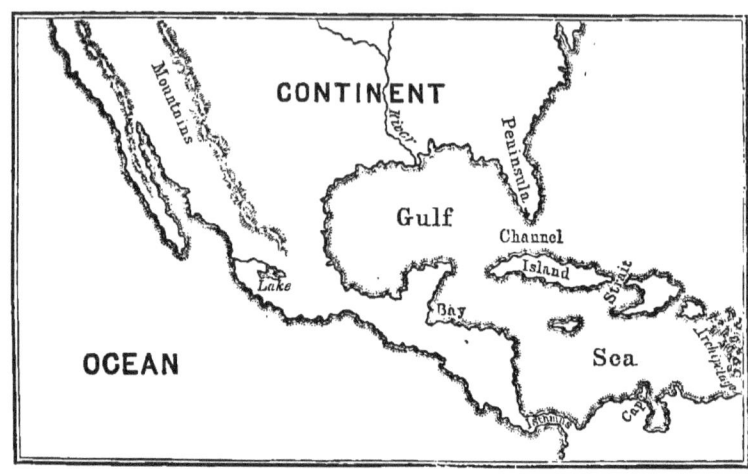

BODIES OF LAND AND WATER.

Q. How are rivers formed?
By a union of rivulets flowing from springs, issuing from high lands, or from lakes or ponds.

Q. Where is the source of a river?
That place from which it begins to flow, as a spring or lake.

Q. What is the mouth of a river?
The place where it discharges its waters.

NOTE. The space occupied by the water of a river is called its bed or channel.

4. MAPS.

Q. Describe a map.
A map is a picture of a part or the whole of the earth's surface, as it would appear if viewed from a place above it.

NOTE. See map of continent, &c., above.

Q. What does a map represent?
The forms of Continents, Oceans, Islands, Lakes, Rivers, &c.

Q. In what direction is the top of the map supposed to be?
North.

Q. The bottom of a map?
South.

Q. The right hand?
East.

Q. The left hand?
West.

Q. What are these directions called?
The cardinal or chief points of the compass.

---

5. HEMISPHERES.*

Q. What does the word Hemisphere signify?
Half of a globe or sphere.

Q. How many Hemispheres are there?
Two, the Eastern and Western.

NOTE. If we take an orange and cut it into halves and place these halves side by side, with their flat surfaces on the wall, they will represent the Hemispheres.

Q. Which is the Eastern Hemisphere?
The one on the right hand.

* See globe or map No. 1

GEOGRAPHICAL DEFINITIONS. 11

Q. What does the map on the Eastern Hemisphere represent?

The Eastern side of the earth; viz: Europe, Asia, Africa, and a part of Oceanica, together with the Indian ocean, and parts of the Northern, Southern, Pacific and Atlantic oceans.

Q. Which is the Western Hemisphere?

The one on the left hand.

Q. What does the map of the Western Hemisphere represent?

The Western half of the earth. It contains North and South America, and the remaining part of Oceanica; also a part of the Northern, Southern, Atlantic and Pacific oceans.

Q. Which Hemisphere contains the most land?

The Eastern.

Q. Which the most water?

The Western.

Q. For what is the Eastern Continent distinguished?

For containing the most land, the highest mountains, and the greatest number of inhabitants.

Q. For what is the Western Continent noted?

For the number and magnitude of its lakes, its extended ranges of mountains, and the length of its rivers.

6. SIZE AND MOTIONS OF THE EARTH, EQUATOR AND CIRCLES.

NOTE. The teacher should use a globe to illustrate this lesson.

Q. What is the size of the Earth?

It is about 25,000 miles in circumference and nearly 8,000 in diameter.

NOTE. The earth is not an exact sphere, the polar diameter being but 7,900 miles, while the equatorial is 7,926.

Q. What is the axis of the Earth?

It is an imaginary line passing through its center, from north to south, upon which it turns.

Q. What are the Poles?

The ends of the Earth's axis.

The northern is called the north Pole, the southern the south Pole.

NOTE. These are also imaginary.

Q. What motions has the Earth?

It has one on its axis, called the diurnal or daily motion, and one around the sun, called the annual or yearly motion.

NOTE. The earth revolves or turns on its axis from west to east, once in twenty-four hours; this causes day and night. It revolves around the sun once in $365\frac{1}{4}$ days. This, with the inclination of its axis to the plane of its orbit, causes the different lengths of days and nights, and the change of the seasons.

NOTE. The earth has other motions, which the pupil will learn about in the study of Astronomy.

Q. What is the Equator?

An imaginary great circle of the earth situated at equal distances from the poles.

Q. How does it divide the earth?

Into two equal parts called the Northern and Southern Hemispheres.

Q. How is the Equator represented on the map of the hemispheres?

By a line crossing it from east to west, and marked 0 on its sides.

Q. What are the Tropics?

Two imaginary small circles parallel to the equator and $23\frac{1}{2}°$ from it.

The northern is called the Tropic of Cancer, and the southern the Tropic of Capricorn.

Q. What are the Polar Circles?

Two imaginary small circles parallel to the tropics and $23\frac{1}{2}°$ from the poles.

The northern is called the Arctic Circle, and the southern the Antarctic Circle.

QUESTIONS ON GLOBE OR MAP No. 1. Point out the North pole. South pole. Equator. Eastern hemisphere. Western hemisphere. Northern hemisphere. Southern hemisphere. Tropics. Polar circles.

7. LATITUDE

Q. What is Latitude?

Distance from the equator either north or south.

Q. How is Latitude represented?

By lines crossing the map from the right to the left, and numbered on its sides.

Q. What are these lines called?

Parallels of Latitude, because they pass around the earth parallel with the equator.

Q. What do the figures attached to the parallels of Latitude show?

The number of degrees of Latitude.

Q. Where do we begin to reckon the degrees of latitude?

At the Equator.

Q. How many degrees between the equator and each of the poles?

Ninety.

Q. What is said of places either north or south of the equator?

Those north of the equator are in North Latitude, and those south, are in South Latitude.

Q. What of places on the equator?

They have no Latitude.

Q. What is the length of each degree of latitude?

Sixty geographical miles, or sixty-nine and a quarter statute miles.

NOTE. The geographical mile must be distinguished from the statute mile. The former may be longer or shorter—the latter is always of the same length.

Q. How then may we learn the distance of a place from the equator?

By determining the number of degrees between it and the equator, and reducing them to miles.

8. LONGITUDE.

Q. What is Longitude?

Distance east or west from some given meridian.

Q. What are Meridians?

Great circles of the earth, extending from pole to pole, cutting the equator at right angles. These circles, marked by lines extending from the top to the bottom of the map, represent Longitude.

Q. From what meridian do we usually reckon Longitude?

That of Greenwich, in England, which is marked 0 on the map, and is called the first meridian.

Q. What is the custom of different nations in this respect?

To reckon Longitude from their capitals, —as the United States from Washington city.

Q. Where are the degrees of Longitude usually marked on the maps?

On the map of the world, they are marked on the equator; but on other maps they are usually placed at the top and bottom.

Q. How many degrees of Longitude are there?

Beginning at the first meridian there are 180 degrees of East Longitude, and 180 degrees of West.

Q. How many degrees, then, around the earth?

Three hundred and sixty.

Q. What Longitude have places on the first meridian?

No Longitude.

Q. How can you tell whether the Longitude of a place be East or West?

If the figures or degrees increase from left to right, the Longitude is East; if they increase from right to left it is West.

Q. What is the length of a degree of Longitude?

It is sixty-nine and a quarter miles on the equator, but the degrees constantly lessen from the equator to the poles, where they cease to have any length.*

9. ZONES.

Q. What are Zones?

Divisions of the earth's surface formed by the tropics and the polar circles.

NOTE. The word Zone means a belt; hence it is applied to those portions of the earth's surface, because they surround the earth like a belt.

* See page 23, Table.

GEOGRAPHICAL DEFINITIONS.

Q. How many Zones are there?

Five.—The North Frigid; the South Frigid; the North Temperate; the South Temperate, and the Torrid Zone.

Q. Which is the North Frigid?

That part of the earth which lies around the North Pole, within the Arctic Circle.

Q. Which is the South Frigid?

That part of the earth which lies around the South Pole, within the Antarctic Circle.

Q. What is the climate of these Zones?

They are the coldest parts of the earth, being covered with snow and ice nearly all the year. Hence they are called the Frigid Zones.

Q. Do they produce any grain or fruits?

Neither grain nor esculent fruits are cultivated, and the trees are few and small.

Q. What animals are found?

Only the most hardy kinds, as the white bear, musk ox, reindeer and seal.

Q. What can you say of their inhabitants?

No inhabitants have been found in the South Frigid Zone. Those of the North Frigid Zone are few in number, and generally uncivilized.

Q. What part of the earth's surface is embraced by the North Temperate Zone?

That part situated between the Tropic of Cancer and the Arctic Circle.

Q. What part by the South Temperate Zone?

That part situated between the Tropic of Capricorn and the Antarctic Circle.

Q. What is the climate of the Temperate Zones?

Generally mild and pleasant, but in some parts variable.

Q. What can you say of their productions?

They are numerous and important.— Among them are the various grains, such as wheat, rye, oats, Indian corn, cotton, rice, and the sugar cane; also many other useful and beautiful productions of the vegetable kingdom.

Q. What animals are found in great numbers and variety?

The domestic,—as the horse, ox, cow, sheep, goat, swine, &c.

Q. What may be said of their minerals?

They are rich and abundant, embracing almost every variety.

Q. For what is the North Temperate Zone more particularly distinguished?

For containing the most important countries, the most powerful nations, and the largest portion of the inhabitants of the earth.

Q. How may the inhabitants of these Zones be characterized?

By their possessing fairer complexions, more regular features, stronger intellects, and greater energy of character, than the inhabitants of either of the other zones.

Q. Where is the Torrid Zone situated?

On both sides of the equator, between the Tropics of Cancer and Capricorn.

Q. What is its climate?

It is the warmest part of the earth. Snow and ice are here never seen, except on the tops of the highest mountains. For this reason it is called the Torrid Zone.

Q. What are the productions of this Zone?

Tea, coffee, pepper, spice, cloves, nutmegs, rice, oranges, lemons, and various other fruits.

Q. What animals are peculiar to this Zone?

The largest and most powerful in the world, —as the elephant, the lion, camelopard, rhinoceros, tiger, hippopotamus, camel, &c.

Q. Describe its inhabitants?

They are generally of a dark complexion, and, with a few exceptions, deficient in intelligence, industry, and enterprise.

Q. To what is the Torrid Zone subject?

The most violent storms of wind, which often prostrate every thing in their way. Also to destructive earthquakes and deadly diseases.

THE WORLD.

SQUARE MILES, 190,000,000. POPULATION, 1,000,000,000.

KEY TO MAP NO. 1.*

GRAND DIVISIONS.

1 NORTH AMERICA,
2 SOUTH AMERICA,
3 EUROPE,
4 ASIA,
5 AFRICA,
6 OCEANICA.

POLES, CIRCLES AND ZONES.

7 NORTH POLE,
8 SOUTH POLE,
9 EQUATOR,
10 TROPIC OF CANCER,
11 TROPIC OF CAPRICORN,
12 ARCTIC CIRCLE,
13 ANTARCTIC CIRCLE,
14 TORRID ZONE,
15 NORTH TEMPERATE ZONE,
16 SOUTH TEMPERATE ZONE,
17 NORTH FRIGID ZONE,
18 SOUTH FRIGID ZONE.

OCEANS.

1 NORTHERN OR ARCTIC,
2 ATLANTIC,
3 PACIFIC,
4 INDIAN,
5 SOUTHERN OR ANTARCTIC.

SEAS, GULFS AND BAYS.

6 BAFFIN'S BAY,
7 HUDSON'S BAY,
8 GULF OF ST. LAWRENCE,
9 GULF OF MEXICO,
10 CARIBBEAN SEA,
11 BAY OF PANAMA,
12 GULF OF CALIFORNIA,
13 KAMTCHATKA SEA,
14 SEA OF OKHOTSK,
15 *Sea of Yesso,*
16 SEA OF JAPAN,
17 YELLOW SEA,
18 *Eastern Sea,*
19 CHINA SEA,
20 *Gulf of Siam,*
21 BAY OF BENGAL,
22 SEA OF ARABIA,
23 *Persian Gulf,*
24 RED SEA,
25 GULF OF GUINEA,
26 MEDITERRANEAN SEA,
27 BAY OF BISCAY,
28 NORTH SEA,
29 BALTIC SEA,
30 WHITE SEA,
31 *Gulf of Obi,*
32 BLACK SEA,
33 CASPIAN SEA,
34 *Aral Sea.*

STRAITS AND CHANNELS.

35 BEHRING'S STRAIT,
36 DAVIS'S STRAIT,
37 HUDSON'S STRAIT,
38 MAGELLAN STRAIT,
39 *Torres Strait,*
40 *Bass Strait,*
41 *Sunda Strait,*
42 MALACCA STRAIT,
43 BAB-EL-MANDEB STRAIT,
44 MOZAMBIQUE CHANNEL,
45 STRAIT OF GIBRALTAR,
46 ENGLISH CHANNEL.

ISLANDS.

47 PRINCE WILLIAM'S,
48 GREENLAND,
49 *Iceland,*

---

* In the key to each map, the most important objects are in Roman letters and to be learned first.

THE WORLD.

50 NEWFOUNDLAND,
51 AZORES,
52 BERMUDAS,
53 WEST INDIA,
54 CAPE VERDE ISLANDS,
55 *Joannes*,
56 *Falkland*,
57 TERRA DEL FUEGO,
58 *South Georgia*,
59 SANDWICH LAND,
60 *South Orkney*,
61 *South Shetland*,
62 *Graham's Land*,
63 *Victoria Land*,
64 *Balleny Islands*,
65 JUAN FERNANDEZ,
66 *St. Felix*,
67 GALLIPAGOS,
68 ALEUTIAN,
69 SANDWICH,
70 *Palmyras*,
71 MARQUESAS,
72 *Pitcairn's*,
73 SOCIETY,
74 NEW ZEALAND,
75 NAVIGATOR'S,
76 FRIENDLY,
77 NEW CALEDONIA,
78 NEW HEBRIDES,
79 SOLOMON,
80 MULGRAVE,
81 RADACK,
82 SPITZBERGEN,
83 NOVA ZEMBLA,
84 *New Siberia*,
85 *Kourile*,
86 SAGHALIEN,
87 YESSO,
88 NIPHON,
89 *Magellan's Archipelago*,
90 LOO CHOO,
91 FORMOSA,
92 PHILIPPINE,
93 LADRONE,
94 CAROLINE,
95 *New Ireland*,
96 *New Georgia*,
97 NEW GUINEA,
98 LOUISIADE,
99 AUSTRALIA,
100 VAN DIEMAN'S LAND,
101 SPICE,

102 CELEBES,
103 BORNEO,
104 JAVA,
105 SUMATRA,
106 CEYLON,
107 MADAGASCAR,
108 *Mascarentia*,
109 *St. Paul's*,
110 *Kerguelen*,
111 *Crozet*,
112 ANTARCTIC CONTINENT,
113 *Enderby Land*,
114 *Tristan*,
115 ST. HELENA,
116 ASCENSION,
117 *Canary*,
118 MADEIRA,
119 GREAT BRITAIN,
120 IRELAND.

CAPES AND PENINSULAS.

121 PT. BARROW,
122 CAPE FAREWELL,
123 CAPE RACE,
124 CAPE SABLE, N. S.
125 PENINSULA OF FLORIDA,
126 CAPE SABLE, F.
127 CAPE ST. ROQUE,
128 CAPE HORN,
129 CAPE BLANCO,
130 *Cape St. Lucas*,
131 PENINSULA OF CALIFORNIA,
132 PENINSULA OF ALASKA,
133 CAPE PRINCE OF WALES,
134 *Cape East*,
135 CAPE NORTH,
136 *Cape North-East*,
137 *Peninsula of Kamtchatka*,
138 *Peninsula of Corea*,
139 PENINSULA OF MALACCA,
140 CAPE COMORIN,
141 CAPE GUARDAFUI,
142 CAPE GOOD HOPE,
143 CAPE VERDE.

MOUNTAINS AND DESERTS.

144 ROCKY,
145 ALLEGHANY,
146 ANDES,

147 Geral,
148 Brazilian,
149 SCANDINAVIAN,
150 URAL,
151 ALTAI,
152 STANOVOI,
153 THIAN SHAN,
154 Kuen Lun,
155 Meling,
156 HIMALAYA,
157 HINDOO KOOSH,
158 CAUCASUS,
159 CARPATHIAN,
160 ALPS,
161 APENNINES,
162 PYRENEES,
163 ATLAS,
164 KONG,
165 Moon,
166 Crystal,
167 Snow,
168 DESERT OF COBI,
169 ARABIAN DESERT,
170 SAHARA DESERT.

LAKES.

171 GREAT BEAR,
172 GREAT SLAVE,
173 ATHABASCA,
174 WINNIPEG,
175 SUPERIOR,
176 MICHIGAN,
177 HURON,
178 ERIE,
179 ONTARIO,
180 Titicaca,
181 Tchany,
182 Baikal,
183 Tchad,
184 Ukerewe,
185 Maravi.

RIVERS.

186 MACKENZIE'S,
187 ST. LAWRENCE,
188 MISSISSIPPI,
189 OHIO,
190 MISSOURI,
191 ARKANSAS,
192 RIO GRANDE,
193 COLORADO,
194 COLUMBIA,
195 ORINOCO,
196 AMAZON,
197 NEGRO,
198 UCAYALE,
199 MADEIRA,
200 TOCANTINS,
201 ST. FRANCISCO,
202 RIO DE LA PLATA,
203 PARANA,
204 PARAGUAY,
205 OBI,
206 YENISEI,
207 LENA,
208 AMOOR,
209 HOANG HO,
210 YANG TSE KIANG,
211 Cambodia,
212 Irrawaddy,
213 Brahmapootra,
214 GANGES,
215 INDUS,
216 EUPHRATES,
217 AMOO,
218 URAL,
219 VOLGA,
220 DON,
221 DANUBE,
222 NILE,
223 Zambeze,
224 Orange,
225 Congo,
226 NIGER,
227 Senegal.

RELATIVE HEIGHT OF SOME OF THE PRINCIPAL MOUNTAINS ON THE GLOBE.

1	Mt. Everest,	Asia,	29,002 feet.	10	Mt. Teneriffe,	Canary Isles,	12,200 feet.
2	Aconcagua,	S. America.	23,910 "	11	Pike's Peak,	N. America,	11,500 "
3	Chimborazo,	S. America,	21,424 "	12	Ætna, Vol.,	Europe,	10,870 "
4	Cotopaxi, Vol.,	S. America,	18,875 "	13	Sinai,	Asia,	7,500 "
5	Mt. St. Elias,	N. America,	17,900 "	14	Mt. Washington,	N. America,	6,234 "
6	Popocatapetl, Vol.,	Mexico,	17,700 "	15	Katahdin,	N. America,	5,385 "
7	Mt. Ararat,	Asia,	17,300 "	16	Hecla, Vol.,	Iceland,	5,110 "
8	Mt. Blanc,	Europe,	15,810 "	17	Vesuvius, Vol.,	Europe,	3,968 "
9	Mt. Hooker,	N. America,	15,690 "				

QUESTIONS ON THE MAP OF THE WESTERN HEMISPHERE.

SEAS, GULFS AND BAYS.

Describe a sea. What sea north of South America? 10. Describe a bay. What two large bays in the northern part of North America? 6, 7. Describe a gulf. What large gulf on the southern coast of North America? 9. What gulf west of the island of Newfoundland? 8. What gulf on the western coast of North America? 12. What bay south of the Isthmus of Darien? 11.

STRAITS.

Describe a strait. What strait separates North America from Asia? 35. What strait connects Baffin's Bay with the Atlantic Ocean? 36. What strait at the southern extremity of South America? 38.

ISLANDS.

Describe an island. What island west of Baffin's Bay? 47. What island east of Baffin's Bay? 48. What island east of Greenland? 49. What island east of the Gulf of St. Lawrence? 50. What two clusters of islands in the Atlantic Ocean east of North America? 51, 52. Where are the West India Islands? 53. What island does the Strait of Magellan separate from South America? 57. What islands east of Terra del Fuego? 56, 58. Where are the islands of Juan Fernandez? 63. What is the principal group of islands in the Pacific Ocean north of the Equator? 69. Which is the most southern island in Oceanica? 74.

CAPES AND PENINSULAS.

Describe a cape. Which is the most western cape in North America? 133. Which is the most eastern cape in the Western Hemisphere? 127. Which is the most southern cape in the Western Hemisphere? 128 What is the most western cape of South America? 129. What cape west of the Gulf of California? 130. What cape forms the southern point of Greenland? 122. What two capes does Behring Strait separate? 133, 134. Describe a peninsula. What peninsula east of the Gulf of Mexico? 125.

MOUNTAINS.

Describe a mountain. What range of mountains on the Atlantic coast of North America? 145. What range of mountains extends the whole length of North America? 144. What mountains extend the whole length of South America? 146.

LAKES.

Describe a lake. What five large lakes in North America are connected, and discharge their waters into the Gulf of St. Lawrence? 175-179.

RIVERS.

Describe a river. What river flows into the Northern Ocean? 186. What large river flows into the Gulf of St. Lawrence? 187. Of what lakes is it the outlet? 175-179. What two rivers flow into the Gulf of Mexico? 188, 192. What three principal branches has the Mississippi? 189-191. What large rivers in South America flow into the Atlantic Ocean? 195, 196, 202. What river flows into the Rio de la Plata? 203. What river flows into the Parana? 204. What river flows into the Gulf of California? 193. What river of North America flows into the Pacific Ocean? 194.

QUESTIONS ON THE MAP OF THE EASTERN HEMISPHERE.

SEAS, BAYS AND GULFS.

What seas on the eastern coast of Asia? 14-19. What sea on its southern coast? 22. What sea between Asia and Africa? 24. What Sea between Europe and Africa? 26. Europe has three seas on its northern coast; give their names. 28-30. Where is the Black Sea? 32. What two seas east of the Black Sea? 33, 34. What sea south-east of the island of Nova Zembla? 31. What bay south of Asia? 21. What bay west of Europe? 27. Where is the Gulf of Siam? 20. What gulf has Africa on its western coast? 25.

THE WORLD.

CHANNELS AND STRAITS.

In what part of Africa is the Mozambique Channel? 44. What strait west of the peninsula of Malacca? 42. What strait between the island of Sumatra and Java? 41. What strait at the entrance of the Red Sea? 43. What strait at the entrance of the Mediterranean? 45.

ISLANDS.

What islands in the Northern Ocean? 82–84. Where are the Koorile Isles? 85. What islands east of the sea of Japan? 87, 88. What empire do they form? Ans. Empire of Japan. What island does the Tropic of Cancer cross? 91. Mention the principal islands south-east of Asia in Oceanica. 102–105, 97, 99. What island south of Hindostan? 106. What large island on the eastern coast of Africa? 107. What land in the Southern Ocean? 113. Where is the Island of St. Helena? 115. For what is it remarkable? Ans. As the place of Napoleon's exile and death. What islands on the coast of Africa near the strait of Gibraltar? 118. What islands west of Europe? 119, 120.

CAPES AND PENINSULAS.

Where is the Cape of Good Hope? 142. What cape east of Africa? 141. What peninsula forms the most southern point of Asia? 139. What peninsula east of the Sea of Okhotsk? 137. Where in Europe is Cape North? 135.

MOUNTAINS.

What are the principal ranges of mountains in Asia? 151–157. In Africa? 163–167. What two ranges form a part of the boundary line between Europe and Asia? 150, 158. In what particular do the mountains on the Eastern Continent differ from those on the Western? Ans. Those on the Eastern Continent have the general direction of east and west, while those on the Western run north and south.

LAKES.

From what lake does the Yenisei flow? 182. What lakes in Africa? 183–185.

RIVERS.

What three large rivers flow into the Northern Ocean? 205–207. What two large rivers flow into the Yellow Sea? 209, 210. What three principal rivers flow into the Bay of Bengal? 212–214. Into what does the River Indus flow? 22. The Persian Gulf receives the waters of what river? 216. Into what does the Nile flow? 26. What rivers on the western coast of Africa? 225–227. What two large rivers flow into the Caspian Sea? 218, 219. What river flows into the Black Sea? 221.

QUESTIONS ON BOTH HEMISPHERES.

In what latitude is North America? South America? Europe? Asia? Africa? Australia? What is the latitude of Cape Farewell? Cape Horn? Cape of Good Hope? Behring's Strait? Borneo?

What is the longitude of the Isthmus of Darien? Isthmus of Suez? Cape St. Roque? Cape Horn? Cape of Good Hope? Madagascar?

In what zones is North America? South America? Europe? Asia? Africa?

What grand divisions are crossed by the Equator? 2, 5, 6. What by the Tropic of Cancer? What by the Tropic of Capricorn? What by the Arctic Circle? What islands are crossed by the Equator? 67, 101–103, 105. What two large islands by the Tropic of Capricorn? 99, 107. Are any divisions crossed by the Antarctic Circle? What lands in the South Frigid Zone?

What grand divisions border on the Atlantic Ocean? On the Pacific? On the Indian? Bound North America. South America. Europe. Asia. Africa.

Name the seas, gulfs and bays tributary to the Atlantic Ocean? 6–10, 25–29. To the Pacific? 11–13, 20. What bay in the northern part of North America? 7. What sea between North and South America? 10. What seas between Europe and Asia? 32, 33.

Name the straits in the Eastern Hemisphere. 39–46.

Name the islands in the North Frigid Zone? 48, 82–84. What islands between North and South America? 53. What island east of Greenland? 49.

Name the rivers that flow into the Northern Ocean. 186, 205, 206, 207. On which side of the Western Hemisphere are the rivers the largest? Why?

GEOGRAPHICAL DEFINITIONS.

THE RACES OF MEN.

10. RACES OF MEN.

Q. How are mankind divided?

Into five races of men, viz.: the European or Caucasian, the Asiatic or Mongolian, the American, the Malay, and the African.

Q. How is the European race distinguished?

By fair, or white complexion, and regular features.

Q. What nations are included in the European race?

The people of Europe, excepting Laplanders; those of Western Asia, Northern Africa, and the white inhabitants of America.

Q. How is the Asiatic race distinguished?

By a yellow complexion, flat forehead, and small eyes.

Q. What nations does it include?

Those of Eastern Asia, excepting the Malays; the Finns, Laplanders, Greenlanders, and Esquimaux.

Q. How is the American Indian race distinguished?

By the red complexion, straight black hair and high cheek bones.

Q. What nation does it include?

All the Indians of America except the Esquimaux and those of Greenland.

Q. How is the Malay race distinguished?

By a brown complexion and large features.

Q. What nations are included in this race?

The people of Malacca, Malaysia and the Asiatic isles.

Q. How is the African, or black race distinguished?

By a brownish black color, low forehead, dark woolly hair and thick lips.

Q. What nations does it include?

The negroes of Africa, Australia and New Zealand.

11. STAGES OF SOCIETY.

Q. On what does the social condition of men depend?

On their progress in knowledge, learning and refinement; and on their skill in the mechanical arts.

Q. What do the different degrees of advancement among men in these particulars form?

Various stages of society.

Q. How many of these are there?

GEOGRAPHICAL DEFINITIONS.

Four, viz.: savage, or barbarous, half-civilized, civilized and enlightened.

Q. What can you say of savage nations?

They live by hunting, fishing, and plunder; dwell in huts or caverns, and dress in the skins of animals; as the American Indians.

Q. What is the condition of half-civilized nations?

They understand agriculture and many of the arts tolerably well. They have written languages, and some knowledge of books. Example; Chinese.

Q. What nations are civilized?

Those which have a knowledge of the arts and the sciences; and who derive their subsistence from agriculture, manufactures and commerce.

Q. Give examples?

The natives of Mexico, Paraguay, &c.

Q. For what are enlightened nations noted?

Intelligence, enterprise, industry and their great skill in the arts and sciences. They are also more courteous than other nations, and treat their females with respect and politeness.

Q. What nations are enlightened?

The United States, Great Britain, and the northern and central European States.

Q. How are enlightened and civilized nations distinguished?

By the number and variety of their public buildings, and their works of national utility, as colleges, hospitals, libraries, bridges, canals, railroads, &c.

12. GOVERNMENT.

Q. What are the different forms of Government?

Monarchy, Aristocracy and Democracy.

Q. What is Monarchy?

It is a government in which the power is vested in a king, or emperor, who usually rules during life.

NOTE. Monarchies are of two kinds, Absolute and Limited.

Q. What is an Absolute Monarchy?

It is one where the will of the monarch is law; as China, Persia.

Q. What is a Limited Monarchy?

That in which the power of a monarch is limited by a constitution or law. Great Britain is a Limited Monarchy.

Q. What is an Aristocracy?

A government by the nobles.

Q. What is a Democracy?

A government by the people.

NOTE. In a Democracy, the supreme power is usually placed in the hands of rulers chosen by, and from the whole body of the people, or by their representatives in a national assembly.

13. POLITICAL DIVISIONS.

Q. What are the Political Divisions of the earth?

Empires, Kingdoms, Republics, &c.

Q. What is an Empire?

A country controlled or governed by an emperor. Example; Russian Empire.

Q. What is a Kingdom?

A country governed by a king or queen.

Q. What is a Republic?

A country governed by men who are chosen by the people.

Q. What is the chief officer of a Republic called?

A president.

Q. How are Empires, Kingdoms, and Republics subdivided?

Into Departments, Cantons, Provinces, States, Territories, Parishes, Districts, &c.

NOTE. States are subdivided into Counties, Parishes, or Districts, and these into Cities, Towns and Villages.

14. RELIGION.

Q. What are the principal systems of Religion?

Christian, Mohammedan, Jewish and Pagan.

Q. What nations are called Christian?

GEOGRAPHICAL DEFINITIONS.

Those that believe in Jesus Christ as a Saviour.

Q. How are Christians divided?

Into Protestant, Greek and Roman Catholic.

Q. Who are Mohammedans?

Those who believe in Mohammed who lived about 600 years after Christ.

Q. Who are the Jews?

Those who believe in the Old Testament but reject the New, and expect a Saviour yet to come.

Q. Who are Pagans?

Those who believe in false gods and practice idolatry.

QUESTIONS ON THE MAP OF THE WORLD.

In what latitude is North America? South America? Europe? Asia? Africa? Australia? What is the latitude of Cape Farewell? Cape Horn? Cape of Good Hope? Behring's Strait? Borneo?

What is the longitude of the Isthmus of Darien? Isthmus of Suez? Cape St. Roque? Cape Horn? Cape of Good Hope? Madagascar?

In what zones is North America? South America? Europe? Asia? Africa? What seas and bay in the Torrid Zone? What sea and bays in the North Temperate Zone? What bay in the North Frigid Zone? What is the width of the Torrid Zone? Of the North Temperate?

TABLE OF LONGITUDE.

The following Table shows the number of miles in a degree of longitude on a parallel of latitude for every five degrees from the Equator to the Poles,—sixty geographical miles being taken equal to sixty-nine and a quarter statute miles.

Degree of Latitude.	Geographical Miles.	Statute Miles.	Degree of Latitude.	Geographical Miles.	Statute Miles.
0	60.00	69.25	50	38.57	44.43
5	59.77	68.85	55	34.41	39.64
10	59.09	68.06	60	30.00	34.56
15	57.95	66.76	65	25.36	29.21
20	56.38	64.95	70	20.52	23.64
25	54.38	62.64	75	15.52	17.89
30	51.96	59.85	80	10.42	12.00
35	49.15	56.62	85	5.23	6.02
40	45.96	52.94	90	0.00	0.00
45	42.43	48.88			

TABLE OF RACES.

European, or Caucasian,	420 millions.
Asiatic, or Mongolian,	460 millions.
African, or Negro,	60 millions.
Malay,	40 millions.
American, or Indian,	20 millions.

TABLE OF PREVAILING SYSTEMS OF RELIGION.

Jews,	5 millions.
Christians,	300 millions.
Pagans,	595 millions.
Mohammedans,	100 millions.

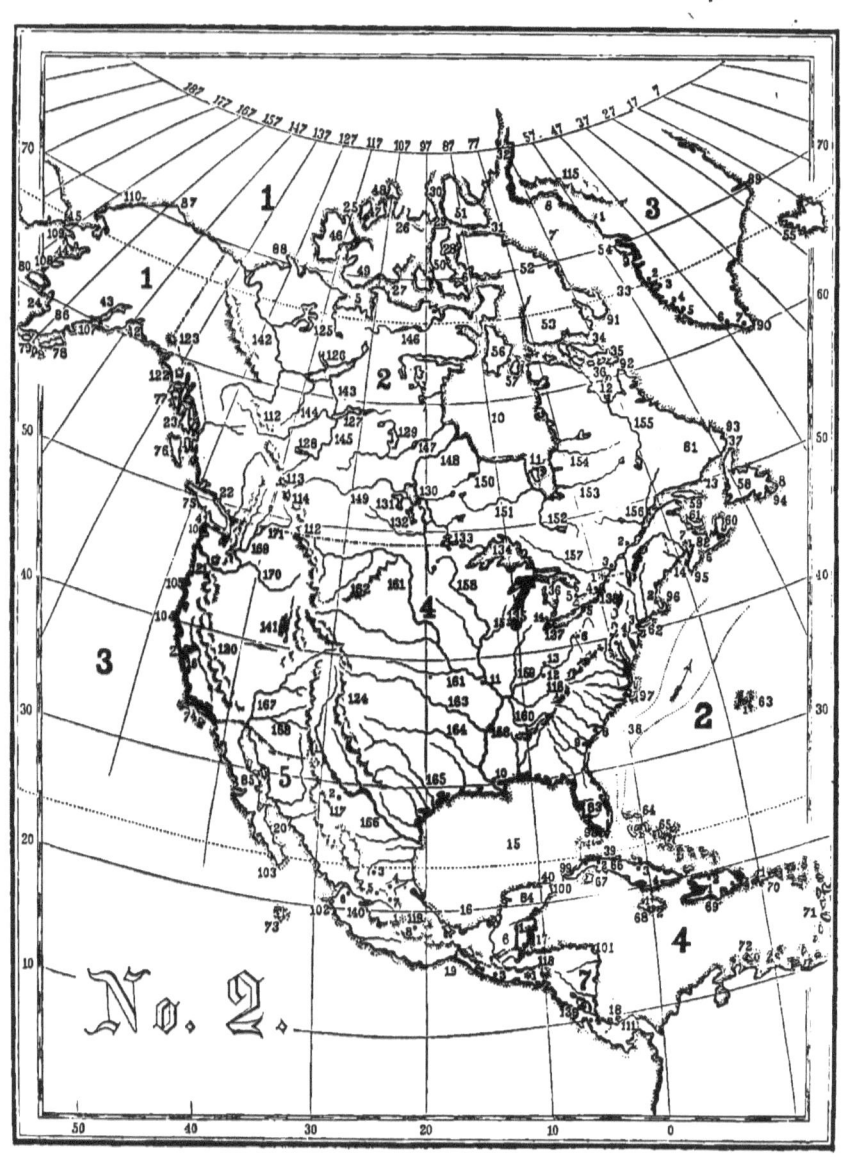

No. 2.

NORTH AMERICA.

SQUARE MILES, 8,370,000.   POPULATION, 40,000,000.

KEY TO MAP NO. 2.

COUNTRIES, CAPITALS, CHIEF TOWNS.

1 Russian America, 1 SITKA.

2 British America.

   Labrador.

   Canada,   1 OTTAWA, 2 Quebec, 3 Montreal, 4 Kingston, 5 Toronto.

   Nova Scotia, 6 HALIFAX.

   New Brunswick, 7 FREDERICTON.

   Newfoundland, 8 ST. JOHN'S.

3 Greenland, 1 UPERNAVIK, 2 *Holsteinburg,* 3 *Sukkertop,* 4 *New Hernhut,* 5 *Lichtenfels,* 6 *Julianshaab,* 7 *Lichtenau.*

4 United States, 1 WASHINGTON, 2 Boston, 3 New York, 4 Philadelphia, 5 Buffalo, 6 Pittsburg, 7 Baltimore, 8 Charleston, 9 Savannah, 10 New Orleans, 11 St. Louis, 12 Louisville, 13 Cincinnati, 14 Detroit, 15 Chicago, 16 San Francisco.

5 Mexico, 1 MEXICO, 2 *Chihuahua,* 3 Zacatecas, 4 *San Luis Potosi,* 5 Guanajuato, 6 *Guadalajara,* 7 *Queretaro,* 8 Puebla, 9 *Merida.*

6 Balize, 1 BALIZE.

7 Central America, 1 SAN SALVADOR, 2 Old Guatemala, 3 New Guatemala, 4 *San Jose.*

OCEANS, SEAS, GULFS AND BAYS.

1 ARCTIC,
2 ATLANTIC,
3 PACIFIC,
4 CARIBBEAN SEA,
5 *Coronation Gulf,*
6 *Boothia Gulf,*
7 BAFFIN'S BAY,
8 *Melville Bay,*
9 *Disco Bay,*
10 HUDSON'S BAY,
11 JAMES'S BAY,
12 *Ungava Bay,*
13 ST. LAWRENCE GULF,
14 BAY OF FUNDY,
15 GULF OF MEXICO,
16 BAY OF CAMPEACHY,
17 BAY OF HONDURAS,
18 *Bay of Guatemala,*
19 GULF OF TEHUANTEPEC,
20 GULF OF CALIFORNIA,
21 SAN FRANCISCO BAY,
22 GULF OF GEORGIA,
23 *Prince of Wales Archipelago,*
24 *Bristol Bay.*

STRAITS, CHANNELS AND SOUNDS.

25 *Bank's Strait,*
26 *Melville Strait,*
27 *Victoria Strait,*
28 PRINCE REGENT'S INLET,
29 BARROW'S STRAIT,
30 *Wellington Channel,*
31 LANCASTER SOUND,
32 *Smith's Sound,*
33 DAVIS'S STRAIT,
34 CUMBERLAND STRAIT,

NORTH AMERICA.

35 *Frobisher Strait,*
36 Hudson's Strait,
37 Bellisle Strait,
38 Gulf Stream,
39 Florida Strait,
40 Channel of Yucatan,
41 *Strait of Juan de Fuca,*
42 *Prince William's Sound,*
43 *Cook's Inlet,*
44 *Norton Sound,*
45 Behring's Strait.

ISLANDS.

46 Baring,
47 *Melville,*
48 *North Georgia,*
49 Victoria Land,
50 Boothia,
51 North Devon,
52 Prince William's Land,
53 *Cumberland,*
54 *Disco,*
55 Iceland,
56 Southampton,
57 *Mansfield,*
58 Newfoundland,
59 Anticosti,
60 Cape Breton,
61 Prince Edward's,
62 Long Island,
63 Bermuda Islands,
64 Bahama Islands, 1 Nassau.
65   Guanahani,
66 Cuba,   1 Havana, 2 Matanzas, 3 *Puerto Principe,* 4 *Santiago de Cuba.*
67 Isle of Pines,
68 Jamaica, 1 Spanish Town, 2 Kingston.
69 Hayti,   1 Port au Prince, 2 *Cape Haytien,* 3 St. Domingo.
70 Porto Rico, 1 St. John's.
71 Caribbees,
72 Lesser Antilles,
73 *Revillagigedo,*
74 *Santa Barbara,*
75 Vancouver's,
76 Queen Charlotte's,
77 Sitka,
78 *Kodiak,*
79 *Shoomagin's,*
80 *Nunivak.*

PENINSULAS, CAPES AND ISTHMUS.

81 Labrador,
82 Nova Scotia,
83 Florida,
84 Yucatan,
85 California,
86 Alaska,
87 Cape Barrow,
88 Cape Bathurst,
89 *Cape Brewster,*
90 Cape Farewell,
91 *Cape Walsingham,*
92 *Cape Chudleigh,*
93 *Cape St. Lewis,*
94 Cape Race,
95 Cape Sable,
96 Cape Cod,
97 Cape Hatteras,
98 Cape Sable, Flor.,
99 Cape St. Antonio,
100 *Cape Catoche,*
101 *Cape Gracias a Dios,*
102 *Cape Corrientes,*
103 Cape St. Lucas,
104 Cape Mendocino,
105 Cape Orford,
106 *Cape Flattery,*
107 *Cape Elizabeth,*
108 *Cape Romanzoff,*
109 Cape Prince of Wales,
110 *Icy Cape,*
111 Isthmus of Darien.

MOUNTAINS.

112 Rocky,
113 Mt. Brown,
114 Mt. Hooker,
115 Arctic Highlands,
116 Alleghany,
117 Sierra Madre,
118 Cosiguina Volcano,
119 Popocatapetl,
120 Sierra Nevada,
121 Cascade Range,
122 Mount Fairweather,
123 Mount St. Elias,
124 Great American Plains.

NORTH AMERICA.

LAKES.

125 GREAT BEAR,
126 GREAT SLAVE,
127 ATHABASCA,
128 Little Slave,
129 Deer,
130 WINNIPEG,
131 Winnipegoos,
132 Manitoba,
133 LAKE OF THE WOODS,
134 SUPERIOR,
135 MICHIGAN,
136 HURON,
137 ERIE,
138 ONTARIO,
139 NICARAGUA,
140 Chapala,
141 GREAT SALT LAKE.

RIVERS.

142 MACKENZIE,
143 SLAVE,
144 Peace,
145 Athabasca,
146 Great Fish,
147 CHURCHILL,
148 NELSON,
149 Saskatchewan,
150 Severn,
151 ALBANY,
152 Abbitibbee,
153 East Main,
154 Great Whale,
155 Koksak,
156 ST. LAWRENCE,
157 OTTAWA,
158 MISSISSIPPI,
159 OHIO,
160 TENNESSEE,
161 MISSOURI,
162 Yellow Stone,
163 ARKANSAS,
164 RED,
165 Brazos,
166 RIO GRANDE,
167 COLORADO,
168 Gila,
169 COLUMBIA,
170 LEWIS,
171 CLARKE'S.

QUESTIONS ON THE MAP OF NORTH AMERICA.

What part of the globe does North America comprise?
The northern division of the Western Continent.
What is its length?
Four thousand eight hundred miles.
What is its breadth?
From two thousand six hundred, to three thousand two hundred miles.
What ocean bounds North America on the north? 1. On the east? 2. On the west? 3. What isthmus connects it with South America? 111. Bound Greenland. Russian America. British America. United States. Mexico. Guatimala. Balize. Name the capital of British America. United States. Mexico. Guatimala.

SEAS, GULFS AND BAYS.

What sea between North and South America? 4.
What large gulf south of the United States? 15. What gulf west of Mexico? 20. West of Newfoundland? 13. On the west coast of British America? 22. What two gulfs has British America on the north? 5, 6.
What bay separates Prince William's Land from Greenland? 7. What two bays in the central part of British America? 10, 11. What bay north of Labrador? 12. What bay between Nova Scotia and New Brunswick? 14. South of the Gulf of Mexico? 16. South of Balize? 17. In the western part of the United States? 21. South-west of Russian America? 24.

NORTH AMERICA.

STRAITS, CHANNELS AND SOUNDS.

What strait between Asia and North America? 45. What straits and inlet north of British America? 25-30. What strait between British America and Greenland? 33.

What sound north of Baffin's Bay? 32. West? 31. What three straits north of Labrador? 34-36. What strait between Newfoundland and Labrador? 37. Between the United States and Cuba? 39. What strait connects the Gulf of Georgia with the Pacific Ocean? 41.

ISLANDS.

What islands in the Arctic Ocean? 46-51. Where is Prince William's Land? 52. What island in Hudson's Bay? 56. East of Greenland? 55. What west? 54. What three islands in the Gulf of St. Lawrence? 59-61. What island east of this gulf? 58. What island upon the eastern coast of the United States near the parallel of 40 degrees north latitude? 62. What group of islands south of Nova Scotia in the Atlantic Ocean? 63.

Which are the four largest islands in the West India group? 66, 68-70. What other islands form a part of this group? 64, 71, 72. Name some of the Caribbee islands. ANS. St. Christopher's, Antigua, Guadaloupe, Martinique, St. Lucia, Barbadoes, St. Vincent, Grenada, Tobago, and Trinidad. What island south of Cuba? 67. North of the Strait of Juan de Fuca? 75. West of British America? 76. What islands near the coast of Russian America? 77-80.

PENINSULAS AND CAPES.

What peninsula south of New Brunswick? 82. East of the Gulf of Mexico? 83. South of the Gulf of Mexico? 84. West of the Gulf of California? 85. South of Russian America? 86. Which is the most northern cape of North America? 87. Which is the most southern cape of Greenland? 90. What cape has Prince William's Land? 91. What two capes has Labrador? 92, 93. What cape east of Newfoundland? 94. What cape has Nova Scotia? 95.

What two capes on the eastern coast of the United States? 96, 97. What cape south of Florida? 98. West of Cuba? 99. What cape has Yucatan? 100. Guatimala? 101. What cape upon the western coast of Mexico? 102. At the southern point of the Peninsula of California? 103. What capes on the western coast of the United States? 104-106. West of Russian America? 108, 109.

MOUNTAINS.

What mountains extend through North America from north to south? 112. What are they called in Mexico? 117. What range of mountains on the eastern coast of the United States? 116. What two ranges in the western part? 120, 121. What two mountains in Russian America? 122, 123. Where is Cosiguina Volcano? 118.

LAKES.

What lakes in British America discharge their waters by the river Mackenzie? 125-128. What by the river Nelson? 130-132. What four great lakes between British America and the United States? 134, 136-138. What large lake wholly in the United States south of Lake Superior? 135. What lake in the United States west of the Rocky Mountains? 141. What lake in Guatimala? 139.

RIVERS.

What large river flows into the Arctic Ocean? 142. What two rivers flow into Lake Athabasca? 144, 145. What rivers flow into Hudson's Bay? 147, 148, 150. What into James' Bay? 151-154. What river flows into Ungava Bay? 155. Into the Gulf of St. Lawrence? 156. What is its principal branch? 157.

What large river flows into the Gulf of Mexico? 158. Mention its principal tributaries. 159, 161, 163, 164. What river forms part of the boundary line between the United States and Mexico? 166. What river flows into the Gulf of California? 167. What is its principal branch? 168. What large river in the United States flows into the Pacific? 169. What are its two principal branches? 170, 171.

NORTH AMERICA.

DESCRIPTIVE GEOGRAPHY.

NORTH AMERICA is the third grand division, in size.

It abounds with noble rivers and lakes; has two extended ranges of mountains, and is well diversified with hills and plains.

The climate is hot in the southern portion, temperate in the middle, and excessively cold in the northern.

Almost every variety of soil is found. Its productions are numerous and valuable. Among them are wheat, Indian corn, rye, oats, grass, potatoes, cotton, sugar, lumber, butter, cheese, and honey.

It is quite rich in minerals, as gold, silver, copper, lead, coal, and iron.

It has a large variety of animals, though the number of wild animals is rapidly diminishing.

North America has seven principal political divisions; viz.: Greenland, Russian America, British America, the United States, Mexico, Balize, and Central America.

Its principal islands are Greenland, Iceland, Newfoundland, and the West Indies.

QUESTIONS.—What is said of the extent of North America? The rivers and lakes? The surface? Climate? Soil? Productions? What minerals are found? What can you say of its animals? How is North America divided? Which are its principal islands?

1. GREENLAND.

Square miles, 380,000. Population, 9,400.

Greenland, a large island north-east of the continent, is a cold, elevated region covered with ice and snow most of the year. It produces lichens, mosses, currants, and a few flowering shrubs. Stinted birch, willow and ash trees are found in small numbers.

SEAL CATCHING.

The wild animals are the reindeer, polar fox and white bear. The only domestic animal is the dog. Sea-fowls, fish, seals, and walrus, abound, and furnish the natives with most of their food and clothing.

Esquimaux Indians inhabit it, with a few Danes. It belongs to Denmark.

QUESTIONS. Describe Greenland. What are its productions? Animals? Who inhabit it? To whom does it belong?

2. RUSSIAN AMERICA.

Square miles, 394,000. Population, 61,000.

Russian America occupies the north-west portion of North America.

It is mountainous, dreary, and but partially explored.

Its climate is cold, and soil, sterile.

The productions are lichens, moss and a few shrubs.

The animals are similar to those of Greenland.

The inhabitants consist of Esquimaux, and a few Russian traders, who reside there for the purpose of collecting furs.

SITKA, its capital, is on a small island near the coast. It is defended by a fort. It contains a foundry and steam engine factory. Several small steam yachts have been built here. There are a number of public schools for the natives and European children.

QUESTIONS. What is the situation of Russian America? What is said of its surface? Climate and soil? Productions? Animals? Who are the inhabitants? Describe Sitka.

3. BRITISH AMERICA.

Square miles, 3,000,000. Population, 2,690,000.

British America is a vast territory embracing all the region north of the United States, excepting Russian America and Greenland.

It includes Hudson's Bay Territory, Labrador, and the provinces of Canada, New Brunswick, Nova Scotia, and Newfoundland.

QUESTIONS. Describe British America. What does it include?

4. HUDSON'S BAY TERRITORY.

Square miles, 2,190,000. Population, 180,000.

The Hudson's Bay Territory comprises the northern and western portions of British America, extending from the Arctic Ocean to the United States, and from Labrador to the Pacific.

With the exception of the region traversed by the Rocky Mountains, this territory is generally level, and contains a great number of lakes and rivers communicating with each other.

The climate in the northern part is almost perpetual winter. In the southern part,

NORTH AMERICA.

the winters are very long and cold, and the summers, short and very warm.

Owing to the severity of the climate, there are few agricultural productions. The principal animals hunted for food, are deer, buffaloes, rabbits and porcupines. Wild fowl are also numerous.

FUR TRADERS.

The principal articles of traffic are the skins of fur-clad animals, of which there is a great variety.

QUESTIONS. What does Hudson's Bay Territory comprise? What is said of its surface? Its lakes and rivers? Climate? Productions? Animals? Articles of traffic?

---

5. LABRADOR.*

Square miles, 450,000. Population, 5,000.

Labrador is an extensive peninsula, lying between Hudson's Bay and the Atlantic, and extending from Hudson's Strait to the Strait of Belle Isle.

The coast is mostly bleak, rugged and desolate. The climate is too cold for most grains, but potatoes and some other vegetables are raised.

The inhabitants, consisting chiefly of Esquimaux, subsist principally by hunting and fishing. The fisheries on the coast are valuable and give employment to a large number of vessels from other provinces and the United States.

Many valuable furs are exported.

QUESTIONS. Describe Labrador. Its coast. Climate. Productions. What is said of its inhabitants? Fisheries? Exports?

For a description of the other British Provinces see Geography of map No. 3.

For description of 4, 5, 6 and 7 see Geography of map No. 4.

GENERAL QUESTIONS ON NORTH AMERICA.

Name the political divisions of North America. Where is British America? Hudson's Bay Territory? Russian America? Greenland? Balize? Mexico? Which is the largest division? The most populous? On what oceans does North America border? What range of mountains in the western part? In the eastern part? In which divisions are volcanoes found? Name the volcanoes?

What lakes are there in North America? Which is the largest? What bays indent the eastern coast of North America? The western? What large gulf south of North America? What large bay in the northern part? Where is Chesapeake bay? What large island north-east of North America? What islands east? South? North? Where are the Bahama islands? Aleutian islands? Newfoundland? Where is Cape Farewell? Cape Sable? Cape St. Lucas? Cape Corrientes?

How does North America rank among other divisions in size? Which division is the most mountainous? The most level? Who inhabit Russian America? What is its capital?

* See Map No. 3.

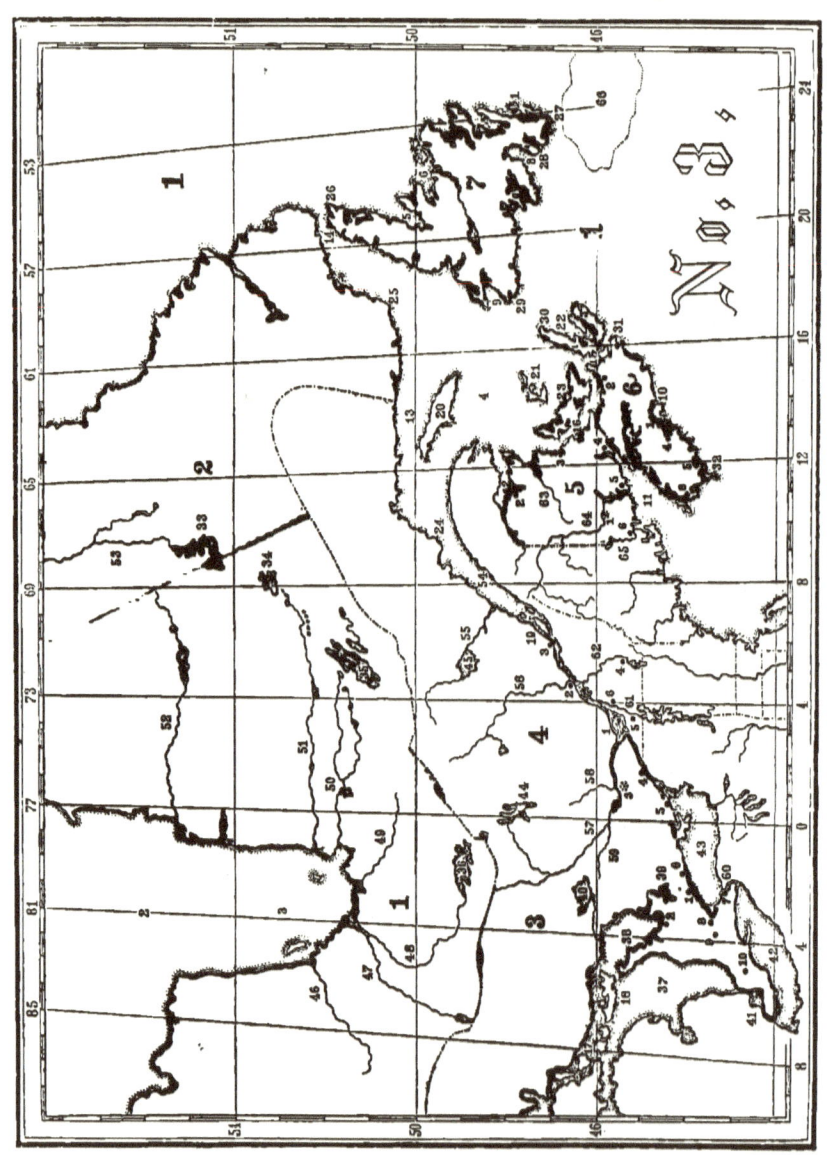

BRITISH PROVINCES.

SQUARE MILES, 3,080,000.   POPULATION, 2,600,000.

KEY TO MAP NO. 3.

COUNTRIES, CAPITALS AND CHIEF TOWNS.
1. **Hudson's Bay Territory.**
2. **Labrador.**
3. **Upper Canada,** 1 Toronto, 2 *Collingwood,* 3 *Ottawa,* 4 *Brockville,* 5 *Kingston,* 6 *Coburg,* 7 *Niagara,* 8 Hamilton, 9 *Brantford,* 10 *London.*
4. **Lower Canada,** 1 Montreal, 2 *Three Rivers,* 3 Quebec, 4 *Sherbrooke,* 5 *St. John,* 6 *St. Hyacinthe.*
5. **New Brunswick,** 1 FREDERICTON, 2 *Bathurst,* 3 *Liverpool,* 4 *Dorchester,* 5 *St. John's,* 6 *St. Andrew's.*
6. **Nova Scotia,** 1 HALIFAX, 2 Picton, 3 Sydney, 4 Lunenburg, 5 *Shelburne,* 6 *Yarmouth.*
7. **Newfoundland,** 1 ST. JOHN'S.

OCEANS, BAYS, &c.
1. ATLANTIC OCEAN,
2. HUDSON'S BAY,
3. JAMES'S BAY,
4. GULF OF ST. LAWRENCE,
5. *White's Bay,*
6. *Notre Dame Bay,*
7. *Bonavista Bay,*
8. *Placentia Bay,*
9. *St. George's Bay,*
10. *Halifax Harbor,*
11. BAY OF FUNDY,
12. *Bay of Chaleur.*

CHANNELS AND STRAITS.
13. CANADIAN CHANNEL,
14. BELLISLE STRAIT,

15. *Gut of Canso,*
16. *Northumberland Strait,*
17. *St. Mary's Strait.*

ISLANDS.
18. MANITOULIN ISLES,
19. ORLEANS,
20. ANTICOSTI,
21. MAGDALEN ISLANDS,
22. CAPE BRETON,
23. PRINCE EDWARD'S.

CAPES.
24. *Des Montes,*
25. *Whittle,*
26. BAULD,
27. RACE,
28. *St. Mary,*
29. RAY,
30. NORTH,
31. *Canso,*
32. SABLE.

LAKES.
33. *Caniopuscau,*
34. *Nitcheguon,*
35. MISTISSINNY,
36. ABBITIBBEE,
37. HURON,
38. GEORGIAN BAY,
39. SIMCOE,
40. NIPISSING,
41. ST. CLAIR,
42. ERIE,
43. ONTARIO,
44. GRAND,
45. ST. JOHN.

*Ottawa is the capital of the whole of Canada.

RIVERS.

46 Albany,
47 Moose,
48 Abbittibbee,
49 Harricanaw,
50 Rupert,
51 East Main,
52 Great Whale,
53 Koksak,
54 St. Lawrence,
55 Saguenay,
56 St. Maurice,
57 Ottawa,
58 Gatineau,
59 Madawaska,
60 Niagara,
61 Sorel,
62 St. Francis,
63 Miramichi,
64 St. John,
65 St. Croix.

QUESTIONS ON THE MAP OF THE BRITISH PROVINCES.

Bound British America.* In what part is Hudson's Bay Territory? Labrador? Bound Upper Canada. Lower Canada. New Brunswick. Nova Scotia. Newfoundland.

OCEANS, SEAS AND BAYS.

What ocean east of the British Provinces? 1. What large bay in the northern part? 2. What is its southern extremity called? 3. What large gulf between New Brunswick and Newfoundland? 4. What bays around Newfoundland? 5-9. What harbor south of Nova Scotia? 10. What bay west of Nova Scotia? 11. What bay north of New Brunswick? 12.

STRAITS AND CHANNELS.

What channel between Canada and Anticosti? 13. What strait between Labrador and Newfoundland? 14. What strait between Nova Scotia and Cape Breton? 15. What strait between Nova Scotia and Prince Edward's? 16. What strait connects Lakes Superior and Huron? 17.

ISLANDS AND CAPES.

What island in the northern part of Lake Huron? 18. What island in the St. Lawrence near Quebec? 19. What island at the mouth of the St. Lawrence?

* See map No. 2.

20. What island east of New Brunswick? 23. What islands north-east of Pr. Edward's? 21. What island north-east of Nova Scotia? 22. What cape south of Labrador? 25. What cape at the northern extremity of Newfoundland? 26. At the southern extremity? 27. At the south-western extremity? 29. North of Cape Breton? 30. At the eastern extremity of Nova Scotia? 31. At the southern extremity? 32.

LAKES.

What lake in Labrador? 33. What two lakes east of James's Bay? 34, 35. What lake is the source of the Abbitibbee? 36. What lakes between Canada and the United States? 37, 41-43. What bay connects with Lake Huron? 38. What lakes wholly in Canada? 39, 40, 44, 45.

RIVERS.

What rivers flow into James's Bay? 46-51. What river in the northern part of Labrador? 53. What river is the outlet of the great lakes? 54. What branches has it on the north? 55-57. Which is the boundary river between Upper and Lower Canada? 57. What river connects lakes Erie and Ontario? 60. Which way does it run? What falls has it? Niagara Falls. What rivers flow into the St. Lawrence from the south? 61, 62. What rivers in New Brunswick? 63, 64. What river is the boundary between New Brunswick and the United States? 65.

PARLIAMENT BUILDINGS AT OTTAWA.

DESCRIPTIVE GEOGRAPHY.

The Province of Canada embraces a section of British America, lying south of the Hudson's Bay Territory and Labrador, extending about 1,400 miles from east to west, and varying in width from 200 to 400 miles.

It was formerly divided into two provinces, Upper Canada, lying on the great lakes and west of the Ottawa river, and Lower Canada, occupying the valley of the St. Lawrence from the mouth of the Ottawa river to the Gulf of St. Lawrence.

The government of Canada is similar to that of Great Britain and Ireland. It consists of a Governor-General appointed by the Crown as its representative, aided by the Executive Council, and a Provincial Parliament.

The prevailing religion of Lower Canada is Roman Catholic, that of Upper Canada, Protestant. There are churches of various denominations in both.

Canada was first settled by the French in 1541. It was acquired by the English in 1760, and has since remained a part of the British Empire.

QUESTIONS. Give the situation and extent of Canada. What is said of its divisions? Government? Religion? History?

3. UPPER CANADA OR CANADA WEST.
Square miles, 148,000. Population, 1,396,000.

Upper Canada has generally a level or slightly undulating surface, with the exception of a table ridge which forms the water shed between Lakes Superior and Huron, and Hudson's Bay.

The soil is fertile, especially on the rich alluvial flats of the river courses.

The climate is affected to some extent by the large lakes. It is healthy, and highly favorable to the growth of grain and the production of the finest fruits. Wheat is the staple product. Peas, rye, barley, oats, buckwheat, Indian corn, potatoes, hemp, and flax, are raised extensively. In the southern part, peaches and apples are produced in great abundance.

Extensive forests of white and red pine, and other forest trees, furnish large quantities of timber for exportation.

Iron of the best quality is found in great abundance. Copper abounds on Lakes Superior and Huron. Silver has been discovered in small quantities, and lead and tin occur in several places.

Whitefish, lake trout and sturgeon of great size abound in the large lakes, and are taken for home consumption and export.

The educational system of Upper Canada is very complete.

OTTAWA is the capital of the whole of Canada. It contains fine public buildings.

Toronto is situated on a circular bay on the north-west shore of Lake Ontario. The streets generally cross each other at right angles. The buildings are mostly of light colored brick, giving the town a pleasant appearance.

The Normal School and Education Office for Upper Canada are located here. These buildings are the most extensive of their kind in North America.

Hamilton is situated on Burlington Bay at the western extremity of Lake Ontario. It contains many fine buildings. It has manufactures of various kinds, and possesses superior commercial advantages.

QUESTIONS. What is said of the surface of Upper Canada? Soil? Climate? Productions? Forests? What are its minerals? What abound in the lakes? What is said of its educational system? Describe Ottawa. Toronto. Hamilton.

4. LOWER CANADA, OR CANADA EAST.
Square miles, 210,000. Population, 1,110,000.

Lower Canada has a broken and irregular surface, and in the eastern part is mountainous, presenting varied and picturesque scenery. The country is well-watered, and though not as fertile as Upper Canada, has a good soil, and some portions of it are highly cultivated. The winters are cold and severe, but during the summers, vegetation is very rapid.

The productions are wheat, corn, rye, oats, peas, flax, and hemp. From the forests, timber of various kinds and maple-sugar are obtained, both for consumption and export.

Iron, copper and gold are the most important minerals.

The majority of the inhabitants are of French origin, and still speak the French language.

FALLS OF MONTMORENCI.

Montreal, on an island of the same name in the St. Lawrence river, is favorably situated for intercourse with both provinces and with the United States. The buildings are principally of a grayish limestone. Some of the public edifices are magnificent structures. Its quays, also built of cut limestone, are unsurpassed in America. The Victoria bridge across the St. Lawrence consists of a wrought iron box twenty feet deep, sixteen feet wide, and seven thousand feet long, supported by towers of stone, and is used for the trains of the Grand Trunk Railway.

Quebec, the most ancient and important port in Canada, is situated on the left bank of the river St. Lawrence, about one hundred and eighty miles north-east from Montreal. It has a picturesque situation, and is divided into the upper and lower towns; the former on the highest part of the promontory of Cape Diamond, the latter at its base.

It is engaged extensively in trade, particularly in the exportation of lumber. The Falls of Montmorenci are about seven miles from the city.

QUESTIONS. What is said of the surface of Lower Canada? Soil? Climate? Productions? Minerals? Inhabitants? Describe Montreal. Quebec.

5. NEW BRUNSWICK.

Square miles, 27,700. Population, 252,000.

The Province of New Brunswick is situated between Maine and the Gulf of St. Lawrence.

The surface is varied; mountain ridges, and sheltered valleys and plains, alternating with each other.

The soil is fertile; the climate is subject to great extremes of heat and cold.

A great part of the province is covered with dense forests which furnish large quantities of timber. Oats, rye, barley, and the fruits of northern New England, are the chief products.

The coal fields are said to extend over 10,000 square miles. Iron and copper are abundant, and large deposits of manganese and plumbago have been discovered.

The rivers, lakes and sea-coasts, abound with fish which are taken in great quantities.

Almost the whole province can be reached by its streams. Several railways are completed, or in progress. The great extent of sea-coast, with its numerous bays, furnishes excellent facilities for commerce.

The affairs of the province are administered by a Lieutenant Governor, aided by an Executive Council, a Legislative Council, and a House of Assembly chosen by the people.

FREDERICTON, the capital, is situated on the right bank of the river St. John. It is regularly laid out, and a place of considerable trade.

St. John's is situated on a rocky peninsula at the mouth of the St. John's river. It stands on a declivity, and presents an imposing appearance to persons approaching from the sea. Its harbor is safe and capacious and never obstructed by ice.

QUESTIONS. How is New Brunswick situated? What is said of its surface? Soil? Climate? Forests? Productions? Coal fields? Minerals? With what do its rivers and lakes abound? What are its facilities for commerce? Government? Describe Fredericton. St. John's.

6. NOVA SCOTIA.

Square miles, 19,000.* Population, 330,000.*

Nova Scotia is a large peninsula lying south-east of New Brunswick, with which it is connected by an isthmus fifteen miles wide. It contains no mountains of great magnitude. A broad belt of high and broken land extends along the Atlantic shores.

The surface is undulating throughout and highly picturesque. The numerous rivers

* Including Cape Breton.

COD AND MACKEREL FISHERIES.

and lakes form an interesting feature in the province.

The soil varies greatly in productiveness. The climate is remarkably temperate, considering its high northern latitude. Dense fogs are prevalent on the Atlantic coast.

The principal productions are wheat, barley, rye, oats, buckwheat, and potatoes.

Large quantities of apples are raised in the western counties.

Coal, iron and copper, are abundant. Silver and lead are found to some extent. Large quantities of gypsum are exported.

Its fisheries give employment to a great number of men and boats.

It has over 1,200 miles of sea-coast, penetrated by the finest bays in the world, which are open to navigation throughout the year, giving it superior commercial advantages.

The eastern arm of the bay of Fundy, called Mines Bay, is remarkable for the height of its tides which sometimes rise sixty or seventy feet.

The inhabitants consist principally of descendants of the English, Scotch and Irish, who now form but one race living in perfect harmony.

It is subject to Great Britain, the government being similar to that of New Brunswick.

Nova Scotia was first discovered by the Cabots in 1497.

HALIFAX is a seaport, situated on Halifax Harbor. Its streets are spacious and cross each other at right angles. It has extensive steam communication with the United States and West Indies, and is the port at which the Cunard mail steamers touch on their voyages to and from Europe. It is also the terminus of the railroad designed to connect Quebec with the Atlantic.

QUESTIONS. How is Nova Scotia situated? What is said of its mountains? What is its surface? Soil? Climate? What are its productions? Minerals? What is said of its fisheries? Describe its sea-coast. Mines Bay. Its inhabitants. Government. When and by whom was Nova Scotia discovered? Describe Halifax.

CAPE BRETON.

Cape Breton has long been celebrated for its fisheries; the principal are cod and mackerel. Large quantities of excellent ship timber are exported.

It is a colony under Nova Scotia, and sends two members to its House of Assembly.

Sydney, in the eastern part of the island, is situated near the famous Sydney coal mines. It has an excellent harbor.

Lunenburg is a place of considerable trade.

QUESTIONS. For what is Cape Breton celebrated? With what province is it united in government? Describe Sydney. Lunenburg.

NOTE. The extent and population of Cape Breton are included in those of Nova Scotia.

7. NEWFOUNDLAND.

Square miles, 36,000. Population, 122,000.

Newfoundland is a large island in the mouth of the gulf of St. Lawrence, and nearer to Great Britain than any other part of America.

It is very irregular in form, its coast being indented with numerous bays and harbors.

The interior of the country has an uneven and rocky surface with numerous rivers and lakes.

The climate is severe but healthful. In May and the beginning of June, dense fogs prevail on the "Banks" and neighboring shores. Much of the soil is unfit for cultivation, though some parts of the island are fertile, producing grain, grapes, and potatoes. The principal forest trees are spruce, birch, larch, willow, and mountain-ash.

The minerals are coal, gypsum, lead, copper, and iron.

The Grand Bank of Newfoundland forms the most extensive submarine elevation on the globe, and swarms with cod and other varieties of fish. The greater part of the population are engaged in the fisheries.

The government is similar to that of the other British North American colonies.

All religious sects are tolerated. Considerable attention has been given to education, and various grades of schools have been established.

A submarine telegraph, eighty-five miles in length, is laid across the Gulf of St. Lawrence, connecting Newfoundland with Nova Scotia, and by continuous lines, with the different parts of the United States.

ST. JOHN'S, the capital, is the most eastern seaport in North America, and only 1665 miles from Galway in Ireland. It has a fine harbor enclosed by two mountains, and defended by numerous batteries and fortifications. The town, consisting principally of one street, has many good buildings, and is improving in regularity and appearance.

QUESTIONS. What is Newfoundland? How is it situated? What is its form? Surface? Climate? Soil? What are its productions? Forest trees? Minerals? What is said of the Grand Bank? Occupation of the inhabitants? Government? Religion? Education? Submarine Telegraph? Describe St. John's.

GENERAL QUESTIONS ON THE BRITISH PROVINCES.

Which province extends farthest east? South? What division lies on both sides of the St. Lawrence?

Where is lake Abbitibbee? Lake Nipissing? Lake St. John? Saguenay River? Ottawa River? St. Francis? St. Croix? Describe the St. Lawrence. Placentia Bay. Bay of Fundy. Bellisle Strait. Manitoulin Isles. Anticosti.

What is the latitude of Montreal? What other cities in and about the same latitude? What is the longitude of Cape Race?

What are the vegetable productions of Upper Canada? In what provinces is iron found? Copper? Coal? What other minerals are found? What are obtained from the forests? From the lakes?

By whom was Canada first settled? To what country does it belong? What language is spoken in Lower Canada? How is Montreal situated? Describe Quebec. St. John's. Halifax. Toronto.

How would you sail from Montreal to Halifax? With what countries has Halifax communication by steam ships?

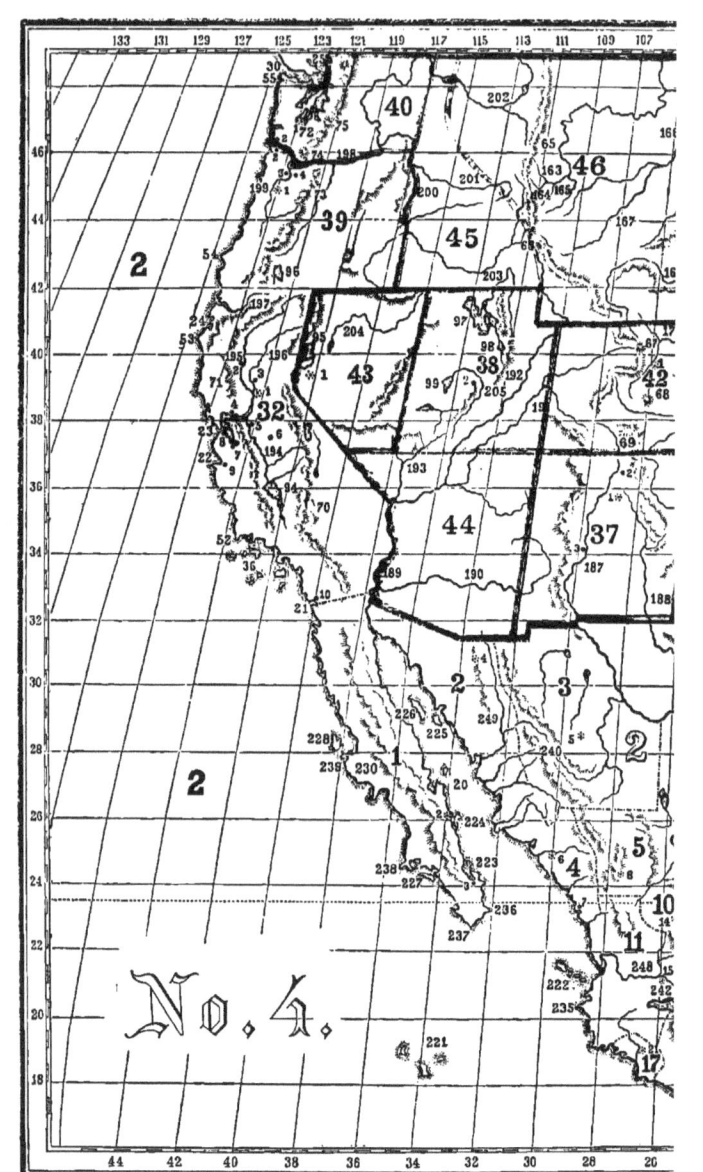

6

UNITED STATES AND MEXICO.

SQUARE MILES, 3,800,000.   POPULATION, 34,600,000.

KEY TO MAP NO. 4.

STATES, CAPITALS AND CHIEF TOWNS.

1 **Maine,** 1 AUGUSTA, 2 Bangor, 3 Eastport, 4 Bath, 5 Portland.

2 **New Hampshire,** 1 CONCORD, 2 Portsmouth, 3 Manchester, 4 Nashua.

3 **Vermont,** 1 MONTPELIER, 2 Burlington, 3 Brattleboro.

4 **Massachusetts,** 1 BOSTON, 2 Lowell, 3 New Bedford, 4 Worcester, 5 Springfield.

5 **Rhode Island,** 1 PROVIDENCE, 2 NEWPORT.

6 **Connecticut,** 1 HARTFORD, 2 NEW HAVEN, 3 New London.

7 **New York,** 1 ALBANY, 2 New York, 3 Brooklyn, 4 Buffalo, 5 Rochester, 6 Syracuse, 7 Utica, 8 Oswego, 9 Ogdensburg, 10 Plattsburg, 11 Whitehall, 12 Troy, 13 Elmira, 14 Dunkirk.

8 **New Jersey,** 1 TRENTON, 2 Paterson, 3 Newark.

9 **Pennsylvania,** 1 HARRISBURG, 2 Philadelphia, 3 Erie, 4 Wilkesbarre, 5 Pottsville, 6 Reading, 7 Lancaster, 8 Carlisle, 9 Lewistown, 10 Somerset, 11 Pittsburg.

10 **Delaware,** 1 DOVER, 2 Wilmington.

11 **Maryland,** 1 ANNAPOLIS, 2 Baltimore, 3 Easton, 4 Cumberland.

12 **District of Columbia,** 1 WASHINGTON.

13 **Virginia,** 1 RICHMOND, 3 Harper's Ferry, 4 Fredericksburg, 5 Petersburg, 6 Norfolk, 7 Lynchburg.

13 ½ **West Virginia,** 1 WHEELING.

14 **North Carolina,** 1 RALEIGH, 2 Edenton, 3 Newbern, 4 Beaufort, 5 Wilmington, 6 Fayetteville.

15 **South Carolina,** 1 COLUMBIA, 2 Abbeville, 3 Camden, 4 Georgetown, 5 Charleston.

16 **Georgia,** 1 MILLEDGEVILLE, 2 Atlanta, 3 Augusta, 4 Savannah, 5 Darien, 6 Columbus, 7 Macon.

17 **Florida,** 1 TALLAHASSEE, 2 Pensacola, 3 Appalachicola, 4 St. Augustine, 5 Key West.

18 **Alabama,** 1 MONTGOMERY, 2 Huntsville, 3 Wetumpka, 4 Tuscaloosa, 5 Mobile.

19 **Mississippi,** 1 JACKSON, 2 Columbus, 3 Natchez, 4 Vicksburg.

20 **Louisiana,** 1 BATON ROUGE, 2 New Orleans, 3 Natchitoches, 4 Shreveport.

21 **Texas,** 1 AUSTIN, 2 Houston, 3 Galveston, 4 Matagorda, 5 Goliad, 6 Corpus Christi, 7 Rio Grande City.

22 **Arkansas,** 1 LITTLE ROCK, 2 Helena, 3 Columbia, 4 Van Buren, 5 Batesville.

23 **Missouri,** 1 JEFFERSON CITY, 2 Independence, 3 Lexington, 4 St. Charles, 5 St. Louis, 6 Potosi.

24 **Tennessee,** 1 NASHVILLE, 2 Knoxville, 3 Murfreesboro', 4 Columbia, 5 Memphis, 6 Jackson.

UNITED STATES.

25 **Kentucky,** 1 FRANKFORT, 2 Louisville, 3 Maysville, 4 Georgetown, 5 Lexington, 6 Bowling Green, 7 Paducah.

26 **Ohio,** 1 COLUMBUS, 2 Toledo, 3 Sandusky, 4 Cleveland, 5 Steubenville, 6 Zanesville, 7 Lancaster, 8 Portsmouth, 9 Chillicothe, 10 Cincinnati, 11 Dayton.

27 **Indiana,** 1 INDIANAPOLIS, 2 Michigan City, 3 South Bend, 4 Madison, 5 New Albany, 6 Evansville, 7 Vincennes, 8 Terre Haute, 9 Lafayette.

28 **Illinois,** 1 SPRINGFIELD, 2 Galena, 3 Chicago, 4 Cairo, 5 Alton, 6 Quincy, 7 Peoria, 8 Rock Island.

29 **Michigan,** 1 LANSING, 2 Saut St. Marie, 3 Detroit, 4 Ann Arbor, 5 Monroe, 6 Adrian, 7 Jackson, 8 Kalamazoo, 9 Grand Haven.

30 **Wisconsin,** 1 MADISON, 2 Green Bay, 3 Fond du Lac, 4 Milwaukee, 5 Racine, 6 Janesville, 7 Prairie du Chien, 8 La Crosse.

31 **Iowa,** 1 DES MOINES, 2 Dubuque, 3 Davenport, 4 Muscatine, 5 Burlington, 6 Council Bluff, 7 Iowa City.

32 **California,** 1 SACRAMENTO, 2 Placer City, 3 Marysville, 4 Benicia, 5 Stockton, 6 Sonora, 7 San Jose, 8 San Francisco, 9 Monterey, 10 San Diego.

33 **Minnesota,** 1 ST. PAUL, 2 St. Anthony.

34 **Nebraska,** 1 OMAHA CITY.

35 **Kansas,** 1 TOPEKA, 2 Wabounse, 3 Leavenworth, 4 Lecompton, 5 Lawrence.

36 **Indian,** 1 TAHLEQUAH.

37 **New Mexico,** 1 SANTA FE, 2 Taos, 3 Socorro.

38 **Utah,** 1 SALT LAKE CITY, 2 Fillmore City.

39 **Oregon,** 1 SALEM, 2 Astoria, 3 Portland, 4 Oregon.

40 **Washington,** 1 OLYMPIA, 2 Pacific City, 3 Ft. Vancouver.

41 **Dakota,** 1 YANKTON.

42 **Colorado,** 1 DENVER CITY.

43 **Nevada,** 1 CARSON CITY.

44 **Arizona.**

45 **Idaho.**

46 **Montana.**

OCEANS, GULFS AND BAYS.

1 ATLANTIC OCEAN,
2 PACIFIC OCEAN,
3 PASSAMAQUODDY BAY,
4 PENOBSCOT BAY,
5 MASSACHUSETTS BAY,
6 NARRAGANSETT BAY,
7 NEW YORK BAY,
8 DELAWARE BAY,
9 CHESAPEAKE BAY,
10 CHATHAM BAY,
11 CHARLOTTE HARBOR,
12 TAMPA BAY,
13 APPALACHEE BAY,
14 PENSACOLA BAY,
15 MOBILE BAY,
16 GALVESTON BAY,
17 MATAGORDA BAY,
18 CORPUS CHRISTI BAY,
19 GULF OF MEXICO,
20 GULF OF CALIFORNIA,
21 SAN DIEGO BAY,
22 MONTEREY BAY,
23 SAN FRANCISCO BAY,
24 HUMBOLDT BAY,
25 GULF OF GEORGIA.

SOUNDS AND STRAITS.

26 LONG ISLAND SOUND,
27 ALBEMARLE SOUND,
28 PAMLICO SOUND,
29 FLORIDA STRAIT,
30 STRAIT OF JUAN DE FUCA.

UNITED STATES.

ISLANDS.
31 Nantucket,
32 Martha's Vineyard,
33 Long Island,
34 Florida Keys,
35 Tortugas,
36 Santa Barbara.

CAPES.
37 Ann,
38 Cod,
39 Malabar,
40 May,
41 Henlopen,
42 Charles,
43 Henry,
44 Hatteras,
45 Lookout,
46 Fear,
47 Canaveral,
48 Florida,
49 Sable,
50 Roman,
51 San Blas,
52 Conception,
53 Mendocino,
54 Orford,
55 Flattery.

MOUNTAINS.
56 Katahdin,
57 White,
58 Green,
59 Catskill,
60 Blue Ridge,
61 Alleghany,
62 Cumberland,
63 Ozark,
64 Black Hills,
65 Rocky,
66   Fremont's,
67   Long's,
68   Pike's,
69   Spanish,
70 Sierra Nevada,
71 Coast,
72 Cascade,

73 Mt. Hood,
74 Mt. St. Helen's,
75 Mt. Ranier,
76 Great American Plains.

LAKES.
77 Red,
78 Lake of the Woods,
79 Rainy,
80 Superior,
81 Michigan,
82 Green Bay,
83 Huron,
84 Georgian Bay,
85 Saginaw Bay,
86 St. Clair,
87 Erie,
88 Ontario,
89 Champlain,
90 Moosehead,
91 Chesuncook,
92 Okechobee,
93 Pontchartrain,
94 Tula,
95 Pyramid,
96 Klamath,
97 Great Salt,
98 Utah,
99 Nicollet.

RIVERS.
100 St. Lawrence,
101 St. John's,
102 St. Croix,
103 Penobscot,
104 Kennebec,
105 Androscoggin,
106 Saco,
107 Merrimac,
108 Connecticut,
109 Hudson,
110   Mohawk,
111 Delaware,
112 Susquehanna,
113 Potomac,
114 Rappahannock,
115 James,

UNITED STATES.

116 Chowan,
117 Roanoke,
118 Tar, or Pamlico,
119 Neuse,
120 Cape Fear,
121 Great Pedee,
122 Santee,
123   Waterree,
124 Savannah,
125 Altamaha,
126   Oconee,
127   Ocmulgee,
128 St. Mary's,
129 St. John's,
130 Scwanee,
131 Appalachicola,
132   Flint,
133   Chattahoochee,
134 Mobile,
135   Alabama,
136   Tombigbee,
137 Pascagoula,
138 Pearl,
139 Mississippi,
140   Yazoo,
141   Ohio,
142   Tennessee,
143   Cumberland,
144   Green,
145   Kentucky,
146   Big Sandy,
147   Kanawha,
148   Monongahela,
149   Alleghany,
150   Muskingum,
151   Scioto,
152   Miami,
153   Wabash,
154   White,
155   Kaskaskia,
156   Illinois,
157   Rock,
158   Wisconsin,
159   Minnesota,
160   Iowa,
161   Des Moines,
162   Missouri,
163   Jefferson,
164   Madison,
165   Gallatin,
166   Yellowstone,
167   Big Horn,

168 Nebraska,
169   North Fork,
170   South Fork,
171 Kansas,
172   Republican Fork,
173   Smoky Hill,
174 Osage,
175 St. Francis,
176 White,
177 Arkansas,
178   Canadian,
179 Red,
180   Washita,
181 Sabine,
182 Neches,
183 Trinity,
184 Brazos,
185 Colorado,
186 Nueces,
187 Rio Grande,
188   Pecos,
189 Colorado,
190   Gila,
191   Grande,
192   Green,
193   Rio Virgen,
194 San Joaquin,
195 Sacramento,
196   Feather,
197 Klamath,
198 Columbia,
199   Willamette,
200   Lewis,
201   Salmon,
202   Clarke's,
203 Bear,
204 Humboldt,
205 Nicollet,
206 St. Joseph's,
207 Grand,
208 St. Clair,
209 Detroit,
210 Maumee,
211 Niagara.

2 MEXICO.*

1 **Lower California,** 2 *Loreto,* 3 *La Paz.*
2 **Sonora,**   4 *Arispe.*
3 **Chihuahua,**   5 *Chihuahua.*

* The States of Mexico may be omitted till the review.

UNITED STATES.

4 Cinaloa,   6 *Culiacan,* 7 *Mazatlan.*
5 Durango,   8 *Durango.*
6 Cohahuila,   9 *Saltillo.*
7 New Leon,   10 *Monterey.*
8 Tamaulipas,   12 *Victoria,* 11 *Matamoras.*
9 San Luis Potosi,   13 *San Luis Potosi.*
10 Zacatecas,   14 ZACATECAS.
11 Jalisco,   15 *Guadalajara.*
12 Guanajuato,   16 GUANAJUATO.
13 Queretaro,   17 *Queretaro.*
14 Vera Cruz,   19 VERA CRUZ, 18 *Jalapa.*
15 Mexico,   1 MEXICO.
16 Michoacan,   20 *Valladolid.*
17 Colima,   21 *Colima.*
18 Guerrero,   22 *Acapulco.*
19 Puebla,   23 PUEBLA.
20 Oajaca,   24 *Oajaca.*
21 Tehuantepec,   25 *Tehauntepec.*
22 Tabasco,   26 *Tabasco.*
23 Chiapas,   27 *Ciudad Real.*
24 Yucatan,   28 *Merida,* 29 *Campeachy,* 30 *Valladolid.*
3 Balize,   1 *Balize.*

BAYS.
212 CAMPEACHY,
213 HONDURAS,
214 TEHUANTEPEC.

ISLANDS.
215 BAHAMA, 1 NASSAU.
216 CUBA, 1 HAVANA, 2 *Matanzas,* 3 *Puerto Principe,* 4 *Santiago.*
217 ISLE OF PINES,
218 HAYTI, 1 PORT AU PRINCE.
219 JAMAICA, 1 SPANISH TOWN, 2 *Kingston.*
220 COZUMEL,
221 *Revillagigedo,*
222 *The Three Marias,*
223 *Espiritu Santo,*
224 *Carmen,*
225 *Tiburn,*
226 *Angelos,*
227 *Margarita,*
228 *Cerros.*

PENINSULAS.
229 YUCATAN,
230 CALIFORNIA.

CAPES.
231 *Roxo,*
232 *Desconocida,*
233 CATOCHE,
234 SAN ANTONIO,
235 *Corrientes,*
236 *Palma,*
237 SAN LUCAS,
238 *San Lazaro,*
239 *Morro Hermoso.*

MOUNTAINS.
240 SIERRA MADRE,
241 POPOCATAPETL.

LAKES.
242 CHAPALA,
243 TERMINOS.

RIVERS.
244 *Santander,*
245 *Tula,*
246 *Usumacinta,*
247 BALSAS,
248 GRANDE,
249 YAQUI.

UNITED STATES.

QUESTIONS ON THE MAP OF THE UNITED STATES.

What country bounds the United States on the north? What ocean on the east? What gulf and country on the south? What ocean on the west? What is the latitude of the United States? What is its longitude?

How many states are there? Name them. How many territories are there? Name them. Bound each state. Give the capital of each. What states border on the Atlantic? On the Gulf of Mexico? On the Pacific? On the great lakes? What states lie west of the Mississippi? What states are separated by the Connecticut? Delaware? Potomac? Savannah? Chattahoochee? Sabine? Ohio? What states touch Lake Michigan?

What territories are bounded north by British America? What border on the Pacific? What territory is bounded by Mexico? What territory south of Oregon? West of Kansas? North of Texas?

GULFS AND BAYS.

What bays on the coast of Maine? 3, 4. What bay on the coast of Massachusetts? 5. South of Rhode Island? 6. What bays on the Atlantic coast south of Connecticut? 7-9. On the west coast of Florida? 10-14. What bay south of Alabama? 15. What bays on the coast of Texas? 16-18. On the Pacific coast? 21-24.

SOUNDS AND STRAITS.

What sound south of Connecticut? 26. What two sounds east of North Carolina? 27, 28.

What strait south of Florida? 29. North-west of Washington Territory? 30.

ISLANDS AND CAPES.

What islands south of Massachusetts? 31, 32. What island south of Connecticut? 33. What reefs south of Florida? 34. Which is the most important island of Florida reefs? Ans. Key West. What islands west of Florida reefs? 35.

What capes has New England? 37-39. What capes at the entrance to the Delaware bay? 40, 41. At the entrance to the Chesapeake? 42, 43. What five capes between Albemarle Sound and Florida reefs? 44-48. Which is the most southern cape of Florida? 49. What four capes on the Pacific coast of the United States? 52-55.

MOUNTAINS.

What mountain in Maine? 56. What mountains in New Hampshire? 57. In Vermont? 58. In New York? 59. What three parallel ranges in the eastern part of the United States? 60-62. What mountains in Missouri and Arkansas? 63. What is the most extensive range of mountains in the United States? 65. Mention the principal peaks. 66-69. What ranges near the Pacific coast? 71, 72. What range between the Coast Mountains and the Rocky Mountains? 70. Mention the principal peaks of the Cascade Mountains. 73-75.

LAKES.

What lakes between British America and the United States? 80, 83, 86-88. What lake between Michigan and Wisconsin? 81. What bay in the western part? 82. What lake between Vermont and New York? 89. What lakes in Maine? 90, 91. What lake in Florida? 92. In Louisiana? 93. In California? 94. What lakes in Utah? 97-99.—Which is the largest? 97.

RIVERS.

What river is the outlet to the Great American Lakes? 100. Which are the seven principal rivers in the New England States? 102-108. Into what do they flow? What river flows into New York Bay? 109. Into Delaware Bay? 111. What four rivers discharge their waters into the Chesapeake? 112-115. What two rivers flow into Albemarle Sound? 116, 117. What two rivers flow into Pamlico Sound? 118, 119.

What are the principal rivers flowing into the Atlantic between Pamlico Sound and Cape Sable? 120-122, 124, 125, 128, 129. What two rivers unite and form the Altamaha? 126, 127.

Which is the largest river flowing into the Gulf of Mexico? 130. Which are the principal rivers flowing into the Gulf of Mexico east of the Mississippi? 130, 131, 134, 137, 138. What large branches has the Apalachicola? 132, 133. What two rivers form the Mobile? 135, 136. Which are the largest eastern branches of the Mississippi? 140, 141, 155-158. What two rivers unite and form the Ohio? 148, 149. What are the main branches of the Ohio? 142-147, 150-153. What are the principal western branches of the Mississippi? 159-162, 175-177, 179. Where does the Missouri rise? What are its main branches? 163-166, 168, 171, 174. Which is the principal branch of the Arkansas? 178. What river between the United States and Mexico? 187. Which are the principal rivers flowing into the Gulf of Mexico between the Rio Grande and the Mississippi? 181-186.

What river from the United States flows into the Gulf of California? 189. What is its principal eastern branch? 190. Which are the principal rivers in California? 194, 195-197. What river in Oregon flows into the Pacific? 198. Which are the two largest branches of the Columbia? 200, 202. What branch has Lewis River? 201. What rivers of Michigan flow into Lake Michigan? 206, 207. What river connects Lake Superior with Lake Huron? Ans. St. Mary's. What rivers between Lake Huron and Lake Erie? 208, 209. What river connects Lake Erie with Lake Ontario? 211. What falls upon it? Ans. Niagara Falls.

QUESTIONS ON MEXICO AND THE WEST INDIES.

What country north of Mexico? What body of water on the east? What Ocean on the south and west? What states of Mexico are bounded north by the United States? Which border on the Gulf of Mexico? What state on the Caribbean Sea? What states border on the Pacific Ocean? What on the Gulf of California? Which is the most south-eastern state? Which is the most north-western? Which states have no sea coast?

What parallel of latitude crosses the northern part of Mexico? What is the latitude of the bay of Tehuantepec? What is the latitude of Cuba? Hayti? What states of Mexico are crossed by the Tropic of Cancer? In what zones is Mexico? In what zone is Cuba? Between what degrees of longitude is Mexico? Cuba? Hayti?

BAYS AND GULFS.

What bay west of Yucatan? 212. What bay on the coast south of Balize? 213. What bay west of Mexico? 21.

What gulf on the southern coast of Mexico? 214.

ISLANDS, CAPES AND MOUNTAINS.

Which is the largest of the West India Islands? 216. What group north-east of it? 215. What large island south-east? 218. What two islands south? 217, 219. What two clusters of islands west of Mexico? 221, 222. What islands in the Gulf of California? 223-226. What islands west of California? 227, 228.

What cape at the north-eastern extremity of Yucatan? 233. What cape west of Yucatan? 232. West of Cuba? 234. West of Mexico? 235. At the southern point of California? 237. What two capes on the western coast of California? 238, 239.

What range of mountains in Mexico? 240. What is the principal volcano? 241.

LAKES AND RIVERS.

What lake in the southern part of Yucatan? 243. What lake near the center of Mexico? 242.

What river between Mexico and the United States? 187. What rivers flow into the Gulf of Mexico? 244-246. What into the Pacific? 247, 248. What into the Gulf of California? 249.

UNITED STATES.

THE CAPITOL AT WASHINGTON.

DESCRIPTIVE GEOGRAPHY.

4. UNITED STATES.

Square miles, 3,000,000. Population, 31,600,000.

THE UNITED STATES comprise a large territory extending from the Atlantic to the Pacific Ocean, and occupying the central portion of North America.

It has a shore line of over 12,600 miles on the Atlantic and Pacific oceans and the Gulf of Mexico.

It may be divided physically into the Northern Lake region, the Atlantic slope, the Gulf region, the Pacific slope, and the Mississippi valley.

It is well watered by numerous large rivers and lakes. Two long ranges of mountains traverse it, between which stretches the great valley of the Mississippi river and its branches.

It possesses a healthful climate, fertile soil, unrivaled facilities for internal navigation, and is one of the most productive countries in the world.

The chief articles of cultivation are Indian corn, wheat, potatoes, oats, rye, cotton, rice, tobacco, and a great variety of fruits.

The most useful minerals abound, such as gold, iron, copper, lead, coal, and lime. There are also quarries of granite, marble, freestone, and slate.

The manufactures are very extensive, embracing a great variety of useful articles. Its commerce extends to all parts of the globe, and is second only to that of Great Britain.

No other nation has so many steam and canal boats traversing its waters, or so many miles of telegraph lines and railroad, either finished, or in course of construction.

UNITED STATES.

The inhabitants of the United States are chiefly of English descent. Some are of Dutch, Irish, and French extraction; and about four millions are of the African race, residing mainly in the southern part.

The people are distinguished for industry, enterprise and intelligence. Schools and colleges are very numerous, and there are few who may not enjoy the means of education.

The prevailing religion is the Protestant, though all sects are tolerated by law.

The government of the United States is a Federal Republic. Each State is independent in its local affairs, and chooses its own officers, but the defence of the country, matters relating to foreign commerce and the general concerns of the nation, are committed by the constitution to the General Government.

The laws are made by Congress, which is composed of a Senate and House of Representatives. The Senate consists of two members from each state, chosen for six years. The representatives are chosen by the people for two years. The President and Vice-President are elected for four years.

In the organized territories, the people choose a legislature to make laws, but the governor is appointed by the President.

The first settlement in the United States was made by the French, in Florida, in 1565; the second, by the English, in Virginia, in 1607.

The colonies were subject to Great Britain till 1776, when the colonists declared themselves free and independent.

The war of the revolution continued seven years, and closed in 1783, when Great Britain acknowledged the independence of the United States.

The states are divided into the Eastern, Middle, Southern, and Western States.

EASTERN STATES.

1 Maine,	4 Massachusetts,
2 New Hampshire,	5 Rhode Island,
3 Vermont,	6 Connecticut.

MIDDLE STATES.

7 New York,	9 Pennsylvania,
8 New Jersey,	10 Delaware.

SOUTHERN STATES.

11 Maryland,	16 Georgia,
12 Dist. of Colum-	17 Florida,
13 Virginia, [bia,	18 Alabama,
13½ West Virginia,	19 Mississippi,
14 North Carolina,	20 Louisiana,
15 South Carolina,	21 Texas.

WESTERN STATES.

22 Arkansas,	29 Michigan,
23 Missouri,	30 Wisconsin,
24 Tennessee,	31 Iowa,
25 Kentucky,	32 California,
26 Ohio,	33 Minnesota,
27 Indiana,	35 Kansas,
28 Illinois,	39 Oregon.

TERRITORIES.

34 Nebraska,	41 Dakota,
36 Indian,	42 Colorado,
37 New Mexico,	43 Nevada,
38 Utah,	44 Arizona.
40 Washington,	45 Idaho.

QUESTIONS. What do the United States comprise? Describe the divisions. Surface. Climate. Soil, &c. What are the chief vegetable productions? Most useful minerals? What can you say of the manufactures and commerce? Steam and canal boats? Telegraph lines and railroads? What is said of the inhabitants? For what are they distinguished? What

UNITED STATES. 51

THE EASTERN STATES.

is said of education? What is the prevailing religion? What is the government? By whom are the laws made? Who compose the senate? How are the representatives chosen? For how long are the president and vice-president elected? How are the organized territories governed? Where and when were the earliest settlements made? When were the colonies declared independent? How long did the revolutionary war continue? Name the Eastern States. Middle. Southern. Western. The territories.

EASTERN, OR NEW ENGLAND STATES.

THE EASTERN OR NEW ENGLAND STATES include Maine, New Hampshire, Vermont, Massachusetts, Rhode Island, and Connecticut, and occupy the north-east portion of the United States.

They were originally settled by the Puritans, at Plymouth, in 1620.

New England is agreeably diversified in surface, has a variable but healthful climate, and has long been distinguished for the intelligence, industry and enterprise of its citizens.

QUESTIONS. How are the Eastern or New England States situated? By whom and when were they settled? What is said of the surface, climate, and people?

1. MAINE.

Square miles, 31,766. Population, 628,000.

Maine, the largest of the New England states, has in general a level or undulating surface, a productive soil, and cold climate.

It abounds with beautiful forests, lakes, and rivers, and its coast is bordered with numerous bays and islands.

Agriculture and lumbering are the leading pursuits, but many of its inhabitants are engaged in manufactures, ship building and fishing. The principal products are grass, Indian corn, rye, oats, barley, potatoes, butter, cheese, maple sugar, and honey.

Large quantities of lumber, lime, hay, and fish, are exported.

AUGUSTA, the capital, is situated on the Kennebec river, fifty miles from its mouth. *Portland* is the largest city in the state. It is built on an elevated site, has a good harbor, and considerable commerce. *Eastport*, on the Passamaquoddy bay, is a place of some trade. Its harbor is remarkable for high tides. *Bangor* is a very flourishing city upon the Penobscot river, and noted for its lumber. *Bath*, on the Kennebec, is well built and enjoys superior advantages for navigation, as the river here is seldom frozen in winter.

QUESTIONS. Describe the surface, soil and climate of Maine. With what does it abound? Mention the chief pursuits of the people. Productions. The exports. What is said of Augusta? Portland? Eastport? Bangor? Bath?

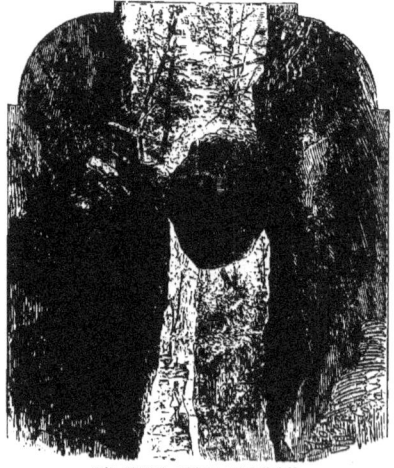

THE FLUME, WHITE MOUNTAINS.

2. NEW HAMPSHIRE.

Square miles, 9,280. Population, 326,000.

New Hampshire has a hilly, and in some portions, a mountainous surface.

The climate is very healthful, and the soil varied, but generally better adapted to grazing than to cultivation.

It has only eighteen miles of sea coast, and but little commerce. Agriculture and manufactures are the principal employments of the people.

The staple productions are wheat, rye, oats, Indian corn, barley, butter, cheese, and maple sugar.

CONCORD, the capital of the state, is a flourishing town, located on the Merrimac river about sixty miles from Boston.

Portsmouth is situated on both sides of the Piscataqua river, three miles from the Atlantic coast, and is the only seaport in the state. It has a fine harbor, a large navy yard, and some commerce. *Manchester*, on the Merrimac river, is the most important city in the state, and is noted for its manufactures. *Nashua* is an important manufacturing town.

QUESTIONS. What can you say of the surface of New Hampshire? Its climate and soil? Sea coast? Employments of the people? Productions? What is said of Concord? Portsmouth? Manchester? Nashua?

3. VERMONT.

Square miles, 10,212. Population, 315,000.

Vermont takes its name from the Green Mountains, which render its surface broken and hilly.

The climate is cold and changeable, but healthful. The soil is rich, affording good tillage and grazing.

This state produces the various grains, potatoes, maple sugar, butter, cheese, and large quantities of wool. Iron ore is abundant and there are extensive quarries of marble.

It has no sea-coast, and its inhabitants are principally engaged in agriculture.

MONTPELIER, situated on the Onion river, is the capital of the state, and a very pleasant town.

Burlington has a beautiful site on the east shore of lake Champlain, commanding a fine prospect. It is the largest town in the state, and is the seat of the University of Vermont.

Brattleboro was the first town settled in Vermont. It has several manufactories.

QUESTIONS. What is the surface of Vermont? Climate and soil? Productions? What is the chief pursuit? Describe Montpelier. Burlington. Brattleboro.

4. MASSACHUSETTS.

Square miles, 7,800. Population, 1,231,000.

Massachusetts is generally level, or slightly uneven in the eastern part; the interior and western portions are hilly and rugged.

The climate resembles that of the other Eastern States, though the coast is subject to cold easterly winds.

The soil is light in the eastern portion and rather sandy; in the middle and western parts more fertile. The farms are highly cultivated, and produce wheat, Indian corn, rye, oats, fruits, butter, and cheese.

Manufactures and commerce chiefly engage the attention of its inhabitants. In cotton and woolen manufactures, Massachusetts is the first state in the Union.

The whale, cod and other fisheries are very valuable.

Massachusetts is also distinguished for the number and excellence of her public schools.

BOSTON is the largest city in New England. It is situated at the head of Massachusetts Bay, and is noted for the wealth and refinement of its citizens, and its numerous scientific and literary institutions. It has a variety of manufactures, and an extensive commerce. The city has many fine buildings.

MANUFACTURES.

Charlestown is situated on a peninsula immediately north of Boston. It contains the Bunker Hill monument, and the United States Navy yard, which occupies an area of more than seventy acres. *Lowell*, on the Merrimac river, is an important manufacturing city. Cotton and woolen goods are produced in great quantities. *Springfield* is one of the most important commercial cities on the Connecticut river. *Worcester*, *Lawrence* and *Lynn* are important manufacturing places. *Salem* holds a high rank as a commercial city. *New*

Bedford is extensively engaged in the whale fishery.

QUESTIONS. Describe the surface of Massachusetts. What is said of its climate? Soil? Productions? Manufactures and commerce? Fisheries? Public schools? Boston? Charlestown? Lowell? Springfield? Worcester, Lawrence and Lynn? Salem and New Bedford?

5. RHODE ISLAND.

Square miles, 1,306. Population, 174,000.

Rhode Island, in extent of territory, is the smallest state in the Union.

The surface is undulating; the soil, fertile on the coast, but barren in the interior, and the climate agreeable.

The productions are grains, fruits, butter and cheese.

This state is largely engaged in manufactures. It has considerable commerce.

PROVIDENCE, one of the capitals, is located on Providence river, and is the seat of Brown University. It has a great variety of manufactures and considerable commerce.

NEWPORT, the other capital, is built on the island of Rhode Island, which lies in Narragansett Bay. This island is a place of great resort in the summer season.

QUESTIONS. What is said of the comparative size of Rhode Island? Surface and soil? Productions? Manufactures? Commerce? Describe Providence. Where is Newport situated?

6. CONNECTICUT.

Square miles, 4,674. Population, 460,000.

Connecticut is, in general, undulating or hilly; the climate is agreeable, and the soil fertile, especially in the valley of the Connecticut River.

Large quantities of grass, potatoes, corn, butter, and cheese, are produced. There are several extensive quarries of granite and freestone. There are also mines of silver, lead, copper and iron.

Its inhabitants are chiefly engaged in agriculture and manufactures.

HARTFORD is situated on the west bank of the Connecticut river, fifty-three miles from its mouth. It is advantageously situated for trade and commerce, and largely engaged in manufactures. It contains Trinity College, the American Asylum for the Deaf and Dumb, a Retreat for the Insane, and a Hospital.

NEW HAVEN is situated at the head of New Haven Bay. It is noted for its literary and educational institutions, of which Yale College is the most important. It is extensively engaged in manufactures and has considerable commerce.

FREE ACADEMY, NORWICH.

New London has a commodious harbor, and is largely engaged in the whale fisheries. *Norwich, Middletown, Bridgeport* and *Waterbury* are the remaining cities.

QUESTIONS. Describe the surface, soil and climate of Connecticut. What are its productions? Mines? Principal employments of its inhabitants? Describe Hartford. New Haven. New London.

UNITED STATES.

NEW YORK CITY.

MIDDLE STATES.

THE MIDDLE STATES are situated south-west of New England. They embrace New York, New Jersey, Pennsylvania and Delaware; and comprise a great variety of surface, climate and soil.

This section is diversified by high and broken ranges of mountains, and numerous rivers and lakes.

The Alleghany is the principal range of mountains. The chief rivers are the Hudson, Delaware, Susquehanna and St. Lawrence.

The Middle States possess superior facilities for commerce and trade. The eastern portion borders New England and the Atlantic, and the north-western, the great lakes, while the interior is traversed by numerous railroads and canals.

QUESTIONS. How are the Middle States situated? Name them. What do they comprise? How are they diversified? What is said of commerce and trade?

7. NEW YORK.

Square miles, 47,000. Population, 3,880,000.

New York is the most wealthy and populous of the United States; hence it is called the "Empire State."

The eastern and northern parts are hilly and mountainous; the western portion spreads out in table-lands, rising from Lake Ontario.

The mountainous sections have a light soil; the more level are usually very rich and fertile.

The climate is healthful, but cold in the northern part. Agriculture is the chief pursuit.

The commerce is larger than that of any other state and extends to all parts of the world, and the manufactures are extensive and constantly increasing.

Wheat is the staple production. Indian corn, and other grains, with potatoes, apples, pears, peaches, maple-sugar, butter, cheese, beeswax, and honey, are the other principal products.

Iron, lead, limestone, and salt springs, abound; also mineral springs, the most noted of which are those at Saratoga, Ballston and Avon.

The natural curiosities of this state are on a grand scale. Among them are the Falls of Niagara, on the Niagara river, which are nearly three quarters of a mile wide, and one hundred and sixty feet high.

Two miles below the cataract, the river is spanned by a magnificent suspension bridge eight hundred feet long, and two hundred and thirty feet above the water, supported by four wire cables, nine and one-fourth inches in diameter.

New York is distinguished for her great commercial advantages, and for her common schools and other educational institutions.

ALBANY, the capital, is situated on the Hudson river, and has a very large inland trade. The Erie Canal here unites with the Hudson. Great numbers of steamboats ply between this city and New York.

New York City, situated on Manhattan island, is the largest and most important city in America, and is the center of trade for the Western Continent. In the extent of its commerce and the amount of its manufactures, it exceeds every other city in the New World. It has many costly and elegant buildings, and numerous literary and benevolent institutions. Broadway, its principal street, and one of the finest to be seen in any city, is eighty feet wide and about three miles in length. The city is supplied with water by means of the Croton aqueduct, which is more than forty miles long.

Brooklyn is on the western extremity of Long Island, opposite New York City, and is extensively engaged in commerce. It contains many fine buildings, and a large Navy Yard. *Buffalo*, on Lake Erie, carries on an extensive trade with the West. Its manufactures are important. It is largely engaged in the converting of wheat into flour. Its principal public buildings are a Court House, Jail, Market House, and several fine churches. *Rochester* is remarkable for its extensive manufacture of flour. *Syracuse* is noted as the seat of the most valuable salt manufactures in the United States. *Troy*, situated on both sides of the Hudson river at the head of steamboat navigation, contains numerous manufactories and has important facilities for commerce.

QUESTIONS. What rank has New York? Describe its surface. Soil. Climate. What is said of agriculture? Commerce and manufactures? Productions? Minerals and springs? Natural curiosities? Suspension bridge? For what is New York distinguished? Describe Albany. New York City. Brooklyn. Buffalo. Rochester. Syracuse. Troy.

---

8. NEW JERSEY.

Square miles, 8,320. Population, 672,000.

New Jersey is hilly in the northern part; in the southern, quite level.

Its climate is mild, and the soil productive, except in the southern portion of the state, where it is sandy.

The inhabitants are chiefly employed in agriculture and the raising of fruit. The finest apples, peaches and garden vegetables, are sent to New York, Philadelphia, and other markets.

New Jersey is extensively engaged in manufactures. Its commerce is small.

It has also valuable shad and oyster fisheries.

Iron ore and zinc are found abundantly in some portions of the state.

Education is receiving increasing attention.

TRENTON, the capital, is situated at the head of tide water on the Delaware river. It is a pleasant city, and the place where General Washington captured the Hessians in 1776.

Newark is the largest city in the state, and largely engaged in manufactures. It is ten miles west of New York City. *Paterson*, at the Passaic Falls, is also a very flourishing manufacturing town.

QUESTIONS. What is said of the surface of New Jersey? Its climate? Soil? Productions? Manufactures? Commerce? Its fisheries? Minerals? Describe Trenton. Newark. Paterson.

---

9. PENNSYLVANIA.

Square miles, 46,000. Population, 2,906,000.

Pennsylvania is a large and important state, distinguished for its mineral resources, manufactures, and internal improvements.

Its eastern section is level or undulating, with a fertile soil and mild climate; the middle is mountainous, and subject to extremes of heat and cold; and the western, hilly, but productive and agreeable.

The people are largely interested in agriculture, manufactures and mining. Wheat, Indian corn, orchard fruits, potatoes, butter, and wool, are the chief products. The farms are generally large and well conducted.

The manufactures are very extensive, and comprise a great variety of articles. In the production of coal and iron, Pennsylvania surpasses any other state in the Union.

Canals and railroads are numerous, greatly increasing the facilities of trade.

This state was settled in 1681, by William Penn, a Quaker, whose kind and liberal treatment of the Indians secured peace to the settlers for seventy years.

HARRISBURG, the capital, is pleasantly located on the Susquehanna river.

MERCHANTS' EXCHANGE, PHILADELPHIA.

Philadelphia, on the west bank of the Delaware river, is, in size, the second city of the United States. It is laid out in squares, is remarkably neat, and is extensively engaged in trade, manufactures and commerce. Many of the public buildings are elegant. It has a mint for coining money, and a Navy Yard. Philadelphia is supplied with water by the Fairmount water-works, which convey the water of the Schuylkill river through the city in iron pipes.

Erie has one of the largest and best harbors on the lake. *Lancaster* is situated in the midst of a populous agricultural district, and has considerable trade. *Pittsburg* is a very flourishing manufacturing town, at the junction of the Alleghany and Monongahela rivers, and has a large inland trade. From its extensive manufactures of iron, it is called the "Birmingham of America." *Pottsville*

UNITED STATES.

THE SOUTHERN STATES.

and *Wilkesbarre* are situated in a coal region.

QUESTIONS. Describe Pennsylvania. What is said of the surface, soil, and climate? Of the pursuits? Productions? Manufactures? Minerals? Canals and railroads? By whom was Pennsylvania settled? What can you say of Harrisburg? Philadelphia? Erie? Lancaster? Pittsburg? Pottsville and Wilkesbarre?

10. DELAWARE.

Square miles, 2,120.   Population, 112,000.

Delaware is the smallest state in the Union except Rhode Island.

It is generally level. Its soil is fertile in the northern part, but sandy in the central and southern portions.

The climate resembles that of New Jersey. The principal pursuits are agriculture and manufactures.

Wheat is the staple production. Apples and peaches are raised in great abundance, and of a fine quality.

DOVER, the capital of the state, is situated on Jones' Creek.

Wilmington, its largest city, is located near the junction of Christiana and Brandywine Creeks. It has considerable commerce, and is engaged extensively in manufactures.

QUESTIONS. How does Delaware compare with the other states in size? What is its surface and soil? Its climate? What are the chief pursuits? Productions? Describe Dover. Wilmington.

SOUTHERN STATES.

THE SOUTHERN STATES are Maryland, Virginia, North Carolina, South Carolina, Georgia, Florida, Alabama, Mississippi, Louisiana, and Texas.

They extend along the Atlantic Ocean and the Gulf of Mexico from Delaware Bay to the Rio Grande.

The coast is level and sandy; the interior is undulating and more fertile. The Alleghany mountains extend through the western portions of Virginia and North and South Carolina.

The inhabitants are mostly of English and French descent.

QUESTIONS. Name the Southern States. What is said of their extent? Describe their surface and soil. What is said of the inhabitants?

11. MARYLAND.

Square miles, 11,124. Population, 687,000.

Maryland comprises a small, well watered country lying on the shores of the Chesapeake bay which divides the state into two parts.

The shores are level, warm, and in summer, unhealthy. The western portion is hilly, and the climate agreeable.

The soil is productive and well adapted to the cultivation of grain and fruits. Wheat and tobacco are raised in large quantities. Indian corn is an important product.

Iron and coal are its most important minerals. Coal is chiefly found in the western part.

Agriculture and commerce are the principal pursuits of the people.

This state was colonized by English Catholics under Lord Baltimore, in 1632. Under his wise administration the colony was very prosperous.

ANNAPOLIS, the seat of government, is situated three miles from Chesapeake bay on the river Severn.

Baltimore is situated on a branch of the Patapsco river, and is the largest city in the state. It has an extensive commerce, and a large trade in flour and tobacco. From the number and elegance of its monuments, it is called the "Monumental city." *Easton* and *Cumberland* are places of some importance. The latter has an extensive trade and several large flouring mills.

QUESTIONS. What does Maryland comprise? Describe its surface and climate. Soil. What are its principal productions? Minerals? Pursuits? By whom was it colonized? What is said of Annapolis? Baltimore? Easton and Cumberland?

12. DISTRICT OF COLUMBIA.

Square miles, 60. Population, 75,000.

The District of Columbia lies on the east bank of the Potomac, one hundred and fifty miles from its mouth, and belongs to the United States.

NOTE. It formerly embraced a tract ten miles square, lying on both sides of the Potomac, and ceded by the states of Maryland and Virginia. The Virginia portion has been ceded back.

SMITHSONIAN INSTITUTION.

WASHINGTON CITY, the capital of the nation, is located here. It was laid out under the direction of General Washington, whose name it bears, and became the seat of government in the year 1800. It contains the Capitol, President's House, General Post Office, Patent Office, and other public buildings.

The Capitol is built of white freestone and marble in the form of a cross. It is a magnificent building, surmounted with domes, and contains the Senate Chamber and Representatives' Hall.

The President's House is also a handsome building of white freestone. It is situated on an eminence about a mile and a half west of the Capitol, and is surrounded by beautiful grounds.

South-west from the Capitol, on a gently rising ground, stands the Smithsonian Institution. It is a noble structure, four hundred and fifty feet long, and built of red sandstone, in the Norman style.

QUESTIONS. Describe the District of Columbia. Washington City. What can you say of the Capitol? The President's House? Smithsonian Institution?

13. VIRGINIA.

Square miles, 38,400. Population, 1,164,300.

Virginia is low and level in the eastern part; the interior and northern parts are hilly and mountainous.

The climate is warm in the lowlands, but mild and healthful in the elevated portions of the state.

The soil is fertile in the valleys, but barren on the mountains.

Tobacco, Indian corn, wheat, and potatoes, are the chief productions.

Gold, iron, lead, copper, and coal, are found; there are also noted mineral springs.

The Natural Bridge, over Cedar Creek, is a solid rock covered with earth and trees, and crosses a chasm two hundred feet deep and sixty feet wide.

RICHMOND, the capital of the state, has a fine site on the James river, one hundred and ten miles from the Chesapeake bay.

Norfolk, on the river Elizabeth, has a very commodious harbor. It is the chief seaport of Virginia.

Petersburg, on the Appomattox, is well situated for trade.

QUESTIONS. What is the surface of Virginia? Climate? Soil? What are the productions? Minerals? Describe the Natural Bridge. Richmond. Norfolk. Petersburg.

13½. WEST VIRGINIA.

Square miles, 22,950. Population, 348,192.

West Virginia is mostly hilly and broken in surface.

The climate is temperate and healthful. The soil is very fertile in the western parts.

The chief agricultural productions are Indian corn, wheat and tobacco. Large numbers of cattle and hogs are fattened for market.

The minerals are coal, iron and salt.

This state was incorporated by act of Congress in December, 1862.

WHEELING, on the Ohio river, has a large trade and extensive manufactures. The hills in the vicinity contain inexhaustible beds of coal.

QUESTIONS. What is the surface of West Virginia? Climate? Soil? What is said of the productions? Minerals? When incorporated? Describe Wheeling.

14. NORTH CAROLINA.

Square miles, 50,704. Population, 992,000.

North Carolina is level and sandy in the eastern part. The sea-coast abounds with swamps, and is bordered by sand bars.

The interior is undulating and productive. The western portion is a broad table land which rises into the Alleghany mountains.

Near the coast the climate is hot, but the elevated portions are cooler and more salubrious.

The chief articles of cultivation are Indian corn, tobacco, sweet potatoes, wheat, oats, cotton, and rice. Its forests furnish large quantities of lumber, turpentine, tar, and rosin.

It has valuable gold mines which are extensively wrought. Iron, copper and coal, are also found.

TURPENTINE DISTILLERY.

Rice, cotton, and naval stores, are the principal exports.

RALEIGH, the capital, has an elevated and healthful situation, and is laid out with great regularity. It contains a fine State House built of granite after the model of the Parthenon.

Wilmington is the largest town in the state. It is located on the Cape Fear river, thirty-five miles from its mouth, and has considerable commerce. *Newbern* and *Fayetteville* are also towns of considerable trade and commerce.

QUESTIONS. What is the surface and soil of the eastern part of North Carolina? Of its interior? Western part? What is the climate? What are the chief productions? What can you say of its gold mines? Other minerals? Exports? Raleigh? Wilmington? Newbern and Fayetteville?

15. SOUTH CAROLINA.

Square miles, 29,385. Population, 703,000.

South Carolina is level and marshy upon the sea-coast. The interior and western portions are undulating.

The soil is in many places sandy and unproductive, but much of it is rich and fertile, especially on the banks of the rivers.

In the lowlands the climate is moist and unhealthful,—in the elevated districts, it is more temperate and agreeable.

The inhabitants are mostly farmers or planters. Cotton, rice, Indian corn, sweet potatoes, wheat, oats, and tobacco, are the principal agricultural productions.

There are several islands along the coast of this state and Georgia, which produce the finest cotton, called "Sea Island Cotton."

The tropical fruits here begin to flourish, as oranges, lemons, figs, &c.

South Carolina has few manufactures, but considerable commerce. Its exports of cotton and rice are extensive.

COLUMBIA, its capital, is pleasantly situated. *Charleston*, at the junction of the Ashley and Cooper rivers, is handsomely built. It has been the principal sea-port of the state. *Camden*, on the Wateree river, is noted for the defeat of General Gates, by Lord Cornwallis, in the Revolutionary War. A battle was also fought here between the Americans under General Greene, and the British under Lord Rawdon. *Georgetown*, situated on Winyaw bay, is a place of some trade.

QUESTIONS. Describe the surface of South Carolina. Soil. Climate. What can you say of its productions? Fruits? Manufactures and commerce? Columbia? Charleston? Camden? Georgetown?

16. GEORGIA.

Square miles, 58,000. Population, 1,057,000.

Georgia is a large state, level on the coast, hilly in the interior, and mountainous in the north.

The Okefenokee Swamp extends from Florida into its southern part, and abounds with alligators and reptiles.

Cotton, rice, sweet potatoes, and Indian corn, are the chief articles of cultivation, but large quantities of wheat, oats, sugar, tobacco, and fruits, are produced.

The manufactures of Georgia are limited, but increasing in importance. Quite a number of railroads are in operation.

Considerable attention is paid to education.

GATHERING COTTON.

MILLEDGEVILLE, the capital of the state, is regularly laid out at the head of steamboat navigation on the Oconee river.

Savannah, is pleasantly located on a high bluff of the Savannah river, eighteen miles from its mouth, has considerable trade, and abounds with a flowering tree, called the "Pride of China." *Augusta* is a beautiful city, one hundred and seventy miles above Savannah, on the Savannah river. *Columbus*, *Macon*, *Darien*, and *Atlanta*, are also thriving towns.

QUESTIONS. What can you say of the size and general features of Georgia? What of the Okefenokee Swamp? Name the chief productions? What is said of manufactures and railroads? Of education? Describe Milledgeville. Savannah. Augusta. What other flourishing towns?

---

17. FLORIDA.

Square miles, 59,268. Population, 140,000.

Florida is a peninsula on the extreme south of the United States, approaching within a degree and a half of the Torrid Zone. The southern portion is covered with marshes and shallow lakes, and is called "The Everglades." The northern and central portions are mostly level. The soil is generally sandy, but productive in many parts. The chief products are cotton, sugar cane, rice, tobacco, Indian corn, and sweet potatoes.

Oranges, dates, figs, and other tropical fruits, abound, with a great variety of blossoming plants.

The forests yield abundantly cedar, and the live oak which is so much used in ship building.

The white inhabitants are chiefly confined to the northern portions of the state.

TALLAHASSEE, the capital, is situated on the Appalachee bay.

St. Augustine was the first town settled in the United States. It has a delightful climate, and is embosomed in orange trees. *Appalachicola*, on the river of the same name, and *Pensacola*, on Pensacola bay, are both thriving places, and have considerable trade. *Key West* is the most populous town in the state, and occupies an island of the same name, four miles long and a mile wide. It has a safe and capacious harbor, and its principal business is derived from salvages and other perquisites of wrecked vessels.

QUESTIONS. What can you say of the situation and surface of Florida? Of its soil? Productions? Of its fruits? Forests? Where do the whites reside? What is said of Tallahassee? St. Augustine? Appalachicola? Pensacola? Key West?

18. ALABAMA.

Square miles, 50,722. Population, 964,000.

Alabama is generally level, except in the northern part, where it is mountainous.

The soil for the most part is productive, and in many places very rich. The climate is quite warm in the southern portion of the state. Snow and ice are occasionally seen in the mountainous districts.

Agriculture principally engages the attention of its inhabitants. Cotton and Indian corn are the great staples. Wheat, oats, sweet potatoes, rice, and tobacco, are also raised.

It has some commerce and manufactures.

MONTGOMERY, the capital, is situated at the head of steamboat navigation on the Tuscaloosa river.

Mobile is the largest city in the state, and its principal seaport. It is pleasantly situated at the head of Mobile bay. *Tuscaloosa*, *Wetumpka* and *Huntsville*, are flourishing towns, possessing considerable trade.

QUESTIONS. What is said of the surface of Alabama? Soil and climate? What are the productions? What is said of commerce and manufactures? Of Montgomery? Mobile? Wetumpka, Tuscaloosa and Huntsville?

19. MISSISSIPPI.

Square miles, 47,156. Population, 791,000.

Mississippi slopes towards the south and west. The southern part is level; the central and northern portions are undulating, and diversified by occasional bluffs and ranges of hills. The western part of the state, upon the Mississippi river, is marshy.

PRODUCTIONS AND EXPORTS.

The climate is warm, and the soil generally rich and highly productive.

The inhabitants are chiefly devoted to the raising of cotton. Indian corn, rice and sugar, are also produced. Fruits, such as figs, peaches and bananas, are abundant.

The plantations of Mississippi are generally large, and often employ several hundred negro slaves each.

Its first settlers were of French descent, who founded the town of Natchez in 1716.

JACKSON is the capital of the state. It is pleasantly situated at the head of steamboat navigation on the Pearl river.

Natchez is one of the pleasantest cities in the western valley. It stands on a high bluff upon the Mississippi, three hundred feet above the surface of the river. Great numbers of steamboats stop here, and a large trade is carried on. *Vicksburg* has a very picturesque site, on the bank of the Mississippi river, the land rising in terraces from the river. *Columbus* is situated on the left bank of the Tombigbee river one hundred and eighty miles from Jackson. It is surrounded by an extensive planting district, and has an active business.

QUESTIONS. What is said of the surface of Mississippi? Climate? Soil? Productions? The plantations? First settlers? Describe Jackson. Natchez. Vicksburg. Columbus.

20. LOUISIANA.

Square miles, 41,255. Population, 708,000.

Louisiana is remarkably level, and abounds with swamps and pine forests, which render much of its surface unfit for cultivation.

The soil on either side of the Mississippi river is very fertile, producing large crops of cotton, sugar, rice, Indian corn, and tobacco. The tropical fruits are abundant.

SUGAR PRESS, FRUITS, CANE AND COTTON.

The climate, in summer, is excessively hot and often sickly. Agriculture is the leading pursuit, but commerce is very extensive and important.

Louisiana formerly belonged to the French, of whom it was purchased by the United States in 1803.

BATON ROUGE, the capital, is situated on the east bank of the Mississippi, one hundred and thirty-one miles above New Orleans. It stands on the first high bank which occurs in ascending the river, and is one of the healthiest towns in the southern portion of the Mississippi valley.

New Orleans is situated on the east side of the Mississippi river about one hundred miles from its mouth. When the river is high, the surface of the water is several feet above the streets of the city, and is kept from overflowing by levees. This city is the great emporium of the south-western and western states, and its harbor is constantly crowded with ships, steamboats and the various river craft of the West. Many of the public buildings and churches of New Orleans are large and costly structures. The custom house, when completed, will be the largest in the Southern States. The benevolent institutions are extensive and well conducted.

Natchitoches is pleasantly situated on Red river, about five hundred miles from New Orleans. It is a place of considerable trade, having regular steam communication with New Orleans. *Shreveport* is a thriving place on the right bank of the Red river, about six hundred and eighty miles by water above New Orleans. It is in the midst of an extensive planting region and advantageously situated for trade.

QUESTIONS. What can you say of the surface of Louisiana? Soil? Productions? Climate? Agriculture and Commerce? Of whom was this State purchased? Describe Baton Rouge. New Orleans. Natchitoches. Shreveport.

21. TEXAS.
Square miles, 237,504. Population, 604,000.

Texas is the largest of the United States in extent of territory. It embraces almost every variety of surface within its limits. It is level in the south-east, undulating in the interior, and mountainous in the west and north west. The Great American Plain extends sixty miles within the bounds of Texas on the north.

The climate is free from the extremes of both the torrid and temperate zones. The heats of summer are much mitigated by the winds which blow steadily from the Gulf of Mexico during that season.

The soil is varied, yet its general character is that of great fertility. Cotton, Indian corn and tobacco are the staple products. Sugar-cane is cultivated in the level country. Oranges, lemons and other fruits grow well. Cayenne pepper is raised in large quantities.

The minerals are gold, silver, salt, copper, and iron. An immense bed of gypsum traverses the north-west portion of the state.

Bisons, wild horses and cattle roam the prairies in large herds.

Texas formerly belonged to Mexico. It declared its independence in 1836, and in 1845 was annexed to the United States.

AUSTIN, the capital, is a flourishing town, situated on the Colorado. The river is navigable to this point during winter. The scenery around Austin is highly picturesque.

Galveston is situated on Galveston island, and is the principal seaport of Texas. It is rapidly increasing in population, and has considerable commerce. *Houston* is located on the Buffalo Bayou about two hundred miles from Austin. It is well situated for trade at the head of steam navigation, and is the principal shipping port for several adjacent counties. *Matagorda* is situated on a bay of the same name at the mouth of the Colorado River. It has considerable trade and is the depot for the produce of one of the richest valleys in the state. The sea-breeze renders this place a favorite summer residence of citizens from the interior.

QUESTIONS. What is said of the comparative size of Texas? Surface? Climate and soil? What are its productions? Minerals? What animals are found here? When was it annexed to the United States? Describe Austin. Galveston. Houston. Matagorda.

NOTE ON THE SOUTHERN STATES.

A portion of the country is at war against the government as this work goes to press, (August, 1862.)

The physical features of the states engaged will remain nearly the same, and any change which may take place in the political condition of the people will be noted in the appendix.

The commerce of the Southern States for the time, is nearly ceased. Means of communication with other nations or with the North, are nearly all cut off. The effects of the war on commerce, manufactures and agriculture, are seen in all the states, and must modify to some extent the descriptions given.

The following states claim to have seceded from the Union:

ALABAMA,	MISSOURI,
ARKANSAS,	NORTH CAROLINA,
FLORIDA,	SOUTH CAROLINA,
GEORGIA,	TENNESSEE,
LOUISIANA,	TEXAS,
MISSISSIPPI,	VIRGINIA.

These states claim to have united under the title of "The Confederate States of America." Their Congress was first held in Montgomery, and afterward removed to Richmond.

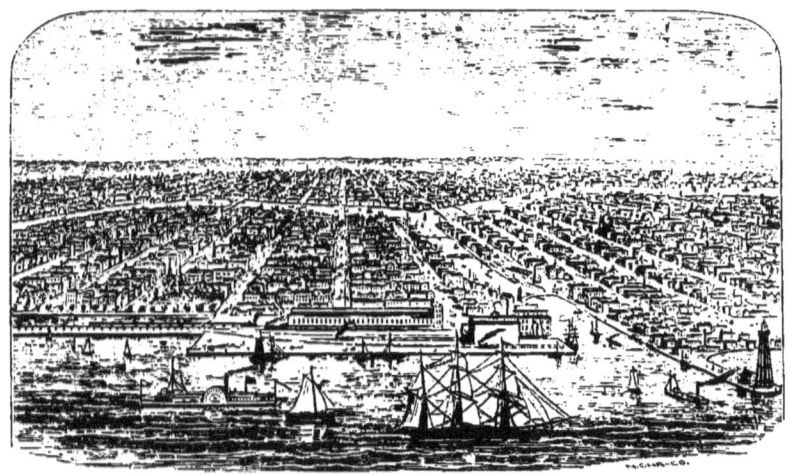

CHICAGO, ILL.

WESTERN STATES.

The Western States are Ohio, Michigan, Indiana, Illinois, Kentucky, Tennessee, Arkansas, Missouri, Iowa, Wisconsin, Minnesota, Kansas, Oregon, and California.

They comprise the greater portion of the valley of the Mississippi and its branches, and abound with extensive forests, vast prairies and majestic rivers. Two of these States lie on the Pacific.

The climate is warmer than in states of the same latitude on the Atlantic coast.

The Western States are rapidly filling up with emigrants from Europe and the older States.

In some of the Western States, a great interest is manifested in the cause of education. Large appropriations have been made for instruction in public schools, and these schools have very much improved.

Colleges and seminaries of learning have been established in important places.

QUESTIONS. Name the Western States. What do they comprise? What is their climate? What is said of emigrants? Education?

22. ARKANSAS.

Square miles, 52,198. Population, 435,000.

Arkansas is marshy in the eastern part, and subject to inundations. The remaining parts are elevated and broken. In the low lands, the climate is unhealthful; in the elevated districts, salubrious.

Near the rivers the soil is generally fertile. Remote from them, it is sterile.

The chief productions are live stock, Indian corn, cotton, wheat, oats, tobacco, and sweet potatoes. It also produces fine fruits.

There are numerous hot springs about fifty miles west of Little Rock, which are much resorted to by invalids. There is a fine cold spring so near one of these warm springs that a person can put one hand into hot and the other into cold water at the same time.

LITTLE ROCK, on the Arkansas river, is the capital and most important town of the state.

Van Buren, on the Arkansas River, is a place of extensive commercial business and some manufactures.

QUESTIONS. What is said of the surface of Arkansas? Climate? Soil? Productions? Describe the springs. Little Rock. Van Buren.

23. MISSOURI.

Square miles, 67,380. Population, 1,182,000.

Missouri is agreeably diversified in surface; the climate is subject to extremes of heat and cold; and the soil is, in general, very productive.

Agriculture and mining are the leading pursuits. The chief productions are Indian corn, wheat, hemp, flax, tobacco, oats, potatoes, butter, and cheese. Great numbers of cattle are reared.

Missouri abounds in mineral treasures. There are several small mountains composed almost entirely of iron ore. Lead is very abundant; also coal, marble and freestone.

JEFFERSON CITY, the capital of the state, occupies a high and commanding position on a bluff of the Missouri River.

St. Louis, the largest city, is situated on the Mississippi river, and possesses great facilities for trade and commerce. It contains many elegant buildings, and is rapidly increasing in wealth and importance. *St. Charles*, near the junction of the Mississippi and Missouri rivers, has a pleasant location and considerable trade. *Independence* is the starting point in the trade with New Mexico and Utah.

QUESTIONS. Describe the surface, climate and soil of Missouri. What are the chief pursuits? Products? Minerals? Describe Jefferson City. St. Louis. St. Charles. Independence.

24. TENNESSEE.

Square miles, 45,600. Population, 1,109,000.

Tennessee is mountainous and rugged in the eastern part; in the western, level or undulating. It is divided by the Cumberland mountains into East and West Tennessee.

It has a mild, agreeable climate, and in general, a fertile soil. Agriculture is the leading pursuit. Cotton, tobacco and Indian corn, are the chief products. Oats, wheat and potatoes, are also cultivated.

Immense numbers of swine and mules are raised in the state.

Iron and coal are found in abundance.

This state also abounds with numerous caves, from which nitrous earth is obtained for the manufacture of saltpetre.

Fossil remains of gigantic antedeluvian animals have been discovered, particularly of the mastodon. Among the Enchanted mountains, so called, are found footprints of animals imbedded in limestone.

NASHVILLE has a pleasant site on the Cumberland river. It is the most wealthy and prosperous city of Tennessee, and is distinguished for its enterprising spirit, literary taste, and polished society.

Memphis, situated on the Mississippi river, is an important commercial town.

QUESTIONS. Describe the surface of Tennessee. Climate and soil. Name the chief pursuit. Productions. What is said of swine and mules? Minerals? Of caves? Fossils? Nashville? Memphis?

25. KENTUCKY.

Square miles, 37,680. Population, 1,155,000.

Kentucky is mountainous in the eastern part. Along the Ohio river it is hilly. The remaining portions are undulating or level.

It has an agreeable and healthful climate, and a very productive soil, adapted to the raising of various kinds of grain.

Wheat, Indian corn, hemp, flax, and tobacco, are the staple productions. Fruits of excellent quality abound. Horses and cattle are reared in great numbers.

Limestone and coal are common, and salt springs are numerous, around which the bones of the mastodon have been frequently found.

Agriculture is the main pursuit, although manufactures and commerce receive much attention.

MAMMOTH CAVE.

Kentucky abounds with numerous caves, of which the "Mammoth Cave" is the most stupendous one known in the world. It has been explored for more than fifteen miles, and contains numerous apartments, magnificent arches, and a navigable stream, abounding with eyeless fish.

Kentucky was settled in 1767, by the renowned Daniel Boone, and a few followers.

FRANKFORT, the seat of government, is beautifully situated on a plain that overlooks the Kentucky river.

Louisville, the largest city of the state, rises gradually from the Ohio river, on which it is situated. It has broad and regular streets, and is extensively engaged in commerce and manufactures. *Lexington* has a very pleasant site, and a number of excellent literary institutions.

QUESTIONS. What is said of the surface of Kentucky? Climate and soil? What are the chief productions? What is said of the minerals? Agriculture, manufactures and commerce? What wonderful cave has Kentucky? When was Kentucky settled, and by whom? Describe Frankfort. Louisville. Lexington.

26. OHIO.

Square miles, 39,964. Population, 2,339,000.

Ohio has no mountains, but the interior is elevated about one thousand feet above the level of the sea. From this, the surface slopes to Lake Erie and the Ohio river.

It has in general a fertile soil, and a mild climate.

Its chief products are wheat and Indian corn, though oats, rye, buckwheat, and tobacco, and the fruits of the Middle States, are raised in abundance. Butter, cheese, and maple-sugar, are produced to some extent. Large numbers of horses and cattle are sent to the eastern markets.

The great lakes, in connection with the rivers, canals and railroads of this state, afford abundant facilities for inland commerce and manufactures, both of which are in a very flourishing condition.

Iron and coal are found extensively.

The state has made very liberal appropriations for her public schools, both for instruction, and for libraries and apparatus.

Ohio was settled in 1788, but it grew very slowly till 1810. Since that time it has increased rapidly in wealth and population.

COLUMBUS, the capital of the state, is finely situated on the east bank of the River Scioto.

It is surrounded by a rich and populous country and is a place of active business.

STATE HOUSE, COLUMBUS.

The capitol is three hundred and eighty-four feet long, by one hundred and eighty-four wide, and is one of the finest buildings in the state. The other principal edifices are the Ohio Lunatic Asylum, Institution for the Blind, Asylum for Deaf and Dumb, and the Penitentiary.

Cincinnati, the largest city in the state, and the "Queen City" of the west, is situated on the Ohio, and rises by terraces from the river's brink. It has grown with great rapidity, and is distinguished for its wealth, and its literary institutions, as well as for its manufactures and trade. *Cleveland* is a beautiful city situated on Lake Erie, possessing great commercial facilities. It has one of the best harbors on the lake. *Sandusky*, situated on Sandusky bay, and *Toledo* on the Maumee river, are both flourishing cities engaged in the commerce of the lakes. *Dayton*, *Zanesville* and *Steubenville* are thriving places and largely engaged in manufactures. *Chilicothe* and *Lancaster* are also important towns.

QUESTIONS. What is said of the surface of Ohio? Soil and climate? Name the chief products. What is said of horses and cattle? Commerce and manufactures? Iron and coal? Of education? Its settlement and growth? Describe Columbus. Cincinnati. Cleveland. Sandusky and Toledo. What other important towns?

27. INDIANA.

Square miles, 33,809. Population, 1,350,000.

Indiana is generally level except in the south-west, which is broken and rocky.

The climate is mild, and the soil exceedingly fertile, especially on the river bottoms.

The inhabitants are principally devoted to agriculture, though the state possesses facilities for manufactures which have been to some extent improved.

Large quantities of Indian corn, wheat, oats, pork, and beef, are exported.

Copper, iron, and coal, are the chief minerals; salt springs are also found, and several interesting caves have been discovered and explored for many miles.

This state has an extensive school fund, and common schools are rapidly increasing.

INDIANAPOLIS, the seat of government, is pleasantly situated near the White river. It is the terminus of several railroads, which give it important facilities for trade. It has an elegant state-house and other public buildings.

New Albany is a flourishing city on the Ohio river, remarkable for its rapid growth and active trade. Steamboat building is carried on very extensively here. *Madison* is advantageously situated for trade, and has a considerable amount of capital employed in manufactures. *La Fayette* is pleasantly situated on the Wabash and is the principal grain market in the state.

QUESTIONS. What is said of the surface of Indiana? Climate and soil? Agriculture and manufactures? Exports? Minerals? Common schools? Indianapolis? New Albany? Madison? La Fayette?

28. ILLINOIS.

Square miles, 55,405. Population, 1,711,000.

Illinois is principally a table land, sloping to the south and west. In climate, soil and productions, it resembles Indiana.

Agriculture is the chief pursuit; and Indian corn, wheat and oats, with a variety of fruits and vegetables, are raised in the greatest abundance.

The prairies afford fine pasture for horses, cattle and sheep, which are reared in great numbers. A large number of hogs are fatted for market.

Lead, coal and iron abound. The lead mines of Galena are very profitable.

Illinois has made ample provision for education, and has an extended system of internal improvements.

SPRINGFIELD, the capital, is a flourishing town near the center of the state. It is surrounded by rich and extensive prairies, which contain large quantities of bituminous coal.

Chicago, on lake Michigan, is the largest city in the state. It has grown with remarkable rapidity, and is the center of a large and greatly increasing trade. It communicates, by means of the chain of lakes and railroads, with the Atlantic cities, and by the Illinois and Michigan canal and by railroads, with the country west and south.

Peoria is a flourishing city beautifully situated on the Illinois river, and has an extensive trade. *Alton*, *Quincy* and *Rock Island* on the Mississippi river, are rapidly increasing in population and importance. *Galena* is the center of mining operations for this state.

QUESTIONS. What can you say of the surface of Illinois? Climate and soil? Agriculture and products? Animals? Minerals? Education and internal improvements? Springfield? Chicago? Peoria? Alton, Quincy and Rock Island? Galena?

29. MICHIGAN.

Square miles, 56,243. Population, 749,000.

Michigan consists of two peninsulas, the northern lying between Lakes Superior and Michigan, and the southern between Lakes Huron, St. Clair and Erie, on the east, and Lake Michigan on the west.

The northern peninsula is rugged, and in some parts, mountainous. The southern consists of an extensive undulating plain seldom broken.

The northern part is cold, with a sterile soil. The southern is mild and very fertile. The staple products are wheat, Indian corn, oats, potatoes, butter, maple-sugar, wool, and live stock.

DETROIT, MICH.

The northern peninsula is very rich in copper. Iron, silver, lead, gypsum, and coal, are found.

Michigan has an efficient common school system, and is doing much for the interests of education.

LANSING, the capital, is situated on the Grand river, one hundred and fifty miles from Detroit.

UNITED STATES.

Detroit, the principal city of the state, is situated on the west bank of Detroit river. It has great advantages for trade and commerce. *Monroe*, on the river Raisin, is connected with the lake by a ship canal, and is the principal market for wheat products in this part of the state. *Ann Arbor, Adrian, Jackson, Kalamazoo, Grand Rapids*, and *Grand Haven*, are important thriving towns, engaged in manufactures and trade.

On the southern shores of Lake Superior are bluffs and precipices, towering to the height of three hundred feet, and overhanging the water. They are called the "Pictured Rocks," because the waters have by their ceaseless surges worn them into various forms of grace and beauty.

QUESTIONS. Of what does Michigan consist? Describe the surface of Michigan. Climate and soil. What are its staple products? Minerals? What is said of education? Describe Lansing. Detroit. Monroe. Other towns. The "Pictured Rocks."

30. WISCONSIN.

Square miles, 53,924. Population, 775,000.

Wisconsin has an undulating, and in some parts, a hilly surface, but no mountains.

Its southern portion has a mild climate, and very productive soil. The northern section is more sterile.

The chief productions are wheat, Indian corn, oats, potatoes, maple sugar, and live stock. Considerable quantities of rye, peas, barley, and buckwheat, are also raised.

It is rich in lead and iron. Copper, zinc, marble, and gypsum, are found to some extent.

Liberal appropriations have been made for the support of common schools.

MADISON, the capital, is pleasantly situated on an isthmus between Third and Fourth lakes. The capitol is a fine limestone structure, surrounded by a public square. The city is well situated for business, and possesses many attractions to those seeking health and pleasure.

Milwaukee is located on the shore of Lake Michigan. The general appearance of the city is peculiar and striking from the color and superior quality of the bricks used in building. They are of a delicate and enduring cream color which is highly agreeable to the eye. It is the center of trade for a rich and rapidly improving country. It has an extensive water power employed in various manufactures. Its commerce is rapidly increasing. *Racine*, situated on the west shore of Lake Michigan, has one of the best harbors on the lake. It is regularly laid out with wide streets, and contains a number of fine public buildings. *Green Bay, La Crosse, Janesville*, and *Fond du Lac*, are flourishing towns.

QUESTIONS. What is the surface of Wisconsin? Climate and soil? What are the chief productions? Minerals? What is said of common schools? Madison? Milwaukee? Racine? Green Bay, &c.?

31. IOWA.

Square miles, 50,914. Population, 675,000.

Iowa is generally composed of rolling prairies crossed by rivers whose banks are skirted with wood. A small portion in the north-east is rugged and rocky.

The soil is exceedingly fertile, the climate, agreeable and healthful. The staple productions are Indian corn, wheat and live stock.

Its lead mines are very rich. Coal, iron, copper, and limestone, abound.

Agriculture and mining are the leading pursuits.

DES MOINES, the capital, became the seat of government in 1857.

Dubuque is the central depot of the mining region of Iowa, and a place of active trade. *Davenport* is a flourishing city on the Mississippi at the foot of the upper rapids. *Muscatine, Burlington, Council Bluff,* and *Iowa City* are important towns.

QUESTIONS. What is said of the surface of Iowa? Soil? Climate? Productions? Minerals? Pursuits? Des Moines? Dubuque? Davenport? Other towns?

33. MINNESOTA.

Square miles, 75,000. Population, 172,000.

Minnesota abounds in lakes and ponds, and though there are no high mountains in the state, it is the most elevated tract of land between Hudson's Bay and the Gulf of Mexico, and from its central heights, sends its waters to every point of the compass.

FALLS OF ST. ANTHONY.

The climate is cold, especially in the Northern part. The soil is various, but generally fertile in the valleys of the rivers.

The agricultural productions are Indian corn, wheat and oats. Copper, lead and iron, are the principal minerals.

Its unsettled portions abound in wild animals, among which the buffalo, elk, deer, and antelope, are found.

ST. PAUL is a flourishing city situated on the Mississippi, nine miles below the falls of St. Anthony. It is at the head of steamboat navigation and a place of active business. Its growth has been rapid.

St. Anthony, situated at the Falls of St. Anthony, is an important place. It has an immense water power, which is being rapidly improved for manufacturing purposes.

QUESTIONS. What is said of Minnesota? Its Climate? Soil? Productions? Minerals? Animals? St. Paul? St. Anthony?

35. KANSAS.

Square miles, 114,798. Population, 107,000.

Kansas is a new state lying west of Missouri.

The eastern part of the state is level or gently undulating; the western is hilly, and sometimes mountainous.

It has numerous rivers. The Missouri forms its north-eastern boundary. The Kansas is the largest river principally within the territory, and is said to be navigable for 900 miles.

The eastern portion and the valleys of the principal rivers are unrivaled in fertility. Its productions are similar to those of Missouri.

It has valuable forest trees and timber, consisting of oak, hickory, ash, cottonwood, and sugar-maple, on the river bottoms, and cedar, pine, and poplar, on the slopes of the mountains.

Kansas was erected into a territory in 1854, and admitted as a state in 1861.

TOPEKA is the capital.

Leavenworth, Lecompton, and *Lawrence* are the principal towns.

QUESTIONS. How is Kansas situated? What is said of the surface? Its rivers? The soil? Productions? Forest trees? History? Towns

SAN FRANCISCO.

32. CALIFORNIA.

Square miles, 155,980. Population, 380,000.

California is the most western of the United States, and extends for seven hundred miles on the shores of the Pacific.

It has an undulating surface with numerous valleys, deep ravines and high mountains.

The climate is warm and dry in summer, and wet in winter.

In the valleys, the soil is very fertile. Barley, wheat, oats, potatoes, and fruits, are the chief products. In the southern parts, the fruits of tropical climates are produced.

The rich deposits of gold make this one of the most important mineral regions in the world. Quicksilver is found in abundance. Copper, silver and platina have been discovered in various places.

California was first colonized by the Spaniards. It became a province of Mexico, and was subject to revolutions and disturbances till by the treaty of peace of 1848, it became a part of the United States.

The discovery of gold in 1847, was the principal cause of the early rapid growth of California, which gained for it admission into the Union as a state, in 1850.

SACRAMENTO is situated on the Sacramento river about one hundred and twenty miles from the ocean, and is extensively engaged in trade. It is accessible for steamers and sailing vessels of a large size, at all seasons of the year. Its streets are well laid out, crossing each other at right angles.

San Francisco lies on the western side of a bay of the same name. It is regularly laid out, has a fine harbor, and considerable commerce. It is the natural market for the state, and one of the finest ports in the world. *Stockton*, near the San Joaquin river, is an important trading point for the southern mines, and *Marysville*, on the Feather river, for the northern mines.

QUESTIONS. How is California situated? What is said of its surface? Climate? Soil? Productions? Minerals? History? Describe Sacramento. San Francisco. Stockton and Marysville.

33. OREGON.

Square miles, 100,000. Population, 52,000.

Oregon lies north of California, on the Pacific Ocean. It is mostly hilly or mountainous. A part of it consists of elevated plateaus-

The climate is mild and healthy. The valleys are very productive. Wheat is the staple; but oats, barley, turnips, and most of the fruits of the Middle States flourish.

Gold and coal have been discovered in Oregon.

The forests abound with wild animals, such as deer, black and grizzly bears, elks, foxes, wolves, and antelopes, and the rivers are well stocked with fish.

SALEM, the capital, is pleasantly situated on the Willamette, in the midst of a fertile country.

CASCADES OF THE COLUMBIA.

Astoria, on the Columbia, ten miles from its mouth, is the principal port of entry. *Portland*, at the head of ship navigation, on the Willamette River, is the largest and most commercial town in Oregon.

QUESTIONS. Where is Oregon situated? What is said of the surface? Climate? Soil? Productions? Minerals? Animals? Salem? Astoria? Portland?

TERRITORIES.

THE TERRITORIES of the United States comprise that portion of the country not yet organized with state governments, and admitted into the confederacy as states. They are mostly thinly settled, or in a wild state.

A portion have territorial governments, and send delegates to Congress. Some of them are rapidly increasing in population and wealth, and will soon be organized as states, and admitted into the Union.

Questions. What constitutes the Territories? What is their condition?

34. NEBRASKA.

Square miles, 75,000   Population, 29,000.

Nebraska includes a large tract of country lying west of the Missouri River, and north of Kansas.

The surface is principally a high prairie land. The climate is mild, and the soil, fertile, especially in the river bottoms.

The timber trees are black walnut, oak, and lime trees.

The principal wild animals are grizzly bears, buffaloes and beavers.

A great number of fossils have been found in this territory.

OMAHA CITY is pleasantly situated on the west bank of the Missouri River.

QUESTIONS. What does Nebraska include? What is said of its surface? Climate? Soil? Timber trees? Wild Animals? Fossils? Omaha City?

36. INDIAN TERRITORY.

Square miles, 71,000.

Indian Territory lies west of Arkansas, between Kansas and Texas.

It is inhabited principally by Indians, many of whom removed from the Southern States east of the Mississippi. The Cherokees, Choctaws, Creeks and Chickasaws are the most improved of the aborigines, and are advancing in civilization. There are good schools and churches among them.

QUESTIONS. Where is Indian Territory? By whom is it principally inhabited? What is said of the Cherokees, &c.

37. NEW MEXICO.

Square miles, 116,000. Population, 83,000.

New Mexico is west of Texas, between Mexico and Colorado.

This territory is principally a high table land traversed by broken ranges of mountains, the most prominent of which is the Sierra Madre.

The soil is generally sterile, except in the valleys of the rivers, which are productive, yielding large crops of wheat, Indian corn, oats and barley, and apples, peaches, melons, and grapes.

The minerals are gold, silver, iron, copper, lead, coal, and gypsum.

The inhabitants are Indians, Mexicans, and Americans.

New Mexico is a part of the tract acquired from Mexico, by the treaty of 1848.

SANTA FE, the capital, is situated on the Santa Fe River, a branch of the Rio Grande. The houses are principally built of adobes, or sun dried bricks. Each house usually forms a square with a court within, upon which nearly all the apartments open. This town is the great emporium of the overland trade from Missouri and Kansas.

QUESTIONS. Where is New Mexico situated? What is its surface? Soil? Minerals? Inhabitants? When was New Mexico acquired? Describe Santa Fe.

38. UTAH.

Square miles, 100,000. Population, 40,000.

Utah Territory is situated west of the Rocky Mountains, and is wholly in the interior.

The eastern part is diversified with hills, mountains and fertile valleys. The western portion, known as the Great or Fremont Basin, is an elevated table land hemmed in by mountains, with its own system of rivers and lakes.

The climate of the plateau, in mid-summer, is dry and hot, with cool mornings and evenings. The winters are mild, and the temperature is generally more uniform than in the eastern states.

WESTERN EMIGRATION.

The greater part of the territory is barren and can not be cultivated with profit. Some of the valleys are fertile, and produce wheat, rye, oats, barley, and Indian corn.

Gold has been discovered in considerable

quantities; and salt is collected from the lakes.

The most extensive lake is the Great Salt Lake. It is about seventy miles long and thirty wide, with no visible outlet. The water is so salt, that no living thing can exist in it.

The Utah lake, about thirty-five miles long, is a fresh water lake stored with fish. It is connected with Great Salt Lake by the Jordan River. The other principal lakes are the Pyramid, Humboldt and Nicollet Lakes; all of them without any visible outlet.

Most of the civilized inhabitants of the territory are Mormons. They are settled in a well-watered fertile district east of the Great Salt Lake.

SALT LAKE CITY is situated near the east bank of the Jordan river. It was laid out in July, 1847.

Fillmore City was the former capital.

QUESTIONS. Where is Utah Territory? What is said of the surface? Climate? Soil? Minerals? Great Salt Lake? Utah Lake? Other principal Lakes? Inhabitants? Salt Lake City?

40. WASHINGTON.

Square miles, 64,000. Population, 11,000.

Washington Territory occupies the northwest portion of the United States, lying on the Pacific, with British America for its northern boundary.

The surface, soil and productions are similar to those in Oregon. The climate is more variable. The highest peaks of the mountains are covered with perpetual snow.

Coal has been found.

OLYMPIA, the capital, is situated at the head of Puget's Sound.

FORT VANCOUVER.

QUESTIONS. What does Washington Territory occupy? What is said of the surface, soil and productions? Climate? What mineral is found? Where is Olympia?

41. DAKOTA.

Square miles, 149,000. Population, 5,000.

Dakota is a new territory lying west of Minnesota, and bounded north by British America.

Its surface is broken by mountains and valleys. The valleys are quite fertile and productive.

In the northern part the climate is cold, and the winters severe; in the southern part it is more mild.

The products are Indian corn, wheat, oats, barley, and potatoes. Timber is scarce in some parts of the territory.

Coal has been found in several places.

There are numerous salt lakes in the northern part.

YANCTON is the capital.

QUESTIONS. Where is Dakota? What is said of its surface? Soil? Climate? Productions? Coal? Salt lakes? Yancton?

42. COLORADO.

Square miles, 100,000. Population, 34,000.

Colorado lies between Kansas and Utah. Its surface is uneven, and, in some parts, mountainous. The Rocky Mountains pass through nearly the center of the territory.

The valleys of most of the rivers are fertile, but much of the soil is unfitted for cultivation.

Gold is produced in large quantities.

DENVER CITY is an important place, and has considerable trade.

QUESTIONS. What is said of Colorado? Its surface? The Rocky Mountains? The valleys? Gold? Denver City?

43. NEVADA.

Square miles, 80,000. Population, 7,000.

Nevada is between Utah and California. Its surface is broken with mountains and valleys. Some of the latter are very fertile. The soil in the northern and western parts is sterile.

The climate is mild and generally healthy. Wheat, barley, oats, potatoes, and fruits, are the chief vegetable products.

It contains rich silver mines.

CARSON CITY, the capital, is pleasantly situated in the Carson Valley.

QUESTIONS. How is Nevada situated? What is said of its surface? Soil? Climate? Productions? Silver mines? Carson City?

44. ARIZONA.

Square miles, 120,000.

Arizona is situated south of Utah, between New Mexico and California.

It consists principally of a table land somewhat broken by mountains.

It contains mines of gold and silver.

QUESTIONS. Where is Arizona situated? Of what does it consist? What does it contain?

5

45. IDAHO.

Square miles, 295,000.

Idaho is situated north of Utah, and includes a complete section of the Rocky Mountains.

The surface is broken and mountainous. This territory contains many gold mines, and has extensive forests of timber.

QUESTIONS. Where is Idaho situated? What does it include? What is said of its surface? Mines and forests?

2. MEXICO.

Square miles, 850,000. Population, 7,662,000.

Mexico occupies the southern portion of North America, and comprises twenty-two states, one federal district, and five territories.

It has in general a very elevated though broken surface; and is traversed by the Sierra Madre, or the southern portion of the Rocky Mountains.

The shores are low, hot, and unhealthy; the table lands, mild and salubrious; the mountainous districts are cold.

There are some barren tracts, but most of the soil is very fertile, producing the grains and fruits of the temperate zone, and, in the lowlands, the most valuable tropical products.

Indian corn, wheat, sugar, coffee, tobacco, and the American aloe, or maguey plant, are the chief vegetable productions.

Agriculture, manufactures and commerce, are all much neglected.

The gold and silver mines of Mexico are exceedingly rich, and constitute its chief resource. Iron, copper and lead are abundant.

The inhabitants consist of whites, Indians, and mixed races. The mass of them are ignorant and insubordinate. The Roman Catholic is the prevailing religion.

THE GREAT SQUARE AND CATHEDRAL, MEXICO.

Mexico, the capital, is a large and wealthy city, situated in a delightful valley, 7,000 feet above the level of the sea. It is regularly laid out, has spacious streets, and contains many costly cathedrals and other buildings.

Guanajuato and Zacatecas are large cities, chiefly important for their rich silver mines. Puebla is a handsome city, containing a few manufactories. Vera Cruz, the principal seaport and commercial town, is situated on the Gulf of Mexico.

QUESTIONS. Where is Mexico situated? What does it comprise? Describe its surface. Climate. Soil. What are its chief productions? What is said of agriculture, manufactures and commerce? Of mines? The inhabitants? Religion? Describe the city of Mexico. Guanajuato and Zacatecas. Puebla. Vera Cruz.

3. BALIZE.

Square miles, 15,000. Population, 11,000.

Balize, or British Honduras, is situated east of Yucatan. Its shores are studded with numerous small islands; along the coast, the land is swampy, and in the interior, wooded. The soil of the valleys is fertile.

The climate is moist, but not unhealthful. The productions are sugar, cotton, coffee, and indigo. Mahogany, logwood, and other dye-woods, are exported.

It is a British Colony.

Balize, the capital, is inhabited principally by blacks, and has considerable trade.

QUESTIONS. How is Balize situated? What is said of its shores? Soil? Climate? Productions? To whom does it belong? Describe Balize.

3. CENTRAL AMERICA.*

Square miles, 200,000. Population, 2,150,000.

Central America is the most southern portion of North America. It is a mountainous country, abounding with elevated plains and numerous volcanoes. The climate is extremely warm on the coast. In the interior, it is temperate and salubrious, resembling perpetual spring. The soil is rich, and yields choice fruits and other tropical products in great abundance; mahogany is also found here in large quantities.

The forests are very extensive and contain many kinds of trees fatal to animal life.

Central America includes the five states of Guatimala, San Salvador, Honduras, Nicaragua and Costa Rica. These were for a time associated in a confederation, similar to that of the United States, but this being

* See Map and Key of North America.

dissolved in 1839, the different states, though nominally republican, have since been in reality ruled by a succession of military despots. Attempts have been made to form other and partial confederations, whose duration, when formed, has been short.

The population consists of three classes; whites and Creoles; Mestizoes, or the descendants of whites and Indians; and aboriginal natives.

SAN SALVADOR is situated on a small stream which flows into the Pacific Ocean. It stands in a well watered vale, several thousand feet above the Pacific. It has greatly suffered by earthquakes, and was nearly destroyed by one in 1854.

GUATIMALA, the capital of the state of Guatimala, is pleasantly situated in a rich and spacious plain. It contains upwards of sixty richly ornamented churches and several public offices. It has a flourishing trade.

QUESTIONS. How is Central America situated? What is said of its surface? Climate? Soil? Productions? Forests? What does it include? Describe its government. Population. San Salvador. Guatimala.

WEST INDIES.*

Square miles, 91,800.

Population, 3,800,000.

THE WEST INDIA ISLANDS are a numerous group lying in the torrid zone, between North and South America.

The larger islands are traversed by ranges of mountains; others contain isolated peaks, many of which are volcanic; while the

* See Map and Key of North America.

smallest are mere islets formed of coral reefs, and uninhabited.

The winters are mild and pleasant. The heat of summer is extreme, though moderated by the mountains and sea-breezes.

Some of these islands are well-watered by mountain streams, and are remarkably fertile, yielding cotton, sugar, maize, coffee, spices, medicinal plants, dye-stuffs, and a great variety of fruits, as oranges, lemons, pine-apples, bread-fruit, tamarinds, and citrons. Cuba, Hayti and Jamaica belong to this class.

The forests abound with mahogany, cedar, and lignum-vitæ. The commerce is important and very flourishing.

The West India Islands are divided into the Greater and Lesser Antilles, Caribbee and Bahamas. All of them are subject to various European powers, except Hayti.

GREATER ANTILLES.

THE EXCHANGE, HAVANA.

Cuba is the largest of the West India Islands, and lies at the entrance of the Gulf of Mexico.

The northern part is generally level and has rich valleys and plains. The central and southern portions are more diversified and in some parts, mountainous.

The productions are tobacco, cotton, sugar, coffee, and tropical fruits.

HAVANA, the capital, is the most important city in the West Indies. It has a secure and commodious harbor.

Matanzas is an important commercial town, and has a flourishing trade with the United States.

Cuba belongs to Spain.

Jamaica is about ninety miles south of Cuba. A chain of mountains crosses the island from east to west.

Its productions are the same as those of Cuba.

The capital is SPANISH TOWN.

Kingston is the chief commercial city.

The island belongs to Great Britain.

Hayti, or St. Domingo, lies east of Cuba. The center of the island is mountainous. The soil is fertile, the climate hot, and during most months of the year, unhealthful to foreigners.

Coffee and cotton are the chief articles of export. Mahogany is abundant.

Porto Rico lies east of Hayti. The surface is varied and well-watered. The soil is fertile, and the climate fine and salubrious.

The principal productions are sugar and coffee.

ST. JOHNS is the capital, and principal sea-port.

This island belongs to Spain.

The Lesser Antilles consist of a number of small islands, which lie off the coast of South America.

The Caribbee Islands lie between the Caribbean Sea and the Atlantic Ocean, and extend from Porto Rico to South America.

The northern are called the Leeward, and the southern, the Windward Isles.

The Bahamas lie north-east of Cuba, and are supposed to number about five hundred.

Many of them are simply coral rocks, not inhabited. The surface of most of the islands is level, and the soil sandy.

The principal product is cotton. Indian corn, and the fruits and vegetables of tropical regions are produced on many of the islands. Salt is also exported.

NASSAU, the capital, is on the island of New Providence.

These islands belong to Great Britain.

QUESTIONS. Where are the West India Islands? Describe their surface. Climate. Soil. What are their productions? With what do the forests abound? What is said of their commerce? How are they divided? To whom subject?

Which is the largest? What is said of its surface? What are its productions? Describe Havana. Matanzas. To whom does Cuba belong?

How is Jamaica situated? What is said of its mountains? Productions? What is its capital? Its commercial city? To whom does Jamaica belong?

Where is Hayti? What is said of it? Its exports?

Describe Porto Rico. Surface. Soil and Climate. What are its productions? Describe St. Johns. To whom does Porto Rico belong?

What are the Lesser Antilles? Where are the Caribbee Islands? Where are the Bahamas? What are many of them? What is said of their surface and soil? What are the products? What is exported? Describe Nassau. To whom do these islands belong?

GENERAL QUESTIONS ON THE UNITED STATES.

How are the United States bounded? What states border on British America? On the Atlantic Ocean? Which are the Gulf States? What states border on the Pacific? What states are bounded on the west by the Mississippi River? What states have no sea coast?

Where are the White Mountains? Green Mountains? Ozark Mountains? Mention the principal peaks of the Rocky Mountains. Of the Cascade Mountains.

Where is the St. Lawrence River? In what direction does it flow? Describe the Connecticut River. The Hudson. Susquehanna. Potomac. Ohio. Sabine. What are the principal rivers flowing into the Gulf of Mexico? Where does the Mississippi river rise? What are its principal tributaries? What rivers west of the Rocky Mountains?

Where is Lake Superior? Lake Michigan? Lake Champlain? Lake Pontchartrain? Great Salt Lake?

Where is Massachusetts Bay? Chesapeake Bay? Tampa Bay? Mobile Bay? Galveston Bay? Gulf of Georgia? Florida Strait? Albemarle Sound? Long Island Sound? Strait of Juan de Fuca?

Where is Nantucket? Long Island? Cape Cod? Cape May? Cape Charles? Cape Hatteras? Cape Mendocino?

Between what parallels of latitude are the United States? What is the latitude of Albany? New York? Philadelphia? Washington? New Orleans? Chicago? San Francisco? What longitude from Greenwich is Washington?* Boston? Philadelphia? St. Louis? San Francisco?

Which of the United States are mostly mountainous? Which states have a level surface? What is the climate of the New England States? Of Louisiana? Of Texas? Of California?

What states produce corn? Of what states is wheat a staple production? Tobacco? Cotton? Rice? Sugar? What are the staple productions of Ohio? Kentucky? Texas? Iowa?

In what states is iron found? Coal? Gold? Silver? Lead? Copper? Locate the principal gold mines in the United States?

Which state has the greatest amount of commerce? Which are the principal manufacturing states? Which is the largest city in the United States? Which is the largest city in the Western States? Which are the principal Atlantic sea ports? What ports on the Gulf of Mexico? On the great Lakes? On the Pacific Ocean? Through what waters would a vessel pass in going from St. Louis to New York? What is the principal natural curiosity of the Middle States? Of the Western States? Of the Southern States.

GENERAL QUESTIONS ON MEXICO AND THE WEST INDIES.

How is Mexico Bounded? What is its Capital? What Mountains in Mexico? What Volcano? Bound Balize.

Where is the river Santander? Tula? Grande? Yaqui? Lake Chapala? What Gulf east of Mexico? Where is the Bay of Campeachy? Honduras? Tehuantepec?

In what direction from Florida is Cuba? The Bahamas? In what direction from Cuba is Hayti? Jamaica? In which direction is Cuba the longest? Where is Cape Catoche? Cape San Antonio? Cape San Lucas?

What is the latitude of Cuba? The City of Mexico? In what zone is Cuba? In what zones is Mexico? What is the climate of Mexico? Of the West India Islands?

What are the productions of Mexico? Of the West India Islands? Where is mahogany found? Coffee? What minerals in Mexico?

Describe Jamaica. The Bahamas. Who inhabit Mexico? Central America? What is said of the government of Mexico? Central America? West Indies?

Describe the city of Mexico. San Salvador. Havana.

* The figures at the top of the Map mark the longitude from Greenwich.

SOUTH AMERICA.

SQUARE MILES, 6,500,000. POPULATION, 18,000,000.

KEY TO MAP NO. 5.

STATES, CAPITALS AND CHIEF TOWNS.

1 **New Granada,** 1 BOGOTA, 2 Aspinwall, 3 Carthagena, 4 *Santa Marta,* 5 *Mompox,* 6 *Socorro,* 7 *Honda,* 8 *Popayan,* 9 *Panama.*

2 **Venezuela,** 1 CARACAS, 2 *Coro,* 3 *Valencia,* 4 La Guayra, 5 Cumana, 6 *Bolivar City,* 7 *Trujillo,* 8 *Maracaybo.*

3 **Guiana,** 1 GEORGETOWN, 2 New Amsterdam, 3 Paramaribo, 4 Cayenne.

4 **Brazil,** 1 RIO JANEIRO, 2 *Macapa,* 3 *Para,* 4 Maranham, 5 *Parnahiba,* 6 *Aracati,* 7 Pernambuco, 8 Bahia or St. Salvador, 9 *Espirito Santo,* 10 *San Paulo,* 11 *Porto Alegre,* 12 *Rio Grande,* 13 *Diamantina,* 14 *Cuyaba,* 15 *Matto Grosso,* 16 *Barra,* 17 *Santarem.*

5 **Paraguay,** 1 ASSUMPTION, 2 Concepcion, 3 *Curuguaty,* 4 *Villa Rica,* 5 *Neembucu.*

6 **Uruguay,** 1 MONTEVIDEO, 2 *Maldonado.*

7 **Argentine Republic,** 1 BUENOS AYRES, 2 *Corrientes,* 3 *Cordova,* 4 *Mendoza,* 5 *Rioja,* 6 *Catamarca,* 7 *Tucuman,* 8 *Santiago.*

8 **Patagonia.**

9 **Chili,** 1 SANTIAGO, 2 *Copiapo,* 3 *Huasco,* 4 Coquimbo, 5 Quillota, 6 Valparaiso, 7 *Concepcion,* 8 Valdivia, 9 *Castro.*

10 **Bolivia,** 1 CHUQUISACA, 2 *La Paz,* 3 Cochabamba, 4 Potosi, 5 *Cobija.*

11 **Peru,** 1 LIMA, 2, *Payta,* 3 *Cazamarca,* 4 *Trujillo,* 5 *Cerro Pasco,* 6 *Callao,* 7 *Huamanga,* 8 Cuzco, 9 *Arequipa,* 10 *Puno,* 11 *Arica.*

12 **Ecuador,** 1 QUITO, 2 *Ibarra,* 3 Guayquil, 4 *Riobamba,* 5 *Cuenca,* 6 *Loja.*

OCEANS, SEAS, GULFS AND BAYS.

1 ATLANTIC OCEAN,
2 PACIFIC OCEAN,
3 CARIBBEAN SEA,
4 GULF OF DARIEN,
5 GULF OF VENEZUELA,
6 *Gulf of Paria,*
7 *Pinzon Bay,*
8 BAY OF ALL SAINTS,
9 *Paranagua Bay,*
10 BLANCO BAY,
11 ST. MATTHIAS BAY,
12 BAY OF ST. GEORGE,
13 *Queen Adelaide's Archipelago,*
14 *Archipelago de Madre de Dios,*
15 *Gulf of Penas,*
16 *Chonos Archipelago,*
17 *Gulf of Guaytecas,*
18 *Concepcion Bay,*
19 GULF OF GUAYAQUIL,
20 BAY OF CHOCO,
21 BAY OF PANAMA.

STRAITS.

22 MARACAYBO,
23 MAGELLAN,
24 *Le Maire.*

ISLANDS.

25 *Curacoa,*
26 *Buen Ayre,*
27 MARGARITA,
28 *St. Vincent,*
29 *Barbadoes,*
30 *Grenada,*
31 *Tobago,*
32 TRINIDAD,
33 JOANNES,
34 *Itamaraca,*
35 *Abrolhos,*
36 *St. Sebastian.*

SOUTH AMERICA.

37 *Cananea,*
38 *St. Catharina,*
39 Falkland,
40 South Georgian,
41 *Staten Land,*
42 Terra del Fuego,
43 Hermit,
44 Wellington,
45 Chiloe,
46 Juan Fernandez,
47 St. Felix,
48 *Lobos,*
49 *Puna,*
50 *Quibo,*
51 *St. Anne.*

ISTHMUS AND CAPES.

52 Isthmus of Darien,
53 Gallinas,
54 *Orange,*
55 *North,*
56 St. Roque,
57 Frio,
58 St. Antonio,
59 *Corrientes,*
60 *Blanco,*
61 Horn,
62 Pillar,
63 Blanco,
64 San Lorenzo,
65 *San Francisco.*

MOUNTAINS AND DESERTS.

66 *Parima,*
67 *Pucaraima,*
68 *Acaray,*
69 Brazilian,
70 *Volcan,*
71 Andes,
72   Aconcagua,
73   *Gualateiri,*
74   *Illimani,*
75   *Sorata,*
76   *Chuquibamba,*
77   Chimborazo,
78   Cotopaxi,
79   *Tolima,*
80 Geral,
81 Desert of Atacama.

LAKES.

82 Maracaybo,
83 *Patos,*
84 *Mirim,*
85 *Ibera,*
86 *Coluguape,*
87 *Bevedero,*
88 *Porongos,*
89 Titicaca,
90 Reyes.

RIVERS.

91 Magdalena,
92   Cauca,
93 Orinoco,
94   *Apure,*
95   *Meta,*
96   *Guariare,*
97   *Curoni,*
98 *Essequibo,*
99 *Demerara,*
100 *Berbice,*
101 *Surinam,*
102 *Marowyne,*
103 *Oyapok,*
104 Amazon,
105   *Trombetas,*
106   *Aniba,*
107   Negro,
108   *Branco,*
109   *Cassiquiare,*
110   *Uaupes,*
111   Caqueta,
112   Putumayo,
113   *Napo,*
114   *Huallaga,*
115   Ucayale,
116   *Javary,*
117   *Jutay,*
118   *Jurua,*
119   Purus,
120   Madeira,
121   Beni,
122   Mamore,
123   *Guapai,*
124   *Guapore,*
125   Topajos,
126   *Arinos,*
127   *Tres Barras,*
128   Xingu,
129   Para.

SOUTH AMERICA.   85

130	TOCANTINS,		145	*Cuyaba*,
131	ARAGUAY,		146	PILCOMAYO,
132	*R. das Mortes*,		147	VERMEJO,
133	*Gurupi*,		148	SALADO,
134	*Maranham*,		149	*Tercero*,
135	PARNAHIBA,		150	SALADO,
136	ST. FRANCISCO,		151	*Dulce*,
137	*Parahiba*,		152	COLORADO,
138	RIO DE LA PLATA,		153	RIO NEGRO,
139	URUGUAY,		154	*Camarones*,
140	PARANA,		155	*Port Desire*,
141	*Tiete*,		156	*Chico*,
142	PARANAIBA,		157	*Santa Cruz*,
143	PARAGUAY,		158	*Biobio*,
144	*Tacuari*,		159	*Desaguadero*.

QUESTIONS ON THE MAP OF SOUTH AMERICA.

BOUND South America. How many square miles has it? Inhabitants? What is its latitude? Longitude? In what zones does it lie?

How many states has South America? Name them. The capital of each. Bound each state. What states border on the Pacific Ocean? The Atlantic Ocean? The Caribbean Sea? Which state has no sea coast? What state entirely west of the Andes? Which is the largest state in South America?

OCEANS, GULFS, BAYS, &c.

What ocean east of South America? 1. West? 2. What sea north? 3. What bay south of the Isthmus of Darien? 21. What gulf north? 4. What gulf north of Venezuela? 5. What three bays on the coast of Brazil? 7-9. What three bays on the Atlantic coast south of Brazil? 10-12.

What archipelagoes on the west coast of Patagonia? 13, 14, 16. What two gulfs on the west coast of Patagonia? 15, 17. What gulf on the coast of Ecuador? 19. What bay on the west coast of New Granada? 20.

ISLANDS.

What islands north of Venezuela? 25-32. What island at the mouth of the Amazon? 33. What five islands near the coast of Brazil? 34-38. What islands east and south of Patagonia? 39-43. What west? 44, 45. West of Chili? 46, 47. What island west of Peru? 48. South of the Isthmus of Darien? 50.

CAPES.

Which is the most northern cape? 53. Which is the most eastern? 56. Southern? 61. Western? 63. What four capes has Brazil? 54-57. What two has the Argentine Republic? 58, 59. What cape at the western extremity of Terra del Fuego? 62. What two capes has Ecuador? 64, 65.

MOUNTAINS.

What mountains between Guiana and Brazil? 67, 68. In the south-eastern part of Brazil? 69. What in the western? 80. What chain of mountains extends the whole length of South America? 71. Mention the principal peaks. 72-79.

LAKES.

What lake in Venezuela? 82. What two lakes in the southern part of Brazil? 83, 84. What lakes in the Argentine Republic? 85, 87, 88. What lake in the southern part of Peru? 89.

RIVERS.

What river in New Granada flows into the Caribbean sea? 91. What river in Venezuela flows into the Atlantic? 93. Which is the largest river in South America? 104. Mention its principal branches. 107, 115, 119, 120, 125, 128. What river flows into the Atlantic about 11° south latitude? 136. What at about 35° south latitude? 138. Mention its principal tributaries. 139, 140.

SOUTH AMERICA.

DESCRIPTIVE GEOGRAPHY.

South America is a vast triangular peninsula, occupying the southern half of the western continent. Its greatest length is 4800 miles, and its greatest breadth, 3230 miles, and it contains 6,500,000 square miles.

It is naturally divided into three great sections, the eastern, or table lands of Brazil; the middle, or valley of the Amazon, La Plata and Orinoco; and the western, or mountainous districts of the Andes.

It is distinguished for its lofty mountains, majestic rivers and extensive plains. Though partly in the Torrid Zone, the climate is not excessively hot, but usually mild and salubrious. The soil is much of it fertile.

The elevated plains and mountain declivities abound with the fruits and vegetables of the temperate zone, and the lower regions yield all the most valuable tropical products.

The vegetation of this country is unsurpassed in its luxuriance and beauty. In many places winter is unknown, and the hills and valleys are clothed with constant verdure.

The potato, maize, cocoa, vanilla, and many other useful plants, are found in their native state. The dense forests contain excellent timber, and remain in their primitive grandeur.

It is rich in mineral productions, among which are gold, silver, copper, iron, lead, and precious stones.

The most ferocious animals of South America are the puma, jaguar and ocelot. The sloth, ant-eater, armadillo, tapir, and antelope, are numerous. The lama, alpaca, and vicuna are useful animals.

A variety of monkeys is found, and birds of the most superb plumage. The condor, the largest bird of flight, inhabits the snowy solitudes of the Andes.

SOUTH AMERICA.

Vultures, harpies, eagles, toucans, orioles, and parrots, abound. There are numerous insects and reptiles. The serpents and alligators are of monstrous size.

The domestic animals were imported from Europe. They have multiplied so rapidly as to relapse into a wild state, and now roam the country in vast herds.

South America was first visited by Columbus in 1498. Soon after, the Spaniards and Portuguese conquered the native Indians, and made numerous settlements.

These settlements or provinces remained subject to Spain and Portugal until the present century, when they threw off the yoke and became republics.

South America comprises the following divisions, viz., New Granada, Venezuela, Guiana, Brazil, Paraguay, Uraguay, Argentine Republic, Patagonia, Chili, Bolivia, Peru, and Ecuador.

QUESTIONS. What is South America? How divided? For what distinguished? What is the climate? Soil? What are the products of the different sections? What is said of the vegetation? What plants are found in their native state? What can you say of the Minerals? Wild animals? Domestic animals? Of the discovery and settlement of South America? What farther of the provinces? Name the divisions.

The lower tracts are hot and unhealthy They abound with the most valuable tropical products. The elevated plains on which most of the inhabitants reside, are cool and salubrious.

Cocoa, coffee, sugar, tobacco, indigo, hides, Brazil and dye woods, are the principal articles of cultivation and commerce.

It has rich mines of gold and silver, also precious stones.

The country is in many parts so rugged as to render the construction of roads impracticable. Travelers are carried in a chair by persons hired for that purpose, or on mules.

Rope bridges, on which the inhabitants pass with ease, are thrown over the chasms.

The Panama railroad, about fifty miles in length, extends across the isthmus from Aspinwall to Panama.

BOGOTA, the capital, is a handsome town, situated in the interior, on an elevation, a mile and a half above the level of the sea. The streets are narrow but regular.

CARTHAGENA.

Carthagena has a fine harbor, and an extensive trade. *Aspinwall*, on the north, and *Panama*, on the south side of the isthmus of Darien, are the principal ports.

QUESTIONS. How many square miles has New Gra-

1. NEW GRANADA.

Square miles, 480,000. Population, 2,360,000.

New Granada is traversed by three ranges of the Andes, and contains several lofty peaks. The scenery among these mountains is extremely grand and beautiful.

nada? What is the population? Surface? Climate? What are the chief articles of cultivation and commerce? In what is it rich? What is said of roads and travelers? Bridges? Railroad? Describe Bogota. Carthagena. Aspinwall and Panama.

2. VENEZUELA.

Square miles, 426,000. Population, 1,400,000.

Venezuela, in the northern part, is traversed by the Andes. The southern portion comprises the vast fertile plains of the Orinoco and its branches.

The climate is extremely hot in the lowlands, but temperate in the higher regions. The soil is very rich, yielding large crops of sugar, tobacco, coffee, cotton, and the tropical fruits.

The plains or llanos are covered with tall coarse grass, on which graze numerous herds of cattle, horses and mules.

CARACAS, the capital, is situated in a pleasant valley, and is subject to earthquakes. It was nearly destroyed in 1812, with 12,000 of its inhabitants. It has since been rebuilt.

La Guayra has an important commerce. *Valencia* and *Cumana* are places of some trade.

The Island of Margarita belongs to Venezuela.

QUESTIONS. What is the number of square miles in Venezuela? The population? What is said of the surface? The climate? Soil and productions? Plains? What animals are found in great numbers? Describe Caracas. La Guayra, Cumana, and Angostura. What island belongs to Venezuela?

3. GUIANA.

Square miles, 163,000. Population, 214,000.

Guiana is a level, fertile country, belonging to the English, Dutch and French. It has two dry seasons and two wet seasons in a year. In the dry seasons the climate is agreeable.

The principal productions are sugar, coffee and maize. Cayenne pepper and cloves are largely exported from Cayenne.

The inhabitants consist of foreign residents, aboriginal tribes and negroes; the latter constituting the majority.

GEORGETOWN, the capital of British Guiana, at the mouth of the Demerara river, is regularly built. Its streets are broad, mostly with canals in the middle, communicating with each other and the river. The low, swampy position of the city renders it unhealthy.

PARAMARIBO, the capital of Dutch Guiana, has a fine harbor, and is the center of trade for the colony.

CAYENNE, the capital of French Guiana, is situated on an island, and is noted for its pepper.

QUESTIONS. Mention the number of square miles in Guiana. The population. Describe Guiana. Its climate. Name its chief products. What is said of the inhabitants? Georgetown? Paramaribo? Cayenne?

4. BRAZIL.

Square miles, 3,000,000. Population, 6,500,000.

Brazil is an extensive country, comprising nearly the whole of the valley of the Amazon, and the country lying on the coast south of it as far as latitude 32°.

It abounds with majestic rivers, extensive plains, and vast forests. A part of it contains low ranges of mountains.

The climate is mild and salubrious in the elevated and southern sections, but hot and unhealthy near the equator. The soil is very fertile, and vegetation, exceedingly luxuriant.

SOUTH AMERICA.

Its staple productions are coffee and sugar, but cotton, rice, tobacco, maize, wheat, ginger, and yams, are found in great abundance. Oranges, lemons and bananas, grow luxuriantly in some parts.

It is also rich in mineral treasures, as gold, silver, diamonds, topaz, and other precious stones.

Wild animals are very numerous, among which are enormous serpents, alligators, and birds of beautiful plumage.

Immense herds of cattle, which are hunted for their hides and horns, graze on the plains. Horses and mules are numerous in the south.

VIEW IN BAHIA.

Agriculture is the leading pursuit. There are few manufactures. It has considerable commerce. Sugar, cotton, hides, horns, coffee, cabinet and dye woods, and gums, are among the chief exports. The government is a hereditary, constitutional monarchy.

The inhabitants consist of Whites, Negroes, mixed races, and several savage tribes of Indians. Labor in the fields and in the mines is performed principally by negro slaves.

Free schools for teaching the rudiments of learning are established.

The religion is Roman Catholic, but other religions are tolerated.

Rio Janeiro, its capital, and the largest city in South America, has a very fine harbor, an extended commerce, and several literary institutions. It contains several public buildings, and is surrounded by varied and picturesque scenery.

Para, Maranham, Pernambuco and *Bahia* are the other principal seaports.

QUESTIONS. How many square miles has Brazil? Inhabitants? What does it comprise? With what abound? What is the climate? Soil? Name the chief products. Minerals. What is said of wild animals? Cattle? Agriculture and manufactures? Commerce? Exports? Government? Inhabitants? Schools? Religion? Rio Janeiro? What are the other principal seaports?

5. PARAGUAY.

Square miles, 84,000. Population, 300,000.

Paraguay occupies the peninsula between the Parana and Paraguay rivers.

It is a small, level state, well watered and fertile. The climate is temperate and healthy, and the productions are various and valuable.

Maize, rice, sugar, drugs, and tropical fruits abound; also matte, or Paraguay tea, used in South America as China tea is used in this country and in Europe.

Large herds of wild cattle roam the plains, and birds of beautiful plumage live in the dense forests.

Its inhabitants are chiefly civilized Indians, and descendants of Europeans, from Spain. They are generally intelligent and industrious.

The government is a republic. The religion, Roman Catholic.

This state became independent in 1813,

and soon after was governed by Dr. Francia, who ruled under the title of Dictator, until his death, in 1840.

He very much improved the condition of the people, and secured to them peace and prosperity, while the neighboring republics were unsettled and distracted.

ASSUMPTION, the capital, is finely situated, but poorly built, and has considerable trade. Foreigners are now admitted, and commerce with other nations is encouraged.

QUESTIONS. Paraguay has how many square miles? What is the population? Describe it. Name the chief products. What abound on its plains and in its forests? What is said of the inhabitants? Government? Religion? What can you say of its history? Of Assumption?

6. URUGUAY.

Square miles, 75,000. Population, 120,000.

Uruguay is a small state lying between the river Uruguay and the Atlantic.

CATHEDRAL AT MONTEVIDEO.

The surface is generally level, and the climate agreeable. The soil is fertile, but remains for the most part uncultivated.

The principal productions are wheat, maize and beans. Melons are raised in abundance.

Hides, horns and tallow are its chief exports.

The government is republican.

This republic, formerly known as the Banda Oriental, belonged to the United Provinces of Buenos Ayres. On account of its commercial facilities, Brazil laid claim to it; but after a protracted war both parties assented to its independence.

MONTEVIDEO, the capital, is situated on the Rio de la Plata, which is here eighty miles wide. It has a fine cathedral, a good harbor and an important trade.

QUESTIONS. What is the number of square miles and the population of Uruguay? Describe its situation. Surface, soil and climate. Mention its productions. Its exports. What is its Government? History? Describe Montevideo.

7. ARGENTINE REPUBLIC.

Square miles, 900,000. Population, 1,300,000.

The Argentine Republic occupies a section drained by the waters of the Paraguay and Colorado.

The northern part is mountainous and barren. The central and southern portions are fertile, and consist principally of immense plains called Pampas. These have few trees and are covered with tall grass that affords fine pasture.

The plains are extremely warm; the coast and elevated tracts are cool. The climate is remarkable for its dryness.

The productions are sugar, cotton, tobacco, maize, wheat, and the various fruits of the temperate and torrid zones.

It has rich mines of gold, silver, copper, iron, and coal.

On the plains, are vast herds of horses and cattle, which are taken by the Indian with his lasso, a leathern thong. Deer, jaguar, and the American ostrich also abound.

Wool, hides, horns, and tallow, are the chief articles of export.

The government is nominally a republic, but the president, or director, possesses in reality the powers of a dictator.

The religion is Roman Catholic. Education throughout the province is in a low state.

This Republic became independent of Spain in 1816. It has taken, at different times, the names of the United Provinces of the Rio de la Plata, the Argentine Republic, and Buenos Ayres.

BUENOS AYRES, the capital, is strongly fortified, and has an extensive commerce, somewhat impeded by the difficulty of navigating the La Plata. The houses are mostly built of brick, and whitewashed. It contains fine public buildings, a good college well endowed, normal and other schools.

PUBLIC SQUARE AT MENDOZA.

Mendoza is well built and has an extensive trade with Chili, carried on by means of mules.

QUESTIONS. Give the number of square miles in the Argentine Republic. Its population. Describe its situation. Surface. Climate. Name its products. Minerals. Animals. Articles of export. What is said of its Government? Religion? Education? History? Names? Of Buenos Ayres? Mendoza?

---

8. PATAGONIA.

Square miles, 350,000. Population, 120,000.

NATIVES OF PATAGONIA.

Patagonia comprises the southern portion of the western continent, extending from the Atlantic to the Pacific ocean.

The Andes pass through it, rendering its surface mountainous and rugged. The greater part of it is cold and barren, only a very small portion being under cultivation.

Fish abound on the coast.

It is thinly inhabited by independent tribes of Indians, who are said to be excellent horsemen.

QUESTIONS. How many square miles and inhabitants has Patagonia? What does Patagonia comprise? What is its surface and climate? What abound on its coasts? Who inhabit it?

9. CHILI.

Square miles, 170,000. Population, 1,200,000.

Chili is a long, narrow tract of land, lying between the Andes and the ocean. It has a mountainous surface, is subject to violent earthquakes, and has several volcanoes constantly burning.

COSTUMES OF THE CHILIANS.

The climate is equable and very salubrious. Numerous mountain streams, which flow into the Pacific, fertilize the soil, especially in the southern part, where it is productive; the northern part is barren.

Fruits, grains, and vegetables, are abundantly raised, but the rearing of cattle is the most important branch of industry.

Mines of gold, silver, and copper, are extensively worked.

The Chilians are courteous, humane, and industrious.

The general government is administered by a president elected for five years. He is assisted by a council of eight members. The legislature consists of two houses, the Senate and House of Deputies.

The established religion is Roman Catholic. Other religions are tolerated.

Chiloe and its adjacent islands, also those of Juan Fernandez, belong to Chili. Juan Fernandez is celebrated as the residence of Alexander Selkirk, a Scotch sailor. His adventure gave rise to the story of Robinson Crusoe.

SANTIAGO, the capital, is beautifully situated.

Valparaiso, its port, has a fine harbor, and an extensive trade with Europe, the United States and China. *Quillota* has remarkably rich mines of copper. *Valdivia* and *Coquimbo* possess good harbors.

QUESTIONS. What is the area of Chili? Population? Surface? Its climate and soil? What is said of fruits, grains, &c.? The rearing of cattle? Mines? Chilians? Government? Religion? What islands belong to Chili? What can you say of Juan Fernandez? Santiago? Valparaiso? Quillota? Valdivia and Coquimbo?

10. BOLIVIA.

Square miles, 375,000. Population, 1,700,000.

Bolivia is an extensive republic situated north of Chili and the Argentine Republic, and west of Brazil.

The surface is mountainous and greatly elevated. The climate is generally temperate.

Rye, maize, potatoes, cotton, rice, indigo, and cocoa, are the chief productions.

This country is noted for its valuable mines of gold and silver. The silver mines of Potosi are the richest in the world. They were discovered by Hualpo, a Peruvian Indian, in 1545, while climbing a mountain in pursuit of some goats. Laying hold of a shrub to assist his ascent, it was torn up by the roots, exposing the silver beneath.

Bolivia was a Spanish province till 1825, when it achieved its independence under General Bolivar, from whom it derives its name.

The constitution, which was drawn up for the new state by him, and adopted by congress in 1826, makes ample provision for personal and political liberty, securing religious toleration and the freedom of the press.

The religion is Roman Catholic.

THE GRAND PLACE AT CHUQUISACA.

CHUQUISACA, the capital, has a university and several fine buildings.

Potosi is situated 13,000 feet above the level of the sea, in a region cold and barren, but rich in silver mines. *Cochabamba* has considerable trade in grain and fruits.

QUESTIONS. What is the area of Bolivia? Population? What is said of its situation? Surface? Climate? Productions? For what is it noted? Who discovered its mines? When and under whom did it become independent? What is said of the government? Religion? Describe Chuquisaca. Potosi. Cochabamba.

11. PERU.

Square miles, 400,000. Population, 2,300,000.

Peru is an irregular country, traversed by two ranges of the Andes. On the coast the climate is very hot, and the soil arid. The table lands have a cool climate and fertile soil.

The chief productions are cotton, maize, sugar, coffee, and Peruvian bark. There are also rich mines of gold, silver, and mercury, or quicksilver.

Agriculture and manufactures are neglected.

The country is almost destitute of roads and bridges. Transportation is carried on principally by means of lamas and mules.

A railroad between Lima and Callao has been completed, and another from Arica to Tacna has been commenced.

The native Peruvians were a peaceable race, who understood agriculture and the arts, and worshiped the sun.

The present inhabitants are supposed to be about one-half Indians, one-fourth white persons, or Creoles, and the rest colored people of mixed breeds.

The Peruvians achieved their independence in 1824. They possess a good degree of enterprise, wealth and refinement.

The government is popular and representative. The president is elected for six years.

The dominant religion is Roman Catholic but other creeds are tolerated.

LIMA, the capital, is a wealthy city, remarkable for its magnificent public build-

THE CONVENT OF SAN FRANCISCO, LIMA.

ings. It has several manufactories, and a large trade through the port of Callao.

Cuzco, was the capital of the ancient Peruvian empire, and the residence of the Peruvian Incas. It was founded by Manco Capac, the first Inca of Peru, in 1043, and contains numerous elegant palaces and temples. In 1534 it was taken by the Spaniards, under Pizarro, who cruelly put to death the reigning Incas, and pillaged the city.

QUESTIONS. What number of square miles has Peru? Inhabitants? Describe its surface, climate and soil. What are its productions? What is the state of agriculture and manufactures? What is said of roads and bridges? What can you say of its inhabitants? When did Peru become independent? What is said of the government? Religion? Lima? Cuzco?

12. ECUADOR.

Square miles, 240,000. Population, 620,000.

Ecuador is situated on the coast of the Pacific, north of Peru, and directly under equator.

It is remarkable for its lofty mountains, elevated plains and varied climate. Vegetation is luxuriant, and the forests are covered with perpetual green.

All the tropical fruits abound. Cocoa, rice, pepper, sugar-cane, Indian corn, cotton, wheat, and barley, are also produced.

Earthquakes and violent tempests are frequent.

Some of the most elevated peaks of the Andes are found in this country; among which are Mount Chimborazo and the volcanoes Cotopaxi and Pichincha.

The form of government is republican, with a president and vice-president as the head.

The religion is Roman Catholic.

Education is in a very backward state.

CATHEDRAL AT GUAYAQUIL.

QUITO, the capital, is a beautiful city, built on the side of a volcano, 8000 feet above the level of the sea. It is well built and has several handsome squares. Eleven snow-capped mountains may be seen from the city.

SOUTH AMERICA.

Guayaquil has a fine harbor and an extensive commerce. It is well laid out and has some good public edifices; but it is mostly built of wood, on low ground, and is ill supplied with water.

QUESTIONS. Number of square miles in Ecuador? Population? Describe its situation. Surface. Vegetation. Productions. To what is it subject? What is said of its mountain peaks? Government? Religion? Education? Describe Quito? Guayaquil.

GENERAL QUESTIONS ON SOUTH AMERICA.

How is South America bounded? What is its general form? In which direction is it the longest? What divisions border on the Caribbean Sea? What on the Atlantic Ocean? What on the Pacific? Which division has no sea coast? Which is the largest division? Which is the smallest?

What range of mountains extends the whole length of South America? Mention the principal peaks of the Andes. In what state are the highest peaks? What other mountains in South America? What states are mostly level?

Which are the three largest rivers of South America? In what direction does each flow? Why are there no large rivers flowing into the Pacific? What are the principal tributaries of the Orinoco? Of the Amazon? Of the La Plata? Where is Lake Maracaybo? Lake Titicaca? Into what does the river Dulce flow?

Where is the gulf of Darien? The gulf of Venezuela? The gulf of Guayaquil? The bay of All Saints? Blanco Bay? The bay of St. George? The bay of Panama? Straits of Maracaybo? Straits of Magellan?

Where is the island of Curacoa? Trinidad? Joannes? Where are the Falkland Islands? South Georgian? Where is Terra del Fuego? Chiloe? Juan Fernandez? Cape Gallinas? Cape St. Roque? Cape Frio? Cape Horn? Cape Blanco?

What is the latitude of Cape Gallinas? Cape Horn? Of the island of Juan Fernandez? Of the mouth of the Amazon? Of the mouth of the Orinoco? Of the mouth of the La Plata? Of Quito? Rio Janeiro? Buenos Ayres? Lima?

What is the longitude from Greenwich of the Isthmus of Darien? Of Cape St. Roque? Of Bogota? Of Rio Janeiro? Chuquisaca? The mouth of the Amazon? The mouth of the Orinoco?

What countries of South America are crossed by the equator? What by the Tropic of Capricorn? In what zones is South America? What countries are in the Torrid Zone? What in the South Temperate Zone? In which zone is vegetation most luxuriant? What, besides distance from the Equator, affects the climate of the countries of South America?

Which division of South America has the coldest climate? In what divisions is the climate very warm? What divisions have a temperate climate? What are the seasons in Guiana? What is the general character of the soil in the valleys of the northern and middle countries? What are the vegetable productions of New Granada and Venezuela? In what country is ginger produced? From what country is Cayenne pepper exported? In what countries are coffee and sugar found? Cotton? What country exports dye woods and gums? In what countries are there large numbers of cattle?

Where is gold found? Silver? Copper? Mercury? In what country are the richest silver mines? Where are diamonds found? What is the government of Brazil? Of most of the other countries? What is the prevailing religion in South America?

Which is the largest city in South America? What has it? How is Bogota situated? What are the principal sea ports in South America? For what is Lima remarkable? What has Chuquisaca? What does Buenos Ayres contain? How is Quito situated? In what direction from New York is Rio Janeiro? How would you sail from Buenos Ayres to San Francisco, Cal.? How is transportation carried on in Peru? How do people travel in New Granada?

220
12
205
20

EUROPE.

SQUARE MILES, 3,800,000.   POPULATION, 276,000,000.

KEY TO MAP NO. 6.

COUNTRIES, CAPITALS, CHIEF TOWNS.

1 **Norway,** 1 CHRISTIANA, 2 Drontheim, 3 *Konigsburg,* 4 *Bergen.*

2 **Sweden,** 1 STOCKHOLM, 2 *Gefle,* 3 *Falun,* 4 *Upsal,* 5 *Kalmar,* 6 *Carlscrona,* 7 *Gothenburg.*

3 **Russia,** 1 ST. PETERSBURG, 2 *Archangel,* 3 *Kasan,* 4 *Saratov,* 5 *Astrakhan,* 6 Sevastopol, 7 *Kherson,* 8 *Odessa,* 9 *Ismail,* 10 *Kiev,* 11 *Minsk,* 12 *Vilna,* 13 Riga, 14 *Revel,* 15 *Abo,* 16 *Cronstadt,* 17 *Novgorod,* 18 *Yaroslav,* 19 *Tver,* 20 *Moscow,* 21 *Kalooga,* 22 *Orel,* 23 *Smolensk.*

RUSSIAN PROVINCES.

4 **Lapland,** 1 KOLA, 2 *Tornea.*

5 **Poland,** 1 *Cracow,* 2 *Warsaw,* 3 *Lublin.*

6 **Austria,** 1 VIENNA, 2 *Prague,* 3 *Brunn,* 4 *Olmutz,* 5 *Wieliczka,* 6 *Bochnia,* 7 *Lemberg,* 8 *Cronstadt,* 9 *Hermanstadt,* 10 *Temesvar,* 11 *Agram,* 12 *Ragusa,* 13 *Cattaro,* 14 *Trieste,* 15 *Laybach,* 16 *Gratz,* 17 *Lintz,* 18 *Presburg,* 19 *Buda,* 20 *Pesth,* 21 *Debreczin.*

7 **Turkey,** 1 CONSTANTINOPLE, 2 *Belgrade,* 3 *Widin,* 4 *Bucharest,* 5 *Brahilov,* 6 *Jassy,* 7 *Silistria,* 8 *Shoomla,* 9 *Varna,* 10 *Adrianople,* 11 *Gallipoli,* 12 *Seres,* 13 *Salonica,* 14 *Larissa,* 15 *Arta,* 16 *Yanina,* 17 *Scutari,* 18 *Bosna-Serai,* 19 *Sophia.*

8 **Greece,** 1 ATHENS, 2 *Corinth,* 3 *Nauplia,* 4 *Tripolitza,* 5 *Patras.*

ITALY, OR ITALIAN STATES.

9 **Sardinia,** ⎧ 1 TURIN, 2 *Milan,* 3 *Parma,* 4 *Modena,*
10 **Venice,**   ⎪ 5 *Florence,* 8 *Mantua,* 9 *Verona,*
11 **Parma,**   ⎨ 10 *Padua,* 11 *Venice,* 24 *Leghorn,*
12 **Modena,**   ⎪ 25 *Genoa,* 26 *Nice,* 27 *Sassari,* 28
13 **Tuscany,** ⎩ *Cagliari.*

14 **States of the Church,** 6 ROME, 12 *Bologna,* 13 *San Marino,* 14 *Ancona.*

15 **Kingdom of Naples,** 7 NAPLES, 15 *Bari,* 16 *Taranto,* 17 *Reggio,* 18 *Messina,* 19 *Catania,* 20 *Syracuse,* 21 *Trapani,* 22 *Palermo,* 23 *Salerno.*

16 **France,** 1 PARIS, 2 *Brest,* 3 *Rennes,* 4 *Cherbourg,* 5 *Caen,* 6 *Havre,* 7 *Rouen,* 8 *Calais,* 9 *Lille,* 10 *Amiens,* 11 *Rheims,* 12 *Metz,* 13 *Nancy,* 14 *Strasburg,* 15 *Dijon,* 16 *Lyons,* 17 *Bastia,* 18 *Ajaccio,* 19 *Toulon,* 20 *Marseilles,* 21 *Montpelier,* 22 *Toulouse,* 23 *Bayonne,* 24 *Bordeaux,* 25 *Nantes,* 26 *L'Orient,* 27 *Angers,* 28 *Tours,* 29 *Orleans,* 30 *Troyes,* 31 *St. Etienne,* 32 *Limoges.*

17 **Spain,** 1 MADRID, 2 *Compostela,* 3 *Corunna,* 4 *Ferrol,* 5 *Gijon,* 6 *Bilbao,* 7 *Barcelona,* 8 *Tortosa,* 9 *Valencia,* 10 *Alicante,* 11 *Murcia,* 12 *Cartagena,* 13 *Granada,* 14 *Malaga,* 15 *Gibraltar,* 16 *Cadiz,* 17 *Seville,* 18 *Cordova,* 19 *Badajos,* 20 *Toledo,* 21 *Salamanca,* 22 *Leon,* 23 *Valladolid,* 24 *Burgos,* 25 *Saragossa.*

18 **Portugal,** 1 LISBON, 2 *Braga,* 3 *Oporto,* 4 *Coimbra,* 5 *Elvas,* 6 *Evora,* 7 *Setubal.*

19 **England,** 1 LONDON, 2 *Newcastle,* 3 *York,* 4 *Hull,* 5 *Norwich,* 6 *Cambridge,* 7 *Dover,* 8 *Portsmouth,* 9 *Southampton,* 10 *Plymouth,* 11 *Bristol,* 12 *Birmingham,* 13 *Liverpool,* 14 *Manchester,* 15 *Leeds,* 16 *Sheffield.*

20 **Wales,** 1 *Caernarvon,* 2 *Merthyr Tydvil,* 3 *Cardigan.*

21 **Scotland,** 1 EDINBURGH, 2 *Wick,* 3 *Inverness,* 4 *Aberdeen,* 5 *Dundee,* 6 *Perth,* 7 *Paisley,* 8 *Glasgow.*

EUROPE.

22 Ireland, 1 DUBLIN, 2 *Londonderry*, 3 *Belfast*, 4 *Waterford*, 5 *Cork*, 6 *Limerick*, 7 *Galway*, 8 *Sligo*.

23 Belgium, 1 BRUSSELS, 2 Ghent, 3 Antwerp, 4 *Liege*,

24 Holland, 1 HAGUE, 2 Amsterdam, 3 *Groningen*, 4 *Rotterdam*.

25 Denmark, 1 COPENHAGEN, 2 Elsinore, 3 *Flensborg*, 4 *Sleswick*.

26 Prussia, 1 BERLIN, 2 *Stettin*, 3 *Colberg*, 4 Dantzic, 5 Konigsberg, 6 *Memel*, 7 *Thorn*, 8 *Posen*, 9 Breslau, 10 *Liegnitz*, 11 *Halle*, 12 *Magdeburg*, 13 *Potsdam*, 14 *Elberfield*, 15 Cologne, 16 *Aix la Chapelle*.

27 German States,[*]1 FRANKFORT, 8 Bremen, 9 Hamburg, 10 Lubeck.

28 Mecklenburg, 2 SCHWERIN.

29 Hanover, 3 HANOVER, 11 Gottingen.

30 Saxony, 4 DRESDEN, 12 Leipsic.

31 Bavaria, 5 MUNICH, 13 Nuremburg, 14 *Augsburg*.

32 Wirtemburg, 6 STUTTGART, 15 Ulm.

33 Baden, 7 CARLSRUHE, 16 *Manheim*.

34 Switzerland, 1 BERNE, 2 *Basel*, 3 Zurich, 4 Geneva.

OCEANS, SEAS, GULFS AND BAYS.

1 ATLANTIC OCEAN,
2 ARCTIC OCEAN,
3 WHITE SEA,
4 ONEGA GULF,
5 *Tcheskaya Gulf*,
6 CASPIAN SEA,
7 AZOF SEA,
8 BLACK SEA,
9 *Gulf of Burgas*,
10 SEA OF MARMORA,
11 ARCHIPELAGO,
12 MEDITERRANEAN SEA,
13 ADRIATIC SEA,
14 GULF OF TARANTO,
15 GULF OF GENOA,
16 GULF OF LYONS,

17 BAY OF BISCAY,
18 *Galway Bay*,
19 *Donegal Bay*,
20 IRISH SEA,
21 NORTH SEA,
22 *Murray Firth*,
23 *Firth of Forth*,
24 ZUYDER ZEE,
25 BALTIC SEA,
26 GULF OF RIGA,
27 GULF OF FINLAND,
28 GULF OF BOTHNIA,
29 *Faxe Bay*,
30 *Brede Bay*.

STRAITS AND CHANNELS.

31 SKAGER RACK,
32 CATTEGAT,
33 THE SOUND,
34 STRAIT OF YENIKALE,
35 CHANNEL OF BOSPORUS,
36 STRAIT OF DARDANELLES,
37 STRAIT OF OTRANTO,
38 STRAIT OF MESSINA,
39 STRAIT OF BONIFACIO,
40 STRAIT OF GIBRALTAR,
41 ENGLISH CHANNEL,
42 STRAIT OF DOVER,
43 BRISTOL CHANNEL,
44 ST. GEORGE'S CHANNEL,
45 NORTH CHANNEL.

ISLANDS.

46 ICELAND,
47 LOFFODEN ISLANDS,
48 *Soroe*,
49 *Magroe*,
50 CYPRUS,
51 *Rhodes*,
52 *Scarpanto*,
53 *Samos*,
54 *Scio*,
55 *Mitylene*,
56 *Stalimni*,
57 NEGROPONT,
58 *Cyclades*,
59 CANDIA,

---

[*] Comprising only the smaller German States not otherwise numbered. Frankfort, Bremen, Hamburg and Lubeck, are free cities.

EUROPE.

IONIAN ISLANDS,
60 *Cerigo*,
61 *Zante*,
62 CEPHALONIA,
63 CORFU,
64 SICILY,
65 MALTA,
66 LIPARI ISLANDS,
67 ELBA,
68 CORSICA,
69 SARDINIA,
70 MINORCA,
71 MAJORCA,
72 IVICA,
73 *Jersey*,
74 *Guernsey*,
75 WIGHT,
76 SCILLY ISLANDS,
77 GREAT BRITAIN,
78 IRELAND,
79 *Anglesea*,
80 *Isle of Man*,
81 HEBRIDES ISLANDS,
82 ORKNEY ISLANDS,
83 SHETLAND ISLANDS,
84 FAROE ISLANDS,
85 ZEALAND,
86 FUNEN,
87 *Laaland*,
88 *Falster*,
89 *Rugen*,
90 *Bornholm*,
91 OLAND,
92 GOTHLAND,
93 *Oesel*,
94 *Dago*,
95 ALAND.

PENINSULAS

96 CRIMEA,
97 MOREA.

CAPES.

98 NORTH,
99 SVIATOI,
100 MATAPAN,
101 SPARTIVENTO,
102 PASSARO,
103 *Teulada*,
104 CORSO,
105 *San Martin*,
106 *Palos*,
107 GATA,
108 TRAFALGAR,
109 ST. VINCENT,
110 FINISTERRE,
111 ORTEGAL,
112 LA HAGUE,
113 LAND'S END,
114 CLEAR,
115 *Wrath*,
116 THE NAZE.

MOUNTAINS.

117 SCANDINAVIAN,
118 URAL,
119 CAUCASUS,
120 CARPATHIAN,
121 BALKAN,
122 ALPS,
123   MOUNT BLANC,
124 APENNINES,
125 MOUNT VESUVIUS,
126 MOUNT ÆTNA,
127 SIERRA NEVADA,
128 SIERRA MORENA,
129 CANTABRIAN,
130 MONTSERRAT,
131 PYRENEES,
132 *Cevennes*,
133 *Auvergne*,
134 *Grampian Hills*,
135 MOUNT HECLA.

LAKES.

136 WENER,
137 WETTER,
138 MAELAR,
139 *Purus*,
140 *Sego*,
141 *Vigo*,
142 ONEGA,
143 LADOGA,
144 *Ilmen*,
145 *Peipus*,
146 *Platten Zee*,
147 CONSTANCE,
148 GENEVA.

EUROPE.

RIVERS.

149 *Drammen,*
150 *Glommen,*
151 *Klar,*
152 Dahl,
153 *Indal,*
154 *Umea,*
155 *Skelleftea,*
156 *Lulea,*
156 Tornea,
158 *Keni,*
159 Onega,
160 Dwina,
161   *Sookhona,*
162   *Vitchegda,*
163 *Mezene,*
164 Petchora,
165   *Oosa,*
166 Ural,
167 Volga,
168   *Samara,*
169 Kama,
170   *Bielaya,*
171   *Viatka,*
172 Oka,
173 *Sura,*
174 *Kooma,*
175 *Terek,*
176 *Kooban,*
177 Don,
178   *Manitch,*
179   *Khoper,*
180   *Donets,*
181 Dnieper,
182   *Desna,*
183   *Pripets,*
184 Bog,
185 Dniester,
186 Danube,
187 Pruth,
188 Theiss,
189 Drave,
190 Save,
191 *Maritza,*
192 Po,
193 *Tiber,*
194 Rhone,
195   *Saone,*
196 Ebro,
197 Guadalquiver,
198 Guadiana,
199 Tagus,

200 Douro,
201 *Minho,*
202 Garonne,
203   *Dordogne,*
204 Loire,
205 Seine,
206 *Meuse,*
207 Rhine,
208 *Weser,*
209 Elbe,
210 Oder,
211   Wartha,
212 Vistula,
213   *Bug,*
214 Niemen,
215 Duna,
216 Nena,
217 *Volkho,*
218 *Sveer,*
219 *Hunnber,*
220 Thames,
221 Severn,
222 Shannon.

AFRICA ON THE MAP OF EUROPE.

COUNTRIES, CAPITALS AND CHIEF TOWNS.

1 **Morocco,**   1 Morocco, 2 *Rabat,* 3 *Mequinez,* 4 *Fez.*

2 **Algiers,**   1 Algiers, 2 *Oran,* 3 *Constantine,* 4 *Bona.*

3 **Tunis,**   1 Tunis, 2 *Kairwan.*

4 **Beled el Jereed,** 1 Touggoort.

5 **Tripoli,**   1 Tripoli, 2 *Mesurata.*

6 **Barca,**   1 Derne, 2 *Bengazi.*

7 **Egypt,**   1 Cairo, 2 *Alexandria,* 3 *Rosetta,* 4 *Damietta.*

ASIA ON THE MAP OF EUROPE.

COUNTRIES AND CHIEF TOWNS.

11 **Persia,**   2 *Tabreez.*

12 **Arabia,**   5 *Petra.*

13 **Turkey,**   1 Smyrna, 2 *Brusa,* 3 *Trebizond,* 4 *Erzroom,* 5 *Kars,* 6 *Diarbekir,* 7 *Mosul,* 8 *Bagdad,* 9 *Bassorah.*

14 **Syria,**   1 Aleppo, 2 *Damascus,* 3 *Jerusalem,* 4 *Beyroot.*

EUROPE.

QUESTIONS ON THE MAP OF EUROPE.

Bound Europe. How many square miles has it? Inhabitants? What is its latitude? Longitude? In what zones is it? What are its principal political divisions? Which is the most Northern? Eastern? Southern? Western?

Bound Norway. Sweden. Russia. Austria. Turkey. Greece. Italy. France. Spain. Portugal. England. Wales. Scotland. Ireland. Belgium. Holland. Denmark. Prussia. Germany. Switzerland. Name the capitals of each.

OCEANS, SEAS, BAYS AND GULFS.

What ocean west of Europe? 1. North? 2. What sea in the north of Russia? 3. North of Prussia? 25. East of Great Britain? 21. West? 20. What sea separates Europe from Africa? 12. What two seas south of Turkey? 10, 11. What three south of Russia? 6-8. What bays west of Ireland? 18, 19. What bay west of France? 17.

What gulf north of Russia? 5. What three gulfs west? 26-28. What two gulfs south and west of Italy? 14, 15. What gulf south of France? 16. North of Holland? 24.

STRAITS AND CHANNELS.

What three channels at the entrance of the Baltic Sea? 31-33. What two channels between great Britain and Ireland? 44, 45. What channel between England and France? 41. In the south-west of England? 43.

What strait separates England from France? 42. What strait is the entrance to the Mediterranean Sea? 40. What strait between the islands of Sardinia and Corsica? 39. Sicily and Italy? 38. Italy and Turkey? 37. What strait connects the Sea of Marmora and the Archipelago? 36. The sea of Marmora and the Black Sea? 35. The Black Sea and the sea of Azof? 34.

ISLANDS.

What islands off the west coast of Norway? 47, 48. What large island west of Norway? 46. What group south-east of Iceland? 84. To what country do they belong? To Denmark. What islands north of Scotland? 82, 83. What west? 81. What islands in the Irish Sea? 79, 80. What large island west of Great Britain? 78. What islands between England and France? 73-75. What islands between Sweden and Denmark? 85-88. What islands in the Baltic Sea? 89-95. What three islands east of Spain? 70-72. What islands south of Italy? 64, 66-69. What island south of Sicily? 65. To what government does it belong? To England. What islands west of Greece? 61, 62. What large island south of the Archipelago? 59. What two islands south of Turkey in Asia? 50, 51.

PENINSULAS AND CAPES.

What peninsula south of Russia? 96. Which is the most northern cape of Europe? 98. What cape south of Norway? 116. South-west of England? 113. South of Ireland? 114. Of Portugal? 109. What two capes has Spain on the north-west? 110, 111. What cape south of Greece? 100.

MOUNTAINS.

What mountains between Europe and Asia? 118. Between Norway and Sweden? 117. What mountains in Austria? 120. Turkey? 121. Switzerland? 122. Italy? 124. Spain? 127-130. France? 132, 133. What mountains separate France and Spain? 131.

What volcano in Iceland? 135. In Italy? 125. Sicily? 126.

LAKES.

What are the three principal lakes of Sweden? 136-138. What lakes has Russia? 139-145. What two lakes in Switzerland? 147, 148. What lake in Austria? 146.

RIVERS.

What rivers flow into the Arctic Ocean? 163, 164. Into the White Sea? 159, 160. What rivers of Russia flow into the Caspian Sea? 166, 167. Into the Sea of Azof? 177. Into the Black Sea? 181, 184, 185. What river from Turkey flows into the Black Sea? 186. Mention its principal branches. 187-190. What two rivers in Italy? 192, 193. What are the rivers of Spain and into what do they flow? 196-201. What are the principal rivers of France? 194, 202, 204, 205. What rivers flow into the North Sea? 206-209. Into the Baltic Sea? 210, 212, 214. What river flows into the Gulf of Riga? 215. What rivers flow into the Gulf of Bothnia? 152-158. What river flows from Lake Ladoga to the Gulf of Finland? 216. What three rivers in England? 219-221. What river in Ireland? 222.

EUROPE.

DESCRIPTIVE GEOGRAPHY.

Europe is the least of the grand divisions in size, but the first, in social, political, and commercial importance.

Numerous seas, gulfs and bays penetrate its coast; and the surface is agreeably diversified with mountains, hills, valleys, and plains.

The climate is cold in the north and east, generally temperate and healthful in the middle and west, and warm in the south.

The soil is mostly fertile, producing the most important grains in the north, while in the south, the vine, olive, orange, lemon, and other tropical fruits, are found in abundance.

Coal, iron, copper, lead, tin, zinc, mercury, and salt, are abundant. Gold, silver and precious stones, are found in the Ural mountains.

Europe has comparatively few wild animals, but domestic animals thrive in great numbers and variety.

Agriculture, manufactures and the arts are carried to a high degree of perfection, and its commerce is extensive.

The population is chiefly of Caucasian descent, and great inequalities in society exist.

The lower classes are often extremely ignorant and degraded, and the masses are unable to read and write. The nobility live in great luxury and often oppress the poor.

In many of the European states, common schools are unknown, but universities and colleges abound, which are more liberally endowed with funds and libraries than those of our own country.

Great improvements have been made in popular education during the present century.

The Roman Catholic, Protestant and Greek are the prevailing religions. The governments are chiefly monarchical. A few are small republics.

The principal political divisions of Europe are Norway, Sweden, Russia, Austria, Turkey, Greece, Italy or the Italian States, France, Spain, Portugal, England, Scotland, Ireland, Belgium, Holland, Denmark, Prussia, the German States, and Switzerland.

QUESTIONS. What is the rank of Europe among the grand divisions? What is said of its coast and surface? Climate? Soil? What minerals are abundant? What is said of the animals? Agriculture, &c.? Population? What is the condition of the people? Of education? What religions prevail? Government?, Name the principal political divisions.

1. NORWAY.

Square miles, 123,000.   Population, 1,328,000.

BERGEN.

Norway is a rough, mountainous country, abounding with cataracts and precipices, and presents much romantic scenery.

The winters are long and severe; the summers short, and very hot. The soil is rocky and barren, and but a small part of it suitable for cultivation.

Potatoes, barley, rye, and other kinds of grain, are raised, but the rearing of cattle, mining, and the manufacture of lumber, are the chief occupations of the people.

Norway is rich in mines of lead, iron, copper, and silver.

The Norwegians are well educated, frank, hospitable and industrious, manufacturing their clothing, furniture and tools.

Norway has a legislature of its own, but is subject to Sweden.

The Lutheran is the religion of the state and is professed by the great body of the people.

Education is very generally diffused; instruction is gratuitous, and children are required to attend school.

Norway was united with Sweden in 1814.

CHRISTIANIA, the seat of government, has a picturesque situation and a fine harbor. It is regularly laid out, and built wholly of stone and brick.

Drontheim was the residence of the ancient kings, and is one of the most northern towns in Europe.

Bergen has a good harbor, and is surrounded by mountains on the land side.

QUESTIONS. How many square miles has Norway? Inhabitants? What is its surface? Climate? Soil? What can you say of its products and pursuits? Mines? The Norwegians? Government? Religion? Education? When was Norway united with Sweden? Describe Christiania. Drontheim. Bergen.

2. SWEDEN.

Square miles, 170,000.   Population, 3,482,000.

Sweden is situated east of Norway, and with it forms the peninsula of Scandinavia.

It has in general a level surface, and is diversified by numerous beautiful lakes and rivers. The climate is cold but healthy.

EUROPE.

The soil is light, and a part of it only, capable of cultivation. It produces rye, barley, oats, and potatoes.

The chief resources of the people are the forests, fisheries and mines.

There are extensive mines of iron. Copper, silver and lead, are also found.

The inhabitants are industrious, virtuous, and distinguished for their intelligence and independence. From the polish of their manners, they are called the French of northern Europe.

The government is a limited constitutional monarchy.

Great pains is taken in education, and its primary, grammar schools and universities are superior.

The Lutheran religion is professed by the great body of the people, though other religions are tolerated.

STOCKHOLM, the capital, is beautifully situated between lake Maelar and the Baltic sea. It is built partly on the main land, and partly on several islands connected with each other and the main land by bridges. It has an excellent harbor, and considerable commerce. Its royal palace is one of the finest buildings in Europe.

Gothenburg is, next to Stockholm, the most important trading city of the kingdom.

QUESTIONS. How many square miles has Sweden? Inhabitants? How is it situated? What is said of its surface and climate? Soil? Productions? The chief resources? Its mines? Inhabitants? Government? Education? Religion? Stockholm? Gothenburg?

RUSSIAN EMPIRE.

The Russian Empire is the most extensive empire in the world, containing over seven millions of square miles, and sixty-five millions of inhabitants. It embraces Russia in Europe, Russia in Asia, and Russian America.

QUESTIONS. What is the extent of the Russian Empire? What does it embrace?

3. RUSSIA.

Square miles, 2,142,000. Population, 60,000,000.

Russia is a vast plain occupying all the eastern part of Europe, and comprising more than one-half of it. It abounds with lakes, majestic rivers, and immense forests.

The northern part is excessively cold, and only adapted to grazing. The other sections are temperate, with a fertile soil, producing abundantly, wheat, rye, oats, barley, maize, potatoes, flax, hemp, hops, and various kinds of fruits.

Iron, copper, salt, gold, platina, diamonds, and other precious stones, abound.

Cattle and sheep are reared in great numbers.

THE ROYAL PALACE, STOCKHOLM.

GENERAL VIEW OF THE KREMLIN, AT MOSCOW.

Manufactures and the arts are much encouraged, and have rapidly improved within a few years.

Russia has an extensive system of canals, and several railways are completed, or in progress.

The traveling in the winter is principally by sledges drawn upon the snow.

The inland commerce of Russia is extensive, but its foreign commerce is limited, many of its harbors being frozen over most of the year. Tallow, wheat, hemp, flax, flaxseed, timber, and leather, are the chief exports.

The inhabitants belong to the Caucasian and Asiatic races, and speak different languages. The nobility are wealthy, and live in great splendor.

The government is a military despotism, supported by an army of seven hundred thousand men. The emperor, styled the Autocrat of Russia, is at the head of both church and state.

The established religion is that of the Greek church.

St. Petersburg, the seat of government, is situated at the head of the Gulf of Finland. It was founded by Peter the Great, and from the extent and magnificence of many of its buildings, is called the city of palaces. It also contains many elegant churches. In commerce and science it is the first city in Russia.

Moscow is a very populous city, abounding with beautiful palaces and gardens. It was burnt to the ground in 1812, to prevent the army of Napoleon from occupying it, but has been rebuilt with increased splendor. The Kremlin, or ancient citadel of Moscow, is surrounded by an immense white wall.

Sevastopol is an important town and the principal naval station of Russia on the Black Sea. The forts were principally destroyed by the English and French in 1855. *Odessa*, on the Black sea, *Riga*, on the Baltic sea, *Archangel*, on the White sea, and *Cronstadt*, on an island in the gulf of Finland, are important seaports.

EUROPE.

QUESTIONS. What is the number of square miles in Russia? Inhabitants? What is the surface? Climate, soil and productions? What is said of minerals? Cattle and sheep? Manufactures? Canals and railways? Commerce and exports? The inhabitants? Government? The Emperor? Religion? St. Petersburg? Moscow? Sevastopol? Odessa, Riga, Archangel and Cronstadt?

RUSSIAN PROVINCES.

4. LAPLAND.

Lapland is a dreary, mountainous region, lying at the extreme northern part of Europe, and belongs principally to Russia, but a portion of it to Sweden and Norway.

It is intensely cold, and covered with snow two-thirds of the year. Vegetation is scanty, but minerals are abundant.

The Laplanders are a small hardy race, and rude in their customs. They live in huts, in the center of which they build fires, while the smoke escapes through a hole at the top.

The reindeer, of which they own great numbers, draw them over the snow in sledges; while their milk and flesh supplies them with food, and their skins and horns, with clothing and household furniture.

Tornea and *Kola* are the chief towns.

QUESTIONS. What is Lapland? Its climate? Vegetation? What can you say of the Laplanders? The reindeer? Tornea and Kola?

5. POLAND.

Poland, a once powerful country, was conquered in 1795, and divided between Russia, Austria, and Prussia.

The portion that fell to Russia was erected into a kingdom in 1815, but seeking to regain its independence in 1830, it was completely subdued.

The surface is almost a perfect level; the soil very fertile; and the inhabitants, as in Russia, divided into several grades. The Jews are very numerous and enjoy many privileges.

CATHEDRAL AT CRACOW.

Cracow, the ancient capital of Poland, is now under the Austrian Government. It is celebrated for its magnificent cathedral, in which most of the Polish kings and illustrious men are buried.

Warsaw, the last capital of the kingdom of Poland, is the most important commercial city. It has many fine promenades and palaces.

QUESTIONS. When was Poland conquered? What occurred in 1815? In 1830? What is said of the surface and soil? The inhabitants? Describe Cracow. Warsaw.

6. AUSTRIA.

Square miles, 257,000. Population, 36,514,000.

Austria is an extensive empire in Central Europe, embracing portions of ancient Germany and Poland. It ranks among the leading states of Europe.

It is generally mountainous, though there is a great variety of surface.

The climate is very variable.

The soil is good in the valleys and on the plains, but is not well cultivated.

The productions are, in the north, wheat, rye, oats and barley; in the central and southern provinces, the vine, maize and olives, are produced.

Various minerals, as gold, silver, iron, copper, quicksilver, lead, and salt, are found in great quantities.

The commerce of Austria is limited, but its manufactures are of considerable importance. It has but a small extent of sea-coast.

The inhabitants are chiefly Roman Catholics, and the body of them, though possessing a common education, much oppressed. The government is intolerant, restraining the liberty of the press and freedom of speech. The emperor has almost unlimited power.

VIENNA, the capital, is situated in the midst of a beautiful plain on the river Danube. It has many handsome buildings, and is the residence of great numbers of wealthy noblemen.

Prague is peculiar in its architecture, and from its domes has quite an oriental appearance. *Pesth*, on the left bank of the Danube, is an important city. It is regularly laid out, and is the seat of the only university in Hungary. *Debreczin* has extensive manufactures of soap, tobacco pipe bowls and shoes. *Trieste* is the principal seaport of Austria.

QUESTIONS. How many square miles in Austria? Inhabitants? How is it situated? What does it embrace? How does it rank? What are its surface, climate and soil? Productions? What minerals are found? What is said of commerce and manufactures? The inhabitants? Government? Vienna? Prague, Pesth, and Debreczin? Trieste?

VIEW OF TRIESTE.

TURKISH, OR OTTOMAN EMPIRE.

Turkey, or the Ottoman empire, comprises Turkey in Europe, Turkey in Asia, and a large territory in Africa, including Tunis, Tripoli and Egypt, and their dependencies.

It is ruled by the Sultan, or Grand Porte, whom the Turks impiously style the "Shadow of God" —the "Brother of the Sun," &c.

QUESTIONS. What does Turkey comprise? How is it ruled?

7. TURKEY IN EUROPE.

Square miles, 210,000. Population, 15,500,000.

This country is situated on the west of the Black sea and sea of Marmora, and south of Austria.

It is beautifully diversified with mountains, plains and valleys; and the climate, though subject to extremes of heat and cold, is generally healthy.

The valleys are fertile, and yield in profusion wheat, maize, rice, cotton, tobacco, and various fruits, but agriculture is badly conducted.

Immense numbers of silk-worms are reared on the leaves of the mulberry.

Manufactures are much neglected, and the commerce is chiefly in the hands of foreigners. Education and the arts receive little attention.

The Turks are a well formed race, but extremely haughty, grave and indolent. They are rigid Mohammedans, and very superstitious. Their customs and dress are unlike those of other Europeans. They wear turbans, and loose flowing robes, —sit on cushions, and dispense with knives and forks in eating. Bathing and smoking seem to be their favorite employments.

The government has the characteristic features of an Asiatic despotism, but has been very much modified by the influence of European powers, and especially by that of the allied powers of France and England, whose armies occupied the country during the struggle with Russia in the war of 1854-56.

CONSTANTINOPLE is the capital of the Ottoman Empire, and the residence of the Sultan. It is a strongly fortified, populous, and beautiful city, situated on the Bosporus, with considerable commerce. Its harbor, called the *Golden Horn*, is one of the most secure, capacious and beautiful in the world.

Adrianople, the former metropolis, is a flourishing city.

QUESTIONS. How many square miles has Turkey in Europe? Inhabitants? What is its situation? What is said of the surface and climate? Soil and

RUINS AT PHILIPPI.

productions? What is said of manufactures and commerce? Education and the arts? Describe the Turks. Their customs, &c. Government. Constantinople. Adrianople.

8. GREECE.

Square miles, 18,500. Population, 1,002,000.

Greece is a small kingdom south of Turkey, comprising two peninsulas united by a narrow isthmus, and several islands.

The surface is mountainous in the interior, interspersed with fertile vales. There are a few small plains.

The climate is mild but variable. Wheat, maize, rice, cotton, wool, silk, oil, and a variety of fruits, are produced.

The Greeks are an active, brave and polished people, possessing much genius and love of distinction. They have little learning, but are adepts in cunning and intrigue.

Schools and colleges have recently been established, and the inhabitants seem desirous of improvement.

The government is a hereditary monarchy. A constitution was granted in 1844.

The Greek church is the religion established by law.

For several centuries the Greeks were in subjection to the Turks, who took every method to degrade and oppress them. In 1820, they asserted their independence; and after a long and bloody contest, secured it through the mediation of England, France and Russia.

Ancient Greece was one of the most powerful empires in the world. Two thousand years ago it was the land of song, and the seat of learning and the arts. Ruins of architecture and sculpture still remain, and afford the artist many of his finest models.

ATHENS, one of the most famous cities of antiquity, is the capital of modern Greece. Ruins of magnificent temples and theaters still exist, but they render the meanness of its present buildings only the more conspicuous.

Corinth, in remote times, was one of the most flourishing cities of Greece, and proverbial for its luxury. It is now an important port, and its citadel and fortifications are, next to those of Nauplia, the strongest in Greece. *Nauplia*, is a strongly fortified seaport in the Morea.

QUESTIONS. How many square miles has Greece? Inhabitants? What does it comprise? What is its surface? Climate? What are its productions? What is the character of the Greeks? What is said of education? Government? Religion? Of the subjection of the Greeks? Their independence? Ancient Greece? Ruins? Athens? Corinth? Nauplia?

IONIAN ISLANDS.

Square Miles, 1000. Population, 230,000.

The Ionian Republic comprises the islands in the Ionian sea, west of Greece; and is under the protection of Great Britain.

About half the surface is under cultivation, yielding wheat, barley and other grains, wines, olive oil, and currants.

The inhabitants number about two hundred thousand, chiefly Greeks and Italians, and are shrewd, active, and industrious.

CORFU, on the island of Corfu, is the capital.

QUESTIONS. What does the Ionian Republic comprise? What can you say of the surface and productions? Inhabitants? Corfu?

ITALY, OR THE ITALIAN STATES.

Square miles, 119,000. Population, 24,700,000.

Italy is a celebrated country in the south of Europe and consists of a large peninsula and several islands.

Its surface is varied; a range of mountains extending north and south nearly through the peninsula. Between the mountains are numerous fertile valleys, abounding in beautiful scenery. In the north is a large and fertile plain, very productive.

It has an excellent climate; the atmosphere is remarkable for its clearness.

Agriculture is the leading pursuit. Wheat, maize, rye, rice, oil, wine, silk, dates, almonds, figs, and oranges, are the chief products. Manufactures and commerce are in a languishing condition.

It is rich in mineral products, but has few metals except iron and lead.

The Apennines furnish the beautiful marble of Carrara.

The Italians possess ardent feelings, lively imaginations, and much skill in music, painting and sculpture; but are deplorably indolent, ignorant and superstitious. The Roman Catholic is the established religion; and the clergy compose a considerable portion of the population.

THE PONTE SANTA TRINITA &C., FLORENCE.

Italy was once the seat of a mighty empire, and renowned in the arts and sciences. Monuments of its former wealth and magnificence are every where seen.

In modern times, it has been subdivided into a number of independent kingdoms or states. The principal divisions have been the kingdom of Sardinia, the kingdom of Lombardy and Venice, the duchies of Parma and Modena, the grand duchy of Tuscany, the States of the Church, and the kingdom of Naples.

The eastern part of the Lombardo Venitian kingdom is subject to Austria; the other states have been united under one government.

Mount Etna, a burning volcano, is situated on the island of Sicily, and Mount Vesuvius, near the bay of Naples.

Turin is situated in the midst of a fertile plain, and is remarkable for its neatness and regularity.

Milan is one of the most splendid cities in Italy. Its cathedral is a fine structure of pure white marble, containing 4000 statues.

Florence is situated on the river Arno, and is celebrated for its beautiful fountains, churches, palaces, statuary, and paintings.

Rome is situated on the Tiber and built on seven hills. It was once the metropolis of the renowned, ancient Roman empire. It has been celebrated in modern times for the number and grandeur of its fountains and churches. It contains the church of St. Peter, a magnificent temple, erected at an expense of over eighty millions of dollars.

Naples is located at the foot of Mount Vesuvius, on the north side of the bay of Naples. In beauty of situation, clearness of atmosphere, and mildness of climate, it is almost unrivaled.

THE ASINELLI AND GARISENDA TOWERS, BOLOGNA

Bologna is noted for the lofty tower of Asinelli, and for the leaning tower of Garisenda. From the top of the former more than a hundred cities may be seen.

Genoa is a commercial city pleasantly located on the gulf of Genoa.

QUESTIONS. What is the number of square miles in Italy? Inhabitants? Of what does it consist? What is its surface? Climate? What is said of agriculture? What are its chief products? What is said of manufactures and commerce? Minerals? The inhabitants? Religion? The former condition of Italy? How has it been subdivided in modern times? What is said of the government? Of Mount Etna and Mount Vesuvius? Describe Turin. Milan. Florence. Rome. Naples. Bologna. Genoa.

16. FRANCE.

Square miles, 200,700. Population, 37,472,000.

France is an important empire in the west of Europe, extending from the Mediterranean Sea to the Atlantic Ocean.

HOTEL DE VILLE, PARIS.

The surface is level in the north, consisting mostly of an extensive plain, but hilly and mountainous in the south.

The soil is usually fertile, and the climate temperate and agreeable.

It surpasses all the other countries of Europe in the variety of its agricultural products.

The chief productions are wheat, rye, oats, barley, maize, potatoes, and grapes. The grape vineyards cover several millions of acres, and produce large quantities of wine.

Agriculture is in an advanced state, and a chief pursuit. In the variety and value of its manufactures, France is only second to England; and its commerce is very extensive.

Its minerals are lead, iron, coal and salt.

The French are very gay, social and polite, remarkable for their versatility and bravery, and extremely fond of amusements, especially dancing.

Public libraries and colleges are numerous; many of the French are distinguished for their learning and science, and much progress has been made in common education. All religious sects are tolerated, but the people are chiefly Roman Catholics.

The government was formerly one of the most powerful monarchies of Europe. In the revolution of 1848 it became republican in form, and in 1853 was changed to an empire.

PARIS, the capital, situated on the river Seine, is noted for the number and elegance of its public buildings and gardens, and as the seat of literature, science and fashion. It is extensively engaged in man ufactures, and is celebrated for its mathematical and optical instruments.

Lyons is a populous, wealthy and commercial city, celebrated for its manufactures of silk, and gold and silver stuffs. *Marseilles* is the chief seaport on the Mediterranean. *Rouen* is noted for its manufactures; *Bordeaux*, for its wines. *Toulon* and *Brest* are large naval stations. *Havre* has an extensive trade with the United States.

To France also belongs the island of Corsica, in the Mediterranean sea. *Ajaccio*, on this island was the birth-place of Bonaparte.

QUESTIONS. How many square miles has France? Inhabitants? How is it situated? What is said of its surface, soil and climate? Products? Agriculture, manufactures and commerce? Minerals? The French? The state of education? The government? Paris? Lyons? Marseilles? Rouen? Bordeaux? Toulon and Brest? Havre? Corsica? Ajaccio?

17. SPAIN.

Square miles, 188,000. Population, 13,900,000.

Spain occupies the larger part of the peninsula in the south-west of Europe.

Several ranges of mountains render its surface broken, and afford much wild and romantic scenery.

The climate is warm on the coast, but subject to great changes on the table lands. The soil is varied.

In the fertile regions, wheat, rice, maize, and barley, are produced, and various fruits flourish, particularly grapes, oranges, lemons, figs, and melons.

The minerals are numerous and valuable, but at present little worked. They include gold, silver, quicksilver, copper, iron, and zinc.

Manufactures and commerce are greatly neglected; and the people lack a spirit of enterprise and improvement.

The Spaniards are proud, friendly and brave; but ignorant, easily excited and revengeful. They are extremely fond of amusements, among which are dancing, music and bull-fights. In religion, they are Roman Catholics.

THE LEANING TOWER OF SAN FELIPE, SARAGOSSA.

The government is a limited monarchy, and formerly possessed vast territories in North and South America. The only American colonies now subject to Spain are Cuba, Porto Rico, and a few smaller West India islands. Its dependencies in the Mediterranean are the Balearic islands.

MADRID, the capital, is built on low and irregular sand hills, and is surrounded by a barren and extensive plain. It has several fine palaces, churches and public squares, but is almost destitute of manufactures and trade.

Gibraltar, the most strongly fortified city

in the world, is situated at the southern extremity of Spain, on a bold rocky bluff. It has been in possession of the British since 1705. *Cadiz*, on the island of Leon, is the principal seaport. *Saragossa* is noted for the leaning tower of San Felipe.

QUESTIONS. How many square miles has Spain? Inhabitants? How is it situated? What is said of its surface? Climate and soil? Productions? What minerals are found? What can you say of manufactures and commerce? The Spaniards? Government? Madrid? Gibraltar? Cadiz? Saragossa?

18. PORTUGAL.

Square miles, 35,090. Population, 3,471,000.

Portugal is situated in the south-western part of Europe.

THE SQUARE AND FOUNTAIN OF TOWERS AT BRAGA.

It is beautifully diversified with hills and plains, and possesses a mild and agreeable climate.

The soil is fertile, but agriculture is in a very backward state. Wheat, barley, oats, flax, rice, olives, oranges, lemons, and grapes, are the chief products.

The manufactures are limited. The commerce, formerly large, is now less extensive, and mostly in the hands of foreigners.

The Portuguese resemble the Spaniards in their characteristics, but the two nations have a deep rooted antipathy to each other. The government is a limited monarchy. The religion is Roman Catholic.

LISBON, the capital and principal seaport, is situated at the mouth of the river Tagus, and has considerable commerce. It has several fine public buildings and churches.

Oporto is noted for its wines; *Coimbra* for its University; and *Setubal* for its manufacture of salt.

QUESTIONS. What number of square miles in Portugal? Inhabitants? Where is it situated? What is said of its surface and climate? Soil and productions? Manufactures and commerce? The Portuguese? Government? Religion? Lisbon? Oporto, Coimbra, and Setubal?

THE BRITISH ISLES.

Great Britain comprises England, Wales and Scotland; and with Ireland forms "The United Kingdom of Great Britain and Ireland," also called "The British Isles."

Its principal foreign possessions are British America, West Indies, Cape Colony, a large part of India and Australia. These, with other colonies, united with the British Isles, form the British Empire.

Great Britain is distinguished for the enterprise and intelligence of its inhabitants, and is unrivaled in the extent of its manufactures and commerce.

The government is a limited and hereditary monarchy.

QUESTIONS. What does Great Britain comprise? What are the principal possessions of the United Kingdom? What does the whole form? How distinguished? What is the government?

VIEW OF LONDON FROM GREENWICH PARK.

19. ENGLAND.

Square miles, 51,000. Population, 18,949,000.

England comprises the southern portion of the island of Great Britain.

It has a beautifully diversified surface and abounds with picturesque scenery. The climate is mild, but damp, and the soil, though not naturally fertile, has been brought to a high state of cultivation, and yields the various grains and vegetables in abundance.

Coal, iron, copper, tin, lead. and salt, are found in large quantities. Several mineral and hot springs exist, to which throngs of invalids and fashionable people resort.

England has carried agriculture to a very high state of perfection, and excels every other nation in the variety and value of its manufactures.

It is densely populated, but striking differences are seen in the character and social condition of its citizens. The nobility live in affluence and luxury,—the poor, often in great want. As a nation, however, the English may be characterized as grave, honest, industrious, benevolent, and brave.

The universities of England are numerous and distinguished; but many of the poorer classes are entirely destitute of instruction.

The religion is protestant, though all religious sects have perfect freedom.

LONDON is the capital of the British Empire and the largest city in Europe. It is situated on the river Thames, and in wealth and commerce and its literary and benevolent institutions, it surpasses every other city on the globe.

A number of beautiful bridges cross the Thames, and a tunnel forms a passage under the bed of the river. Many of its public buildings are very imposing structures. St. Paul's Church is next to St. Peter's at Rome, in point of magnificence.

Greenwich, a borough and parish adjoining London, contains the royal observatory from which the longitudes in all British charts are reckoned, and it has a magnificent naval hospital, for the maintenance of wounded or unfortunate seamen. Greenwich park contains about two hundred acres of undulating and wooded land, and is a place much resorted to by the inhabitants of London.

WINDSOR CASTLE.

Liverpool, on the river Mersey, is the second commercial city, carrying on an immense trade with all parts of the world. *Bristol* is situated on the Avon, and has an extensive commerce. It was the first port in Britain, whence regular steam communication with the United States was established. *Birmingham* is noted for its iron manufactures, and *Manchester* for its manufactures of cotton. *Portsmouth* and *Plymouth* are important naval stations.

QUESTIONS. How many square miles has England? Inhabitants? What does it comprise? What is the surface? Climate? Soil? What is said of minerals and springs? Of England in respect to agriculture and manufactures? Its citizens? How may the English be characterized? What is said of education? Religion? London? Greenwich? Liverpool? Bristol? Birmingham and Manchester? Portsmouth and Plymouth?

20. WALES.

Square miles, 7,400. Population, 1,111,000.

Wales is situated west of England, and has generally a mountainous surface.

Its climate is similar to that of England, and its soil is fertile.

The principal productions are barley, oats, and potatoes.

Coal, iron, copper, and lead are abundant.

The Welsh are descendants of the ancient Britons, and are an industrious and hospitable people. Until 1283, Wales was an independent kingdom, when it was united to England.

Merthyr-Tydvil is the principal town, and is situated in a mining district.

QUESTIONS. What number of square miles in Wales? Inhabitants? What can you say of its situation and surface? Climate, soil and productions? Minerals? The Welsh? History? Merthyr-Tydvil?

21. SCOTLAND.

Square miles, 30,000. Population, 3,061,000.

Scotland occupies the whole of the northern part of the island of Great Britain.

It has a broken surface and is noted for the wildness and grandeur of its mountain scenery, its rapid streams, and beautiful lakes, called lochs.

The Grampian Hills divide it into two sections, called the Highlands and the Lowlands. The Highlands are cool, and chiefly adapted to pasture; the Lowlands are milder, and productive of various kinds of grain and vegetables.

The principal minerals are coal, iron, lead, and copper. Manufactures are flourishing; and commerce and the fisheries are extensively pursued.

The Scotch are grave, hardy, and enterprising; of a moral and religious turn of mind; and are remarkably well instructed. Schools are established in every parish, and many of the most distinguished scholars, historians, and poets, have sprung from Scotland.

EDINBURGH CASTLE.

EDINBURGH, the metropolis of Scotland, is distinguished for its romantic site, and numerous literary and charitable institutions. *Glasgow* is a large city, with flourishing manufactures, and noted for its university. *Aberdeen* and *Dundee* are very flourishing manufacturing and commercial towns.

The Hebrides, Orkney, and Shetland islands comprise several hundred in number, and belong to Scotland.

Fingal's Cave, a very romantic cavern, is on the island of Staffa, one of the Hebrides. It is composed of basaltic columns, beautifully jointed and of various forms.

QUESTIONS. How many square miles has Scotland? Inhabitants? Where is it situated? What is its surface and for what is it noted? How divided? What is said of the Highlands? Lowlands? Minerals, manufactures and commerce? The Scotch? Schools and scholars? Edinburgh? Glasgow? Aberdeen and Dundee? The islands? Fingal's Cave?

---

22. IRELAND.

Square miles, 32,500. Population, 5,764,000.

Ireland is a large island, west of Great Britain, sometimes called "Green Erin," from the beauty of its verdure.

Its coast is generally bold and rugged. The surface is undulating, a large part of the interior consisting of an expanse of bog, from which peat for fuel is obtained.

The climate is mild; but its great moisture renders the country better adapted to grazing than tillage. Potatoes, oats, flax, wheat, and barley, are the chief products. Linen is the principal article of manufacture. Cotton and woolen goods are made to a limited extent.

The Irish are ardent, brave, generous, and possess a large share of good humor and wit; but the mass of them are in a state of extreme wretchedness and poverty. The majority are Roman Catholics.

The Giant's Causeway, on the north-west coast, consists of perpendicular columns of basaltic rock, extending into the sea from the base of a stratified cliff. It is the most remarkable curiosity in Ireland.

DUBLIN, the capital, abounds with magnificent edifices and handsome streets, and is surrounded by beautiful suburbs. But in the midst of all this splendor, the deepest indigence and distress are to be found.

Cork is the second city in size, and has a capacious harbor with an extensive commerce. Belfast is also a commercial city.

QUESTIONS. Give the number of square miles in Ireland. Inhabitants. What are the surface and soil? What can you say of the climate? Products? Linen, cotton and woolen goods? The Irish? The Giant's Causeway? Dublin? Cork? Belfast?

23. BELGIUM.

Square miles, 11,400. Population, 4,359,000.

Belgium is a small kingdom of Western Europe, situated north-east of France.

Its surface may be regarded as an inclined plane, somewhat rugged, elevated in the south-east and sloping to the north-west.

The climate is temperate and agreeable, but the low flats are considered unhealthy.

The soil is so highly cultivated as to resemble a garden, and agriculture is carried to the highest perfection. Grains, tobacco, flax, hemp, and fruits, grow in great luxuriance.

The mineral kingdom is exceedingly rich in lead, manganese, zinc, iron, and coal, and manufactures and commerce are in a flourishing state.

The roads of Belgium are very superior, and spacious canals connect the principal cities.

The Belgians combine the persevering industry of the Dutch with the vivacity of the French, and are distinguished for mechanical skill. They are rigid adherents of the Catholic religion. The government is a limited monarchy.

BRUSSELS, the capital, is a beautiful city, adorned with elegant palaces, handsome squares, fountains, and shaded walks. It is also noted for the manufacture of laces, carpets and linens.

Ghent has extensive manufactures. The treaty of peace between the United States and Great Britain was signed here in 1814. Antwerp is the chief commercial city of Belgium, and contains one of the most magnificent cathedrals in Europe.

QUESTIONS. How many square miles has Belgium? Inhabitants? What is Belgium? What is said of its surface? Climate? Soil and agriculture? Productions? Mineral kingdom? Manufactures and commerce? Roads and canals? The Belgians? Government? Brussels? Ghent? Antwerp?

24. HOLLAND.

Square miles, 13,000. Population, 3,962,000.

Holland lies on the North sea, east of Belgium.

CANAL AND PALACE, AMSTERDAM.

It is a flat country, and a part of it is lower than the level of the sea, which is kept from overflowing its surface by embankments raised along its coasts.

It has a moist and cool climate, and a surpassingly rich and productive soil. Grains and fruits are raised abundantly; but more attention is paid to the raising of cattle, and the making of butter and cheese.

Commerce and manufactures, though not so extensive as formerly, are in a flourishing condition. Canals are very numerous, and afford the principal means of conveyance.

The Dutch are a remarkably neat, frugal, industrious, patient, and honest people. Protestantism is the prevailing religion. The government is a limited monarchy.

HAGUE, the capital, is handsomely built, and intersected by numerous canals, whose banks are bordered with trees.

Amsterdam, the most populous and chief commercial city of Holland, is built on piles driven into a marsh of the Zuyder Zee. It is divided by canals into ninety islands, which are connected with each other by nearly 300 bridges.

Its stadt-house is a most magnificent building of freestone, resting on piles driven very deep into the ground.

QUESTIONS. What is the number of square miles in Holland? Inhabitants? Where is it situated? What is said of its surface? Climate and soil? Grains and fruits? Cattle? Commerce and manufactures? Canals? The Dutch? Religion? Government? Hague? Amsterdam?

---

25. DENMARK.

Square miles, 23,000. Population, 2,108,000.

Denmark comprises the peninsula of Jutland, and the adjacent islands, lying north of Germany.

It has a moist, but healthy climate. The soil is in general sandy, interspersed with some extensive fertile tracts.

Agriculture is the leading pursuit, and wheat, rye, barley, oats, buckwheat, and peas, are raised in considerable quantities. Cattle and poultry are reared in great numbers. The products of the dairy are important articles of export.

THE EXCHANGE AT COPENHAGEN.

Denmark is favorably situated for commerce and is extensively engaged in the whale and herring fisheries.

The Danes are industrious, honest and well educated. Common schools are very numerous, and the attendance of the children is enforced by law. The Lutheran is the established religion. The government is an unlimited monarchy, but wisely administered.

COPENHAGEN, on the island of Zealand, is the capital. It has an excellent harbor and extensive dockyards, and is adorned with numerous beautiful squares and fine buildings.

The Danish possessions include Greenland, (already described,) Iceland and the Faroe islands.

ICELAND is cold and mountainous, abounding with volcanoes and boiling springs. Vegetation is scanty, and the inhabitants chiefly subsist on cattle, sheep and fish. The Icelanders are simple in their habits, but industrious and well instructed.

QUESTIONS. How many square miles has Denmark? Inhabitants? What does it comprise? What is the climate? Soil? What can you say of agriculture and the products? The situation of Denmark in respect to commerce? The Danes? Common schools? Religion and government? Copenhagen? Danish possessions? Iceland and its inhabitants?

20. PRUSSIA.

Square miles, 109,000. Population, 18,491,000.

Prussia is divided into two sections by the kingdom of Hanover.

COLOGNE.

The principal division is situated between the Baltic sea and Austria. The western division lies south of Holland and Hanover.

The eastern division is very level, abounding in plains, some of them covered with extensive forests. The western division has numerous low mountain ranges enclosing fertile valleys.

The climate is in general healthy. Much of the soil in the eastern section is sandy and unproductive; that of the western is more fertile.

Wheat, rye, barley, oats, potatoes, and cattle, are largely produced. The minerals are iron, coal, copper, zinc, tin, silver, salt, and, on the shores of the Baltic, amber.

The inhabitants are chiefly Protestants, of German descent, and well educated.

Prussia has a well organized and complete system of public instruction, and every child is required by law to attend school.

The government is an absolute monarchy.

BERLIN, the seat of government, is built on a sandy plain, on both banks of the Spree, and is about ten miles in circumference. It is surrounded by a wall sixteen feet high. It is an elegant city, distinguished for the magnificence of many of its public buildings, and for its literary institutions, and possesses extensive manufactures and trade.

Breslau is extensively engaged in manufactures and trade.

Dantzic and *Konigsberg* are the principal seaports.

Cologne, upon the Rhine, is built in the form of a crescent.

QUESTIONS. What is the number of square miles in Prussia? Inhabitants? How is it divided? What is its situation? The surface? Climate? What are produced? What minerals are abundant? What can you say of the inhabitants? System of instruction? Government? Berlin? Breslau? Dantzic and Konigsberg? Cologne?

27. GERMANY.

Square miles, 92,000. Population, 17,592,000.

Germany proper occupies the central part of Europe.

The Germanic confederation comprises one-third of Austria, nearly all of Prussia, the duchies of Holstein and Lauenburg in Denmark, the kingdoms of Bavaria, Hanover, Saxony, and Wurtemburg, with twenty-eight smaller states, or principalities, and four free cities.

The northern section of Germany consists of a plain which is low and sandy; the central part, of a plateau and mountainous region, and the southern, of mountains and valleys.

The climate is remarkably uniform, except in the district south of the Alps.

With the exception of the loftier mountain districts, the soil is fertile, producing the various grains, and hemp, flax, potatoes, tobacco and hops. Grapes are extensively cultivated south of latitude 51° and in the valley of the Rhine.

Iron, copper, coal, gold, silver, and other metals, are found. Agriculture is the leading pursuit. Manufactures are flourishing, but commerce receives little attention.

The Germans have light complexions, and are noted for industry, perseverance, frankness and hospitality. They are generally well educated, imaginative, and fond of music and dancing.

Universities of the highest celebrity, schools and valuable libraries abound, and no nation produces a greater number of authors, or men more distinguished in science, than Germany.

The German Diet, composed of delegates from the several states, holds its sessions at FRANKFORT, on the Maine, a city noted for the amount of business transacted at its semi-annual fairs.

QUESTIONS. How many square miles has Germany proper? Inhabitants? Where is it situated? What does the Germanic Confederation comprise? What is said of the surface of Germany? Climate? Soil and products? Minerals? Pursuits? The Germans? Universities and Schools? The German Diet?

28. MECKLENBURG.

Square miles, 5,600. Population, 641,000.

Mecklenburg is a level, agricultural tract, bordering on the Baltic Sea. Cattle are reared in great numbers. Liquor, distilled from corn, is the principal article of manufacture.

SCHWERIN is the capital, and *Rostwick* the chief seaport.

QUESTIONS. Describe Mecklenburg? Name its capital and seaport?

29. HANOVER.

Square miles, 14,800. Population, 1,819,000.

Hanover is a kingdom in the north-west of Germany.

In the low alluvial flats, the soil is remarkably rich, but it has many barren heaths. Agriculture and manufactures are in a low condition.

Gold, silver, copper, lead, iron, and coal, are found; and mining constitutes a chief branch of industry.

HANOVER, the capital, is built in a sandy plain. It is divided by the Leine, a branch of the Weser, into the old and new town;

the former, ill built and dirty; the latter, regularly laid out.

Gottingen is the seat of a university; the library, observatory and botanical gardens of which, are among the most celebrated in Europe.

QUESTIONS. Where is Hanover situated? What is said of the soil? What is the condition of agriculture and manufactures in Hanover? What minerals are found? What is said of Hanover? Gottingen?

30. SAXONY.

Square miles, 5,000. Population, 2,000,000.

Saxony, a kingdom of central Germany, is situated south of Prussia.

DRESDEN.

The climate in the loftier mountain districts is cold and bleak, but in other parts, it is milder than in most countries of Europe in the same latitude.

This kingdom is distinguished for the productiveness of its soil, the superiority of its cattle and sheep, and the variety and richness of its minerals.

Agriculture, manufactures and trade are in a flourishing condition, and education is universally diffused

Its university, gymnasia and schools have been much celebrated.

Universal toleration is guaranteed to all religious creeds; but the principal religion is Lutheran.

DRESDEN, the capital, is a beautiful city, with superb palaces and churches, and valuable libraries and galleries of paintings.

Leipsic is the second city in Saxony, and one of the chief seats of commerce in Germany. It is noted for its fairs, at which people are congregated from all parts of Europe, and from Asia and America. It is extensively engaged in the manufacture and trade of books. Its university is one of the most distinguished in Germany.

QUESTIONS. Where is Saxony situated? What is said of the climate? For what is it distinguished? What is the state of agriculture, manufactures and trade? What is said of educational institutions? Religion? Describe Dresden? Leipsic?

31. BAVARIA.

Square miles, 20,000.
Population, 4,000,000.

The Kingdom of Bavaria, situated west of Austria, with a small portion of territory west of the Rhine, in extent and population, is the most important state of Germany proper.

The climate is temperate and healthful, though on account of its general elevation, it is colder than the other countries of Germany.

The soil is fertile, the mountains yielding excellent pasturage, while the valleys are productive in grains and fruits.

MUNICH, the capital, is one of the handsomest cities in Germany, and is noted for its literary institutions, and fine galleries of paintings and sculpture.

THE CATHEDRAL OF SPIRES.

Nuremberg has an antique appearance, and is celebrated for the manufacture of watches, and musical instruments, and the ingenuity of its citizens.

QUESTIONS. What is said of Bavaria? Its climate? Soil? Productions? Munich? Nuremberg?

32. WURTEMBURG.

Square miles, 7,500. Population, 1,815,000.

Wurtemburg is a kingdom of Germany, situated west of Bavaria.

Though mountainous, it is one of the most fertile and highly cultivated portions of Germany, producing grain, fruits and wine.

The inhabitants are among the most highly civilized and best educated in Europe. Schools and libraries are very numerous.

STUTTGART is the capital. It is well built, with broad and handsome streets and fine squares. It has an extensive public library and many private libraries.

Ulm is noted for its splendid cathedral.

QUESTIONS. Where is Wurtemburg situated? What is said of its soil? Inhabitants? Schools and libraries? Stuttgart? Ulm?

33. BADEN.

Square miles, 5,900. Population, 1,357,000.

Baden is a narrow, fertile tract, bordering the Rhine. The Black Forest extends over a large part of the state. Many of its hills are covered to their very summits with vineyards. Agriculture, manufactures and trade are in a flourishing state.

CARLSRUHE, the capital, and *Manheim*, are well built towns.

QUESTIONS. What can you say of Baden? Carlsruhe? Manheim?

FREE CITIES.

1. FRANKFORT, 2. BREMEN, 3. HAMBURG, 4. LUBECK.

These are all that remain of the eighty-five cities which were united in the middle ages for mutual assistance, and called the Hanseatic league.

FRANKFORT, on the Maine, the seat of the Germanic diet, is pleasantly situated in a beautiful, but narrow valley. It has a large number of public squares. It is rich in establishments for the promotion of art and literature, and has considerable trade.

Bremen, situated on both banks of the Weser, has an extensive foreign trade, especially with North America. It is the principal German port for the shipment of emigrants.

Hamburg, the largest of the free cities, and the greatest commercial port on the continent of Europe, is situated on the right bank of the Elbe, seventy miles from its mouth.

SENATE HOUSE, MARKET PLACE AND CATHEDRAL, LUBECK.

Lubeck is enclosed by ramparts and a promenade. Its trade is less important than formerly, but is still thriving, especially with the Baltic states.

QUESTIONS. Name the free cities. What is said of Frankfort? Bremen? Hamburg? Lubeck?

34. SWITZERLAND.

Square miles, 15,000. Population, 2,390,000.

Switzerland, a federal republic of central Europe, comprises twenty-two cantons, called the Helvetic Republic.

It is a land of mountains and vales, lakes and streams, presenting some of the wildest, most picturesque, and sublime scenery in the world.

The Alps, which form its southern boundary, are the loftiest mountains in Europe, and extremely rugged. Dazzling glaciers, or fields of ice, crown their summits, and vast avalanches of snow, rushing from their sides into the vales below, sometimes bury whole villages.

Switzerland has a great variety of climate.

The declivities of the mountains are cold, and only adapted to grazing; the vales are warm, and productive of grain and fruits. Cotton goods and watches are the principal manufactures.

A variety of minerals has been found, but none are worked to much extent, except iron.

The cantons are united for mutual defence, but retain their individual independence in regard to all matters of internal administration.

The diet meets alternately at *Berne*, the nominal capital, *Lucerne* and *Zurich*.

The Swiss are well educated and industrious, honest and hospitable, and ardently attached to their country. In religion they

ALPS AND CONVENT OF THE GREAT ST. BERNARD.

are nearly equally divided between the Protestant and Roman Catholic.

BERNE, on a branch of the Rhine, is one

of the finest cities in Europe, and is surrounded by a picturesque country.

Geneva, distinguished for its literary institutions, and the manufacture of watches, is beautifully situated on lake Geneva.

QUESTIONS. How many square miles has Switzerland? Inhabitants? What does it comprise? Describe its surface. The Alps. What is said of the climate? Productions? Manufactures? Minerals? The cantons? The diet? The Swiss? Religion? Berne? Geneva?

GENERAL QUESTIONS ON EUROPE.

How is Europe bounded? Which is the largest division? What divisions border on the Atlantic? What on the North Sea? What on the Baltic Sea? What on the Mediterranean Sea? What divisions have no sea-coast? What two divisions form a peninsula in the northern part? In the south-western part? What divisions are entirely separated from the continent?

Where are the Scandinavian Mountains? Carpathian Mountains? Alps? Apennines? Pyrenees? Where is Mount Vesuvius? Mt. Etna? Mt. Hecla?

Where is Lake Wener? Constance? Onega? Ladoga? What are the principal rivers of England? Of Sweden? Describe the Dwina. Ural. Don. Danube. Guadiana. Rhone. Loire. Rhine. Elbe. Thames. What are the tributaries of the Danube?

What sea between England and Norway? Between Sweden and Russia? Between Italy and Turkey? Between Ireland and Wales? Mention all the seas in and around Russia? What gulfs connect directly with the Baltic Sea? With the Mediterranean? Where is the Bay of Biscay? Galway Bay? Strait of Dardanelles? Strait of Otranto? Strait of Messina? Strait of Gibraltar? English Channel? Bristol Channel? St. George's Channel? The Skager Rack? Cattegat?

Mention the principal islands found in the Mediterranean Sea. In the Archipelago. In the Baltic Sea. Where are the Shetland Islands? Faroe Islands? Orkney Islands? Hebrides? Loffoden Islands? What Peninsula in the southern part of Russia? Where is the North Cape? Cape Matapan? Cape Spartivento? Cape Trafalgar? Cape St. Vincent? Cape Ortegal? La Hague? Lands End?

What is the latitude of London? Paris? St. Petersburg? Rome? Constantinople? Strait of Gibraltar? North Cape? What is the longitude of Paris? Frankfort? St. Petersburg? Constantinople? Madrid? Lisbon? Dublin?

What countries in Europe are about the same latitude as Vermont? As Pennsylvania? In what zones is Europe?

What countries of Europe are mostly mountainous? What countries are level? What is the climate of England? Of Russia? Of Italy? Of Spain? In what countries is agriculture best conducted? What are the vegetable productions of Norway? Of Austria? Of Italy? Of Portugal? Of France? What are the mineral productions of Norway? Austria? France? Spain? England? Scotland? What is the general character of the French? Italians? Spaniards? Scotch? Dutch? Turks? What is the government of Great Britain? France? Austria? Russia? Turkey? Switzerland? What countries of Europe are Roman Catholic? Protestant? Greek Church? What is the religion of Turkey?

Describe London. Paris. Stockholm. St. Petersburg. Constantinople. Athens. Rome. Madrid. What are the most commercial cities of England? France?

How would you sail from New York to London? From London to St. Petersburg? From London to Naples? From Naples to Constantinople? From Constantinople to Copenhagen? What mountains would you pass in traveling by land from Paris to Rome? What cities of interest? In what countries of Europe should we find the best traveling facilities?

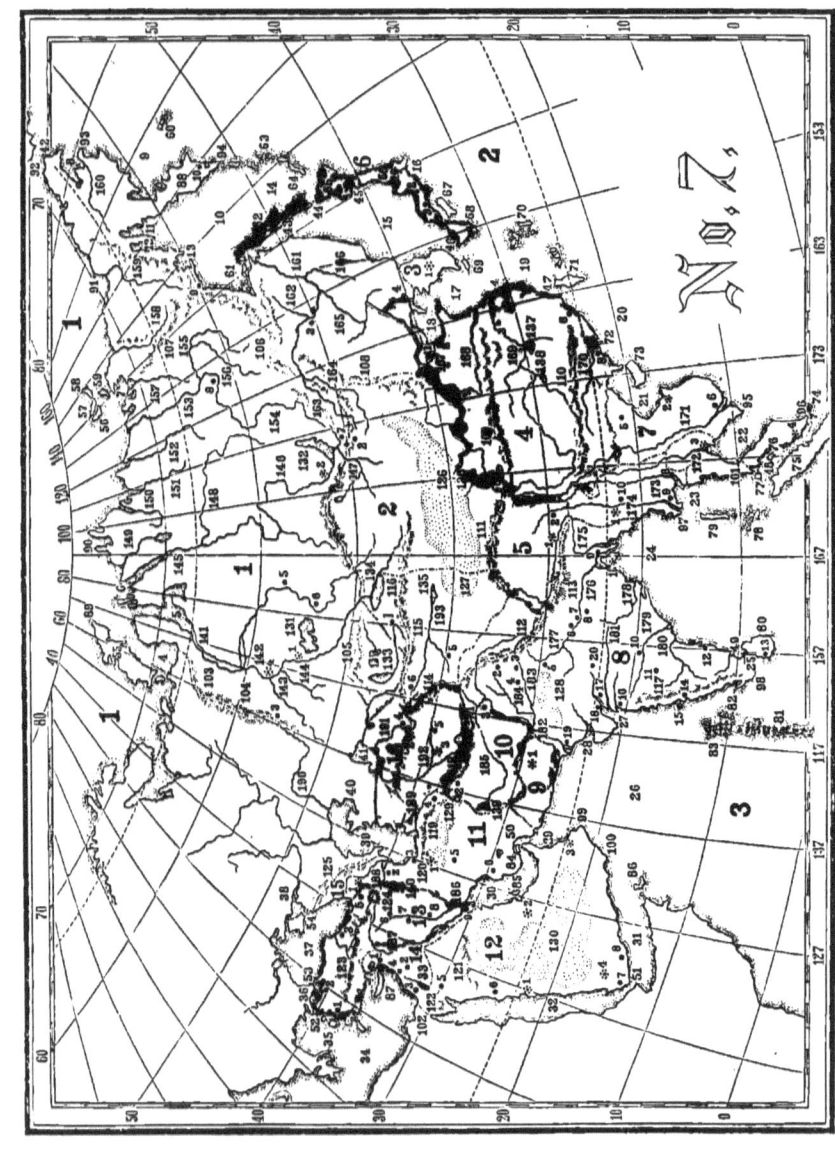

ASIA.

SQUARE MILES, 16,000,000.   POPULATION, 650,000,000.

KEY TO MAP NO. 7.

COUNTRIES, CAPITALS, CHIEF TOWNS.

1 **Siberia,**   1 OMSK, 2 IRKOOTSK, 3 *Yekaterinboorg*, 4 TODOLSK, 5 *Tomsk*, 6 *Barnaul*, 7 *Kiakhta*, 8 *Yakootsk*, 9 *Okhotsk*, 10 *Petropaulovski*.

2 **Chinese Tartary,**
Soongaria, 1 *Eelee*.
Mongolia, 2 *Maimaitchin*.
Mantchooria, 3 *Saghalien*, 4 Chinyang.
Toorkistan, 5 Yarkand, 6 Kashgar.

3 **Corea,**   1 KINGKITAO.

4 **China,**   1 PEKING, 2 *Teentsin*, 3 *Nanking*, 4 Shanghai, 5 *Hang-chow-foo*, 6 Amoy, 7 Canton, 8 *Macao*.

5 **Thibet,**   1 LASSA, 2 *Jiga Gounggar*.

6 **Japan,**   1 YEDDO, 2 *Miako*, 3 *Osaka*.

7 **Farther India,**

Burmah,   1 MONCHOBOO, 9 *Rangoon*, 10 *Amarapoora*.
Anam,   2 HUE, 5 *Ketcho*, 6 *Saigon*.
Siam,   3 BANGKOK.
Malacca,   4 MALACCA, 7 Singapore.
Tenasserim, 8 *Amherst*.

8 **Hindostan,** 1 CALCUTTA, 2 *Cashmere*, 3 *Amritseer*, 4 *Lahore*, 5 Delhi, 6 *Lucknow*, 7 Benares, 8 *Patna*, 9 *Dacca*, 10 *Nagpoor*, 11 *Hyderabad*, 12 Madras, 13 *Colombo*, 14 *Poonah*, 15 Bombay, 16 *Surat*, 17 *Baroda*, 18 *Ahmedabad*, 19 *Hydrabad*, 20 *Oojein*.

9 **Beloochistan,** 1 KELAT.

10 **Afghanistan,** 1 CABOOL, 2 Herat, 3 *Peshawer*.

11 **Persia,**   1 TEHERAN, 2 *Tabreez*, 3 Reshd, 4 *Meshed*, 5 Ispahan, 6 *Sheeraz*.

12 **Arabia,**   1 MECCA, 2 DERAYEH, 3 MUSCAT, 4 SANA, 5 *Petra*, 6 *Medina*, 7 Mocha, 8 Aden.

13 **Turkey,**   1 SMYRNA, 2 *Brusa*, 3 *Trebizond*, 4 Erzroom, 5 *Kars*, 6 *Diarbekir*, 7 *Mosul*, 8 Bagdad, 9 Bassorah.

14 **Syria,**   1 *Aleppo*, 2 Damascus, 3 Jerusalem, 4 Beyroot.

15 **Georgia,**   1 TIFLIS.

16 **Independent Toorkistan,** 1 KHIVA, 2 KHOKAN, 3 BOKHARA, TASHKEND, 5 *Samarcand*.

OCEANS, SEAS, GULFS AND BAYS.

1 ARCTIC OCEAN,
2 PACIFIC OCEAN,
3 INDIAN OCEAN,
4 SEA OF KARA,
5 GULF OF OBI,
6 YENISEI GULF,
7 GULF OF LENA,
8 GULF OF ANADIR,
9 SEA OF KAMTCHATKA,
10 SEA OF OKHOTSK,
11 Penjinsk *Gulf*,
12 Jijiginsk *Gulf*,
13 Tomsk *Gulf*,
14 SEA OF YESSO,

ASIA.

15 SEA OF JAPAN,
16 *Yeddo Bay,*
17 YELLOW SEA,
18 PECHEELEE GULF,
19 EASTERN SEA,
20 CHINA SEA,
21 GULF OF TONQUIN,
22 GULF OF SIAM,
23 GULF OF MARTABAN,
24 BAY OF BENGAL,
25 *Gulf of Manaar,*
26 ARABIAN SEA,
27 GULF OF CAMBAY,
28 *Gulf of Cutch,*
29 GULF OF ORMUS,
30 PERSIAN GULF,
31 *Gulf of Aden,*
32 RED SEA,
33 DEAD SEA,
34 MEDITERRANEAN SEA,
35 ÆGEAN SEA,
36 SEA OF MARMORA,
37 BLACK SEA,
38 SEA OF AZOF,
39 CASPIAN SEA,
40 *Dead Gulf,*
41 ARAL SEA.

STRAITS AND CHANNELS.

42 BEHRING'S STRAIT,
43 CHANNEL OF TARTARY,
44 PEROUSE STRAIT,
45 STRAIT OF YESSO,
46 STRAIT OF COREA,
47 *Strait of Formosa,*
48 STRAIT OF MALACCA,
49 *Palk's Strait,*
50 STRAIT OF ORMUS,
51 STRAIT OF BAB-EL-MANDEB,
52 STRAIT OF DARDANELLES,
53 CHANNEL OF BOSPORUS,
54 *Strait of Yenikale.*

ISLANDS.

55 NOVA ZEMBLA,
56 *Kotelnoi,*
57 *Fadievskoi,*
58 NEW SIBERIA,
59 *Liaghoff,*
60 *Behring's Islands,*
61 *Tchautar,*
62 SAGHALIEN,
63 KOORILE ISLANDS,
64 STATEN ISLANDS,
65 YESSO,
66 NIPHON,
67 SIKOKF,
68 KIOOSIOO,
69 *Quelpaert Islands,*
70 LOO-CHOO ISLANDS,
71 FORMOSA,
72 *Hongkong,*
73 HAINAN,
74 SINGAPORE,
75 SUMATRA,
76 *Penang,*
77 *Junk Ceylon,*
78 NICOBAR,
79 ANDAMAN,
80 CEYLON,
81 MALDIVE ISLANDS,
82 *Coralline Islands,*
83 LACCADIVE ISLANDS,
84 *Kishm,*
85 *Bahrein,*
86 SOCOTRA,
87 CYPRUS.

PENINSULAS, CAPES AND ISTHMUSES.

88 PENINSULA OF KAMTCHATKA,
89 *Cape Zelania,*
90 NORTH EAST CAPE,
91 *Chelagskoy Cape,*
92 EAST CAPE,
93 *Cape St. Thaddeus,*
94 CAPE LOPATKA,
95 CAPE CAMBODIA,
96 CAPE ROMANIA,
97 *Cape Negrais,*
98 CAPE COMORIN,
99 CAPE RASALHAD,
100 *Cape Isolette,*
101 *Isthmus of Kraw,*
102 ISTHMUS OF SUEZ.

ASIA.

MOUNTAINS AND DESERTS.

103 URAL,
104   *Konjakofski*,
105 LITTLE ALTAI,
106 STANOVOI,
107 *Aldan*,
108 *Khingan*,
109 PELING,
110 MELING,
111 KUENLUN,
112 HIMALAYA,
113   KUNCHINJUNGA,
114 *Beloor*,
115 THIAN SHAN,
116 *Peshan Volcano*,
117 GHAUTS MOUNTAINS,
118 HINDOO KOOSH,
119 *Elbrooz*,
120   *Demavend*,
121 *Ramleah*,
122 SINAI,
123 TAURUS,
124 ARARAT,
125 CAUCASUS,
126 GREAT DESERT OF COBI,
127 SANDY DESERT,
128 GREAT SANDY DESERT,
129 GREAT SALT DESERT,
130 DESERT OF AKHAF, OR ARABIAN DESERT.

LAKES.

131 TCHANY,
132 BAIKAL,
133 BALKASH,
134 ZAISAN NOR,
135 *Lop Nor*,
136 *Koko Nor*,
137 *Poyang*,
138 *Ton-Ting Hoo*,
139 *Zurrah*,
140 *Ooroomeeyah*.

RIVERS.

141 OBI,
142 IRTISH,
143   *Tobol*,
144   *Ishim*,
145 YENISEI,
146   ANGARA,
147   *Selenga*,
148   *Toongooska*,
149 *Piasina*,
150 *Khatanga*,
151 *Anabara*,
152 *Olenek*,
153 LENA,
154   *Vitim*,
155   *Aldan*,
156   *Amga*,
157 *Yana*,
158 *Indighirka*,
159 *Kolyma*,
160 *Anadir*,
161 AMOOR,
162   *Chikiri*,
163   *Shilka*,
164   *Argoon*,
165   *Soongari*,
166   *Oosoori*,
167 PEI-HO,
168 HOANG HO,
169 YANG-TSE-KIANG,
170 HONG KIANG,
171 CAMBODIA,
172 MENAM,
173 *Salwin*,
174 IRRAWADDY,
175 BRAHMAPOOTRA,
176 GANGES,
177   *Jumna*,
178 *Mahanuddy*,
179 *Godavery*,
180 *Kristnah*,
181 *Nerbudda*,
182 INDUS,
183   *Sutlej*,
184   *Chenaub*,
185 *Helmund*,
186 TIGRIS,
187 EUPHRATES,
188 *Koor*,
189 *Attruck*,
190 URAL,
191 SIHON,
192 AMOO,
193 *Yarkand*.

ASIA.

QUESTIONS ON THE MAP OF ASIA.

BOUND Asia. What is the number of its square miles? Inhabitants? What is its latitude? Longitude? In what zones is Asia? With what grand divisions is it connected? (See Map of Hemispheres.) Name its political divisions. Their capitals. Which division extends farthest north? South? East? West? What divisions have no sea-coast?

OCEANS, SEAS, GULFS AND BAYS.

What ocean North of Asia? 1. East? 2. South? 3. What sea between Nova Zembla and Siberia? 4. What two seas east of Siberia? 9, 10. What sea east of Chinese Tartary? 15. West of Corea? 17. South of China? 20. West of Hindostan? 26. Between Asia and Africa? 32. West of Turkey? 34. What three seas between Asia and Europe? 36, 37, 39. What sea in Independent Tartary? 41. What is there remarkable in respect to the Caspian and Aral seas? ANS.—Large rivers flow into them, but no outlets have yet been discovered.

What three gulfs north of Siberia? 5-7. What four gulfs on the east? 8, 11-13. What bay in the east of Japan? 16. What gulf south of China? 21. What gulfs south of Farther India? 22, 23. What bay east of Hindostan? 24. What gulfs west of Hindostan? 27, 28. What gulf south of Beloochistan? 29. South of Persia? 30. South of Arabia? 31.

STRAITS AND CHANNELS.

What strait separates Asia from North America? 42. What channel east of Chinese Tartary? 43. What strait between the Sea of Japan and the Sea of Yesso? 44. What strait between Niphon and Yesso? 45. What strait south of Corea? 46. East of China? 47. West of Malacca? 48. South of Persia? 50. South of Arabia? 51.

ISLANDS.

What islands north of Siberia? 55-59. East of Kamtchatka? 60. What island north-east of Chinese Tartary? 62. What islands east of the Sea of Japan? 65, 66. What islands east of China? 67-71. What islands south of China? 72, 73. What island west of Malacca? 75. What islands west of Farther India? 76-79. What large island south of Hindostan? 80. What groups south-west of Hindostan? 81-83.

CAPES AND PENINSULAS.

Which is the most northern cape of Asia? 90. The most eastern? 92. What cape south of the Peninsula of Kamtchatka? 94. East of the gulf of Siam? 95. South of Malacca? 96. South of Burmah in Chin India? 97. What cape south of Hindostan? 98. What isthmus unites Asia to Africa? 102. What peninsula east of the Sea of Okhotsk? 88.

MOUNTAINS AND DESERTS.

What mountains between Asia and Europe? 103. Siberia and Chinese Tartary? 105, 106. What mountains and deserts in Chinese Tartary? 108, 115, 126, 127. What mountains in China? 109, 110. North of Thibet? 111. North of Hindostan? 112. What mountains and desert in Persia? 119, 120. What mountains and desert in Arabia? 121, 130. What mountain near the isthmus of Suez? 122. What mountains in Turkey? 123.

LAKES.

What two lakes in Siberia? 131, 132. What lakes in Chinese Tartary? 133-136. What lake in Afghanistan? 139. What lake in Persia? 140.

RIVERS.

What rivers flow from Siberia into the Arctic Ocean? 141, 145, 149-153, 157-159. Mention the tributaries of the Obi. 142-144. Of the Yenisei. 146-148. Of the Lena. 154-156. What river flows into the Channel of Tartary? 161. What are the principal rivers of China? 167-170. Of Farther India? 171-174. What rivers from Hindostan flow into the Bay of Bengal? 176, 178-180. What into the Arabian Sea? 181, 182. What river flows into Lake Zurrah? 185. What rivers of Turkey flow into the Persian Gulf? 186, 187. What river between Independent Tartary and Russia? 190. What two rivers flow into the Sea of Aral? 191, 192.

ASIA.

DESCRIPTIVE GEOGRAPHY.

Asia is the largest and most populous grand division of the globe.

It contains immense plains and elevated plateaus, traversed by lofty mountains. It has large inland seas or lakes, and numerous rivers.

It is distinguished for its delicious fruits, fragrant spices, and medicinal drugs. Rice, the vine, the tea-plant, and many of the fruits of the torrid zone, are extensively cultivated.

It is rich in gold, diamonds and other precious gems. Silver, copper, iron, tin, and lead, are also found.

The elephant, rhinoceros, lion, tiger, bear, and other wild animals, are numerous. In the southern part, insects and reptiles are abundant—also birds of splendid plumage.

The inhabitants belong chiefly to the Caucasian, Asiatic and Malay races.

The Caucasian race occupies the western part; the Asiatic, the northern and eastern; the Malay race, Malacca, and the Asiatic islands.

The principal nations have their learned men, but the great mass of the population are deplorably ignorant and superstitious. The women are degraded, and often treated like slaves.

Agriculture is pursued in some parts of Asia with great care, but not with the same skill as in Europe. The arts and manufactures are in an imperfect state, though the most superb silks and shawls in the world are manufactured in Asia.

The religion is mostly Pagan and Mohammedan; far the greatest number of people are Pagan.

Asia formerly contained the most wealthy and enlightened nations of the world, and was the seat of the powerful empires of Assyria, Babylonia and Persia.

It has been the theatre of the greatest events that ever transpired on our globe.

Here man was created and placed in the garden of Eden—here he sinned and brought death into the world—here the patriarchs and prophets dwelt—and here, too, was the scene of the birth, crucifixion, and ascension of Christ, the Redeemer of mankind.

QUESTIONS. What is the size of Asia? Mention its natural characteristics. For what is it distinguished? What are cultivated? In what is it rich? What animals are found? Who inhabit it? What is their character? What is said of agriculture and the arts? Religion? What did Asia formerly contain? What has transpired here?

1. SIBERIA.

Square miles, 5,300,000. Population, 3,000,000.

Siberia is a vast country occupying the northern part of Asia, and subject to the Russian government.

It is mostly one immense plain, abounding with numerous marshes and large rivers.

The northern part is excessively cold, scarcely admitting of cultivation. The southern part abounds with extensive forests, and produces grain and potatoes.

The mountainous sections are rich in mines of gold, silver, iron, platina, and in precious stones.

Bears, sables, ermines, beavers, lynxes, and marmots are numerous, furnishing valuable skins and furs for export. The reindeer, sheep and dog, are the principal domestic animals.

The inhabitants consist of wandering native tribes, and exiles who have been banished from Russia for crime. Hunting and mining are their chief employments.

Numerous bones of the mammoth, elephant, and other animals of the torrid zone, are found on the banks of the rivers, and shores of the Arctic Ocean.

OMSK, one of the capitals of West Siberia, has an important military school.

TOBOLSK, the other capital of West Siberia, is situated at the junction of the Irtish and Tobol rivers. It is surrounded by a strong brick wall, and the streets are mostly paved with wood.

Irkootsk, the residence of the governor of East Siberia, is situated on the Angara, thirty miles from lake Baikal. It has several public buildings and numerous schools, and is a place of considerable commerce.

QUESTIONS. How many square miles has Siberia? Inhabitants? Where does Siberia lie, and to whom is it subject? What is said of its surface? Climate and productions? Mines? Animals? Inhabitants? Bones of Animals? Omsk? Tobolsk? Irkootsk?

CHINESE EMPIRE.

Square miles, 5,000,000. Population, 400,000,000.

The Chinese Empire is an immense territory, stretching from the center to the eastern extremities of Asia, and occupying nearly a third of its surface.

It is the most populous empire in the world, and comprises Chinese Tartary, China, Corea, Thibet, and numerous islands.

The government is despotic, and the Emperor is styled the "SON OF HEAVEN," and the "FATHER OF HIS PEOPLE."

QUESTIONS. How many square miles has the Chinese Empire? Inhabitants? Describe it. What does it comprise? What is its government? What is the Emperor styled?

2. CHINESE TARTARY.

This extensive country consists chiefly of elevated table land, abounding with deserts and mountain ranges, and is better adapted to grazing than to tillage.

It is divided into the following provinces, commencing on the east, Mantchooria, Mongolia, Soongaria, and Toorkistan. The last is the most thickly settled. The inhabitants lead a roving life, and raise large numbers of horses and cattle.

YARKAND is the present capital of Chinese Toorkistan. It is enclosed by an earthern rampart, and its houses are built of stone and clay, mostly of one story. It is the chief emporium of trade between the Chinese Empire and the countries west.

Kashgar, the former capital of Toorkistan, is a city of considerable importance. It has manufactures of cotton goods, and articles of gold and jasper.

QUESTIONS. Describe Chinese Tartary. How is it divided? What is said of its inhabitants? Describe Yarkand. Kashgar.

THE GREAT CHINESE WALL.

3. COREA.

Square miles, 80,000. Population, 18,000,000.

Corea is very uneven, being traversed by mountains; the climate is cold. The soil is generally fertile, and the productions are barley in the north; wheat, cotton, rice, millet, and hemp, in the south.

Gold, silver, copper, iron, rock salt, and coal, are found.

KINGKITAO, the capital, is situated on the Kiang river, near the center of the kingdom.

QUESTIONS. How many square miles has Corea? Inhabitants? What is said of the surface, climate and soil? Productions? Minerals? Kingkitao?

4. CHINA.

Square miles, 1,298,000. Population, 367,633,000.

China proper is a large country in the south-east of Asia.

It is mountainous in the interior and western parts, and slopes gradually toward the shore.

The climate is cold in the north, and more mild in the south, though all parts are subject to great extremes of heat and cold.

The soil is fertile, especially in its rich alluvial plains, and is cultivated with great care. The most noted product is tea. Rice, cotton, wheat, barley, and potatoes are also extensively raised.

Gold, silver, copper, iron, and coal, are found to some extent.

The Chinese excel in the manufacture of silk and porcelain. Teas, silks, and China ware, are the principal exports.

China has a very dense population, and is remarkable for the great antiquity of its government, and the peculiarity of its customs.

The inhabitants are mild, intelligent and industrious. Learned men are highly esteemed and much attention is paid to education. The religion of the Chinese is Pagan.

The Chinese wall was built 2000 years since, as a defense against the Tartars. It is 1,500 miles in length, and in some places twenty or thirty feet high, and sufficiently wide for six horsemen to ride abreast.

PEKING, the capital city of China, is situated on a sandy plain, a hundred miles from the Yellow Sea. It consists of two contiguous cities, separately enclosed by lofty walls. The northern, or imperial city, is occupied by the Tartars, and contains several public buildings and magnificent temples. The southern, or Chinese city, contains the largest number of inhabitants. Its entire circuit is twenty-five miles. It has considerable trade and manufactures.

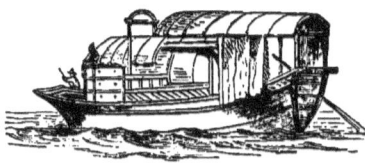

FAMILY BOAT.

Canton is the greatest commercial city in China. It has a large foreign trade, and exports immense quantities of tea. Thousands of its inhabitants live in boats on the river. *Nanking*, a large city and the ancient capital of southern China, is situated near the right bank of the Yang-tse-Kiang, about ninety miles from its mouth. It has important manufactures of crape, satin, Nankeen cloths, artificial flowers, and Indian ink. It contains the celebrated porcelain tower, which was built in the fifteenth century at a cost of over $35,000,000.

The principal Chinese islands are Hainan and Formosa. Large quantities of rice, with camphor, maize, salt, sulphur, fruits, and timber, are exported from the latter.

QUESTIONS. How many square miles has China? What is its population? How is it situated? What is said of its surface? Climate and soil? Productions? Minerals? Manufacture of silk and porcelain? Of exports? For what is China remarkable? What can you say of its inhabitants? Learned men? Religion? The Chinese wall? Describe Peking. Canton. Nanking. The Chinese islands.

---

5. THIBET.

Square miles, 723,000. Population, 8,000,000.

Thibet occupies the southern portion of the great table land of central Asia, and is walled in by lofty mountains.

It has a cold, dry, healthful climate. The soil is poor, and the vegetable productions are very few.

It is rich in mineral productions. Gold, silver, iron, and salt are abundant.

It has large numbers of cattle and sheep. A kind of goat furnishes a very fine hair for the manufacture of cashmere shawls.

LASSA is the capital. The GRAND LAMA resides here, and has a magnificent temple near the city, which is constantly thronged with multitudes of worshipers.

QUESTIONS. Give the number of square miles of Thibet. Population. How is Thibet situated? By what is it walled in? What is said of its climate and soil? Minerals? Animals? Lassa?

ASIA.

6. EMPIRE OF JAPAN.

Square miles, 200,000. Population, 50,000,000.

This empire includes the islands of Yesso, Niphon and Kioosioo, with several small adjacent islands.

The surface is generally uneven. The coasts of the larger islands are extremely irregular, having numerous bays and gulfs.

BAY OF YEDDO.

It has a changeable climate and fertile soil, producing in abundance, rice, cotton, sugar, wheat, tea, and the finest fruits.

Gold, silver, copper, tin, lead, iron, and coal, abound.

Buffaloes and zebus are common, and are used for agricultural purposes. Horses are small but excellent, and are used only by the nobility. There is a great variety of birds and insects.

The Japanese belong to the Mongol race. They are divided into eight classes; princes, nobles, priests, soldiers, civil officers, merchants, artisans, and laborers. Many of them are very intelligent. They are skilled in agriculture and manufactures. Females are treated with great respect.

The government is an absolute hereditary monarchy. The religion consists chiefly in the worship of departed spirits of good men.

YEDDO, the capital, is one of the most populous cities. The houses are usually of one story, but it contains many palaces.

QUESTIONS. What number of square miles has the Empire of Japan? Inhabitants? What does it include? What is said of the surface? Climate, soil and productions? Minerals? Animals? Inhabitants? Government? In what does the religion consist? Describe Yeddo.

INDIA.

India is an extensive and populous country, embracing Chin-India on the east, and Hindostan on the west.

It is distinguished by its numerous rivers, fertile soil, and luxuriant vegetation; and is rich in gold, diamonds, and other precious stones.

Lofty and beautiful forests are numerous. Some of these are rendered almost impenetrable by vines and shrubs, and are called jungles.

The elephant, tiger, lion, panther, leopard, hyena, and rhinoceros, abound—also birds of beautiful plumage, and swarms of insects.

Most of the inhabitants are superstitious pagans, and exceedingly degraded.

QUESTIONS. What is India? By what is it distinguished? In what is it rich? What is said of the forests? What animals are found? Describe its inhabitants.

7. FARTHER INDIA.

Square miles, 1,000,000. Population, 22,000,000.

Farther India, or India beyond the Ganges, is situated between the bay of Bengal and China Sea.

Four parallel mountain chains traverse

this region, from north to south, bounding the great basins of its principal rivers.

It contains many rich valleys, yielding a variety of vegetable products.

The climate is healthful. Agriculture is in a backward state. Rice is the principal product.

Maize, cotton, sugar-cane, ginger, and tropical fruits, are raised to some extent.

In some parts of Farther India, gold, silver, copper, and iron, are found.

Farther India comprises the empires of Anam and Burmah, the kingdom of Siam, the peninsula of Malacca, and the British possessions.

Anam extends from China and the Gulf of Tonquin, to the Gulf of Siam, and includes Tonquin, Cochin China, Champa, and the eastern portion of Cambodia.

Burmah occupies the western part of the peninsula, extending from China to the Gulf of Martaban.

Siam occupies the center of the peninsula, lying between the empires of Anam and Burmah.

Malacca is the most southern portion of Continental Asia, lying between the China Sea and the Strait of Malacca. It was formerly an independent territory, but is now divided between European powers and the king of Siam.

The British possessions embrace a section of country on the east and north of the Gulf of Martaban, the southern portion of Malacca, and the island of Singapore.

Hue, the capital of the empire of Anam, is situated on the Hue river, ten miles from the China Sea. It is surrounded by walls mounting numerous cannon, and its fortress is considered the strongest in Asia.

Bangkok, the capital of Siam, is situated on both banks of the river Menam, twenty miles above its mouth. It has manufactures of tin and iron wares, and leather, and is one of the most commercial cities in Asia.

Monchoboo has recently become the capital of the Burman Empire.

Singapore, situated on the south side of the island of the same name, is one of the principal commercial emporiums of the east. It has an extensive trade with eastern and southern Asia, Great Britain, France, and the United States. The port is free to vessels of all kinds and from all nations.

QUESTIONS. What is the extent of Farther India? Population? How is Farther India situated? What is said of its surface? Soil? Climate? Productions? Minerals? What does it comprise? Describe Anam. Burmah. Siam. Malacca. The British possessions. Hue. Bangkok. Monchoboo. Singapore.

---

8. HINDOSTAN.

Square miles, 1,280,000. Population, 150,000,000.

Hindostan comprises the great central peninsula of Southern Asia. It consists of a vast plain in the north, and high plateaus bounded by mountains in the south. Its soil is very fertile.

The climate in the northern part is mild and agreeable. In the southern, it is oppressively hot and often unhealthy.

Rice, sugar, tobacco, opium, cotton, silk, indigo, and various kinds of grain and spices, are the vegetable productions. The most delicious fruits grow spontaneously.

One of the remarkable vegetable curiosities of Hindostan, is the Banian, or Indian fig tree. Its limbs send downward to the earth numerous shoots, which take root and become large trunks. One tree will sometimes form a grove large enough to shade several thousand persons.

Its minerals are gold, iron, coal, diamonds, and other precious stones.

The Hindoos have excelled in a few manufactures; the embroidered shawls of the province of Cashmere being unrivaled.

The population is dense, and divided into castes, which never associate or intermarry with each other. In some districts, the inhabitants are intelligent and industrious, in others, ignorant and extremely degraded.

PALACE OF THE KING, DELHI.

Their religion is paganism. They worship many thousands of deities—also the river Ganges, and various animals.

The British Government has the control of the larger portion of the country.

The British also possess Ceylon, a beautiful and fertile island, abounding with fruits and spices, and valuable for its pearl fisheries.

CALCUTTA, the capital and largest city in Hindostan, has an extensive commerce, and is thronged with persons from all parts of the globe.

BOMBAY, the capital of Western British India, though inferior to Calcutta and Madras, has an extensive commerce, and is the chief Indian port, connected with the establishment of steam navigation between India and Great Britain.

Madras is situated on a sandy shore on the eastern coast. It has no harbor, but is a place of extensive trade. *Benares* is a wealthy city, situated on the north bank of the Ganges. It is the holy city of the Hindoos, and contains numerous mosques and temples. It is famous for its trade in diamonds.

Delhi was once the largest city in India. It is distinguished for its royal palace.

QUESTIONS. How many square miles has Hindostan? Inhabitants? Where is it situated? What is the surface of Hindostan? What can you say of the soil? Climate? Productions? Banian tree? Minerals? Manufactures? Population? Religion? Who control most of the country? Describe Ceylon. Calcutta. Bombay. Madras. Benares. Delhi.

9. BELOOCHISTAN.

Square miles, 160,000. Population, 2,000,000.

Beloochistan lies west of Hindostan, and extends six hundred miles on the shore of the Arabian sea.

It is a mountainous country, covered chiefly with barren wastes, and thinly populated.

The climate is various, being cold in the elevated parts, and excessively hot in the valleys. In the low and watered plains, rice, sugar-cane, cotton, indigo, and tobacco, are raised; in other parts, wheat, barley, and fruits are the principal products.

The government is despotic, and the religion, Mohammedan.

The inhabitants consist of Belochees and Brahoees. The Belochees are a warlike race, living by plunder. The Brahoees are mild, peaceful, and subsist on their cattle.

KELAT is the principal city and capital.

QUESTIONS. How many square miles has Beloochistan? Inhabitants? Where is it situated? Describe it. Climate. Productions. Government and religion. The inhabitants. Name its chief city.

10. AFGHANISTAN.

Square miles, 300,000. Population, 5,000,000.

Afghanistan lies directly north of Beloo-

NATIVES.

chistan, which it resembles in surface and soil. The summits of the mountains are often covered with snow, while the valleys in summer are extremely hot. It is inhabited by various tribes, of which the Afghans are the chief, and of a brave character.

Arts and manufactures are in a backward state.

CABOOL, the capital, is beautifully situated on the Cabool river in a fertile plain, and has a delightful climate and active trade.

Herat is important for its manufactures and trade.

QUESTIONS. What is the number of square miles in Afghanistan? Population? Describe Afghanistan. Its inhabitants. Arts and manufactures. Cabool. Herat.

11. PERSIA.

Square miles, 450,000. Population, 10,000,000.

Persia extends from the Caspian Sea to the Persian Gulf. It consists of an extensive central plateau, encircled by mountain-chains on three of its sides. These, with vast salt or sandy deserts, and long, arid valleys destitute of streams, are the most striking characteristics of Persia.

The climate is subject to extremes of heat and cold; only in the valleys, is the soil fertile.

Silk of the finest quality, grains, rice, tobacco, cotton, wines, and fruits, are the chief products.

Agriculture receives comparatively little attention. The most elegant silks, shawls, carpets, and porcelain, are manufactured.

MOSQUE OF SULTAN HUSSEIN, ISPAHAN.

The Persians are a handsome, active and warlike people.

Pastoral tribes or shepherds who frequently plunder the more fertile tracts, inhabit the mountainous districts.

In ancient times, Persia was one of the most powerful empires of the East, but its power and influence have been much reduced. The sovereign is an absolute despot.

TEHERAN, the capital, is strongly fortified, and has an unhealthy site. It has manufactures of carpets and iron goods.

Ispahan is a populous city, with a beautiful situation. *Reshd* is a seaport on the Caspian Sea.

QUESTIONS. Give the number of square miles in Persia. Inhabitants. Situation. Striking characteristics. What is said of the climate and soil? Chief products? Agriculture and manufactures? The Persians? Pastoral tribes? Persia in ancient times? Government? Teheran? Ispahan? Reshd?

12. ARABIA.

Square miles, 634,000. Population, 10,000,000.

Arabia occupies a large peninsula in the south-west of Asia.

It consists chiefly of broken mountains and sandy plains or deserts, interspersed with fertile spots; and is almost destitute of streams of water.

The mountainous districts are temperate—the plains are excessively hot, and subject to a pestilential wind, called the Sirocco.

In the fertile regions, coffee and fragrant spices are abundant. Dates, oranges, figs, and melons, grow spontaneously, and furnish the people with much of their food.

The Arabian horse is fleet and beautiful. The camel is the most useful animal. The Arabs are proud, active, intelligent and hospitable to their guests, but rob all whom they meet in the desert.

The Arabs are Mohammedans, and preserve the patriarchal form of government.

The Bedouins are a wandering tribe, who live in the deserts and dwell in tents. They subsist principally on vegetables, and the milk of their camels and asses.

The pearl banks, in the Persian gulf, give employment to nearly thirty thousand men.

MECCA, the birth-place of Mohammed, is considered a sacred city, and resorted to by vast numbers of pilgrims.

Medina contains the tomb of Mohammed, inclosed by magnificent mosques. It is called the "City of the Prophet." *Mocha*

MOCHA.

is the center of trade with Europe, and exports large quantities of coffee. *Muscat*, a seaport on the Indian ocean, is the grand emporium of Eastern Arabia, and a key to the entrance of the Persian Gulf.

QUESTIONS. How many square miles in Arabia? Inhabitants? Where is it situated? Of what does it consist? What is the soil? Climate? Name the products. What is said of the horse? Camel? Describe the Arabs. What is their religion and government? What can you say of the Bedouins? The pearl fisheries? Mecca? Medina? Mocha? Muscat?

13. TURKEY IN ASIA.

Square miles, 538,000. Population, 16,000,000.

Turkey in Asia extends from Arabia to the Black sea, and embraces Asia Minor and Syria.

It is remarkable for having been the seat of the most thrilling occurrences recorded in the Sacred Scriptures.

MOSQUE OF OMAR.

It is still an interesting country, and contains the ruins of the mighty Babylon, of Nineveh, Balbec, and Jerusalem.

It consists of two plateaus and an extensive plain. The larger plateau occupies the whole of its northern portion, and has an elevation of from four to five thousand feet; the other includes Syria and Palestine, and lies to the east of the Mediterranean. The plain forms the lower basin of the Euphrates and Tigris.

The soil and climate present many varieties. The river banks and valleys are very fertile, but in the south are vast arid plains, and but few productions. The summits of the mountains are covered with snow, while the valleys have a tropical climate, and produce the fruits of Southern Asia.

The chief products are grain, cotton, coffee, and tobacco.

Asiatic Turkey was once the seat of powerful empires. It has been conquered by one nation after another, and is now subject to the Turks.

The inhabitants are ignorant and barbarous. They comprise a motley assemblage of Jews, Arabs, Moors, Tartars, Greeks, Turks, Armenians, &c.

Syria is a country of Asiatic Turkey, bounded south by Arabia, and west by the Mediterranean, and a large part of it is very productive. The southern part of Syria is called Palestine.

JERUSALEM, the capital of ancient Palestine, is celebrated as the "Holy City" of the Jews, and the scene of many important events recorded in Scripture. It retains few traces of its ancient grandeur, except the foundation stones of some of its walls, and the remains of arches, acqueducts and subterranean passage ways.

Smyrna is the most populous city of Turkey, and has an extensive trade and commerce. *Damascus* is celebrated for its antiquity, and the fineness of its manufactures. A highly fertile and beautiful country surrounds it.

QUESTIONS. How many square miles has Turkey in Asia? Inhabitants? What is its situation? What does it embrace? For what is it remarkable? What is its surface? Climate and soil? What are its chief products? Of what was it once the seat? Describe the inhabitants. Syria. What can you say of Jerusalem? Smyrna? Damascus?

---

15. GEORGIA.

Square miles, 28,800. Population, 300,000.

Georgia is usually employed to designate the whole territory claimed by the Russians, between the Black and Caspian Seas, and south of the Caucasus mountains.

ASIA.   141

The central part is occupied by a large and fertile valley, having a mild and healthful climate.

The soil in the valleys is very fertile, producing maize, hemp, flax, great quantities of wine and cotton, and also fine fruits.

The natives are distinguished for their fine forms, and for the beauty of the women. The Georgians belong nominally to the Greek Church.

TIFLIS, the capital, is situated in a narrow valley on the Koor. It is the residence of the Russian governor, and is defended by walls and several forts.

QUESTIONS. What is the extent of Georgia? Population? Where is it situated? What is its surface? Soil? What are its productions? For what are the natives distinguished? What is said of the religion? Tiflis?

16. INDEPENDENT TOORKISTAN.

Square miles, 720,800. Population, 4,000,000.

Independent Toorkistan extends from Chinese Tartary to the Caspian Sea, occupying the central portions of Asia.

It has an elevated surface, a mild climate, and abounds with vast deserts.

The southern part of Independent Toorkistan is called Bokhara, and is far the most fertile and best cultivated section. It was formerly the seat of a powerful empire.

The principal productions are cotton, silk, wool, maize, and fruits.

Various independent roving tribes inhabit this country, some of whom subsist by agriculture, but more on their flocks. They are generally Mohammedans.

BOKHARA, the capital of the Khanat of Bokhara, is situated in a flat country, embosomed among the hills, and is enclosed by earthern ramparts. It has long been famous as a seat of Mohammedan learning.

QUESTIONS. How many square miles in Independent Toorkistan? Inhabitants? How is it situated? What is the surface and climate? What abound? What can you say of Bokhara? What are the principal productions of Toorkistan? Who inhabit it? How do they live? Describe the city of Bokhara?

GENERAL QUESTIONS ON ASIA.

In what part of Asia is Siberia? Hindostan? Arabia? What divisions lie south of Siberia? Where are the Ural mountains? Stanovoi? Ghauts? Hindoo Koosh? Elbrooz? Himalaya? Where is Mount Sinai? Ararat?

Where is Lake Baikal? Lop Nor? Zurrah? Where is the river Obi? What are its tributaries? Where is the Amoor? What are the principal rivers of China? Where is the Irrawaddy? Ganges? Indus? Tigris? Ural?

Where is cape Lopatka? Cape Cambodia? Cape Comorin? Isthmus of Suez? Nova Zembla? Formosa? Singapore? Ceylon? Cyprus?

Where is the Gulf of Lena? Gulf of Siam? Gulf of Ormus? Sea of Kara? China Sea? Arabian Sea? Dead Sea? Caspian Sea? Channel of Tartary? Strait of Corea? Strait of Malacca? Strait of Dardanelles? Channel of Bosporus?

What is the latitude of Calcutta? Peking? Mecca? In what zones is Asia? What division of Asia is crossed by the Arctic Circle? What divisions by the Tropic of Cancer? What is the climate of Siberia? What are its minerals? What is the most noted product of China? How is Peking situated? To what race do the Japanese belong? What are the characteristics of the Mongol race? For what is India distinguished? What does Farther India comprise? How is Singapore situated? What remarkable tree is found in Hindostan? In what have the Hindoos excelled? What are the chief products of Persia? The manufactures? For what is Turkey remarkable? What ruins does it contain? By whom is Toorkistan inhabited?

How would you sail from New York to Calcutta? From Calcutta to Constantinople? Which of these three cities is the largest?

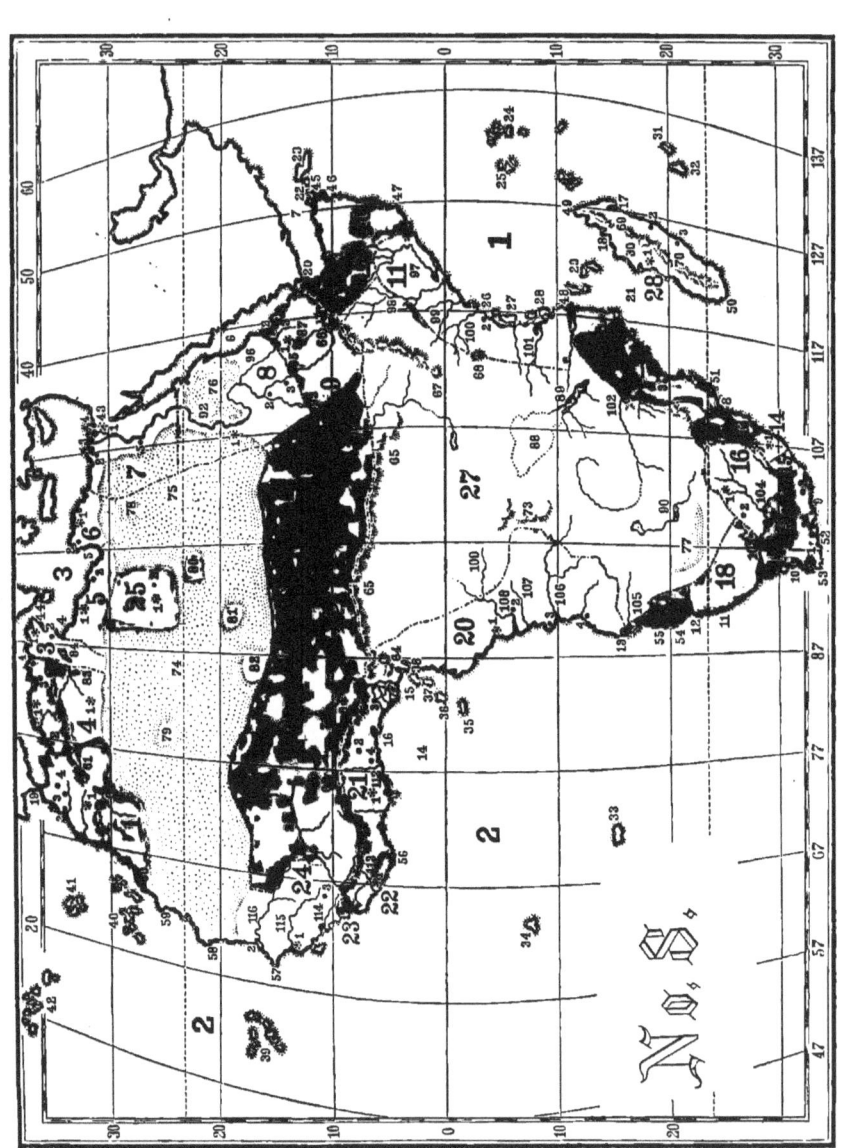

AFRICA.

SQUARE MILES, 12,000,000.   POPULATION, 60,000,000.

KEY TO MAP NO. 8.

COUNTRIES, CAPITALS AND CHIEF TOWNS.

1 **Morocco,** 1 Morocco, 2 *Rabat,* 3 *Mequinez,* 4 *Fez.*
2 **Algiers,** 1 Algiers, 2 *Oran,* 3 *Constantine,* 4 *Bona.*
3 **Tunis,** 1 Tunis, 2 *Kairwan.*
4 **Beled el Jereed,** 1 *Tooggoort.*
5 **Tripoli,** 1 Tripoli, 2 *Mesurata.*
6 **Barca,** 1 Derne, 2 *Bengazi.*
7 **Egypt,** 1 Cairo, 2 *Alexandria,* 3 *Rosetta,* 4 *Damietta,* 5 *Sivot.*
8 **Nubia,** 1 New Dongola, 2 *Khartoom,* 3 *Sennaar.*
9 **Abyssinia,** 1 Gondar, 2 *Massowah,* 3 *Antalo.*
10 **Adel and Ajan,** 1 Berbera, 2 *Zeyla.*
11 **Zanguebar, or Essawahil,** 1 Magadoxo, 2 *Mombas.*
12 **Mozambique,** 1 Mozambique, 2 *Quilimane,* 3 *Sofala.*
13 **Zooloo Country.**
14 **Natal,** 1 Pietermaritzburg.
15 **Kaffraria.**
16 **Bosjesman's Country,** 1 Kurrichane, 2 *Lattakoo.*
17 **Cape Colony,** 1 Cape Town, 2 *Graham's Town,* 3 *Georgetown.*
18 **Hottentot.**
19 **Cimbebas.**
20 **Lower Guinea,** 1 Loango, 2 *San Salvador,* 3 *St. Paul's de Loanda,* 4 *New Benguela.*
21 **Upper Guinea,** 1 Coomassie, 2 *Aboiney,* 3 *Benin,* 4 *Abbeokoota.*
22 **Liberia,** 1 Monrovia.
23 **Sierra Leone,** 1 Freetown.
24 **Senegambia,** 1 Bathurst, 2 *St. Louis,* 3 *Teemboo.*
25 **Fezzan,** 1 Moorzook, 2 *Zueela.*
26 **Soodan,** 1 Kemmoo, 2 Sego, 3 Timbuctoo, 4 Saccatoo, 5 Kobbe, 6 Obeid, 7 Booda, 8 Katunga, 9 *Kano,* 10 *Angornou.*
27 **Ethiopia.**
28 **Madagascar,** 1 Tananarivoo, 2 *Tamatav,* 3 *Mananzary.*

OCEANS, SEAS, GULFS AND BAYS.

1 Indian Ocean,
2 Atlantic Ocean,
3 Mediterranean Sea,
4 Gulf of Cabes,
5 Gulf of Sidra,
6 Red Sea,
7 Gulf of Aden,
8 *Delagoa Bay,*
9 *Algoa Bay,*
10 *St. Helena Bay,*
11 *Cruz Bay,*
12 *Walvisch Bay,*
13 *Great Fish Bay,*
14 Gulf of Guinea,
15 *Bight of Biafra,*
16 *Bight of Benin,*
17 *Antongill Bay,*
18 *Bembatooka Bay.*

AFRICA.

STRAITS, CHANNELS AND SOUNDS.
19 Strait of Gibraltar,
20 Strait of Bab-el-Mandeb,
21 Mozambique Channel.

ISLANDS.
22 Abd-el-Curia,
23 Socotra,
24 Seychelles Islands,
25 Amirante Islands,
26 Pemba,
27 Zanzibar,
28 Monfia,
29 Comoro,
30 Madagascar,
31 Mauritius,
32 Bourbon,
33 St. Helena,
34 Ascension,
35 Annobon,
36 St. Thomas,
37 Prince's,
38 Fernando Po,
39 Cape Verde Islands,
40 Canary Islands,
41 Madeira Islands,
42 Azores Islands.

ISTHMUS AND CAPES.
43 Isthmus of Suez,
44 Bon,
45 Guardafui,
46 Orful,
47 Basmas,
48 Delgado,
49 Ambro,
50 St. Mary,
51 Corrientes,
52 Agulhas,
53 Good Hope,
54 Cross,
55 Frio,
56 Palmas,
57 Verde,
58 Blanco,
59 Bojador,
60 Noon.

MOUNTAINS, DESERTS AND OASES.
61 Atlas,
62   Miltseen,
63 Kong,
64 Cameroon's,
65 Mts. of the Moon,
66 Abba Yaret,
67 Kenia,
68 Kilimandjaro,
69 Radama,
70 Red,
71 Lupata,
72 Snow,
73 Crystal,
74 Sahara Desert,
75 Libyan Desert,
76 Nubian Desert,
77 Desert of Challedenga,
78 Oasis of Seewah,
79 Oasis of Tuat,
80 Oasis of Tibesti,
81 Oasis of Bilmah,
82 Oasis of Agadez.

LAKES.
83 Melgig,
84 Sibkah,
85 Tchad,
86 Fittre,
87 Dembea,
88 Ukerewe,
89 Nyassi, or Maravi,
90 Ngami,
91 Debo.

RIVERS.
92 Nile,
93   White,
94   Gojeb,
95   Blue,
96   Tacazze,
97 Haine,
98 Juba,
99 Ozi,
100 Sabaki,
101 Matoni,
102 Zambezi,
103 Orange,

104 *Vaal,*
105 *Bembaroughe,*
106 *Coanza,*
107 *Ambriz,*
108 Congo,
109 *Umbre,*
110 Niger,
111 *Chadda,*

112 *Volta,*
113 *St. Paul's,*
114 Rio Grande,
115 Gambia,
116 Senegal,
117 *Yeoo,*
118 *Shary.*
119 *Misselad.*

QUESTIONS ON THE MAP OF AFRICA.

Bound Africa. In what zones is it situated? Point out its chief divisions on the map. What states border on the Mediterranean Sea? On the Red? On the Indian Ocean? Atlantic? What states have no sea-coast? What states are crossed by the Equator? What by the Tropic of Cancer? What by the Tropic of Capricorn?

OCEANS, SEAS, GULFS AND BAYS.

What ocean east of Africa? 1. West? 2. What sea north? 3. Between Africa and Asia? 6. What gulfs north of Africa? 4, 5. What gulf north of Adel and Ajan? 7. What bay south of Mozambique? 8. South of Cape Colony? 9. West? 10. West of Hottentot Country? 11. West of Lower Guinea? 13. What gulf south of Upper Guinea? 14. What strait at the entrance of the Mediterranean Sea? 19. Red? 20. What channel between Mozambique and Madagascar? 21.

ISLANDS.

What island at the entrance of the Gulf of Aden? 23. What large island south-east of Africa? 30. What two clusters of islands north-east of Madagascar? 24, 25. What islands east? 31, 32. What islands between Madagascar and the continent? 29. What islands in the Gulf of Guinea? 35-37. What island in the Atlantic Ocean between ten and twenty degrees south latitude? 33. Between the Equator and ten degrees south latitude? 34. What cluster of islands west of Senegambia? 39. South-west of Morocco? 40. North-west? 41, 42.

ISTHMUS AND CAPES.

What isthmus connects Africa with Asia? 43. Which is the most northern cape of Africa? 44. Eastern? 45. Southern? 52. Western? 57. What capes on the eastern coast south of Cape Guardafui? 46-48, 51. Which is the most northern cape of Madagascar? 49. Southern? 50. What capes on the coast of Cimbebas? 54, 55. On the coast of Liberia? 56. On the western coast north of Cape Verde? 58-60.

MOUNTAINS, DESERTS AND OASES.

What mountains in the north of Africa? 61. What mountains in the east? 66-68, 71. North of Ethiopia? 65. In Cape Colony? 72. East of Lower Guinea? 73. North of Upper Guinea? 63. What mountains on the island of Madagascar? 69, 70.

What large desert north of Soodan? 74. South of Barca? 75. In Nubia? 76. Mention the principal oases in the Desert of Sahara. 79-82. What desert in the southern part of Ethiopia? 77.

LAKES AND RIVERS.

Which is the largest lake in Soodan? 85. In Ethiopia? 89.

What river flows into the Mediterranean? 92. What are its principal branches? 93, 95, 96. What are the principal rivers flowing into the Indian Ocean? 98-102. What river between Cape Colony and Hottentot Country? 103. What river forms the northern boundary of Cimbebas? 105. What three rivers from Lower Guinea flow into the Atlantic? 106-108. What large river from Soodan flows into the Gulf of Guinea? 110. What rivers in Senegambia? 114-116. What rivers flow into Lake Tchad? 117, 118. What one into Lake Fittre? 119.

AFRICA.

DESCRIPTIVE GEOGRAPHY.

AFRICA is wholly surrounded by water, except where the Isthmus of Suez connects it with Arabia.

It has a coast line of upwards of fifteen thousand miles, but it is nowhere indented by any great gulf or bay, except by the Gulf of Guinea on the west coast.

It is about 5000 miles in extreme length, and 4,800 in its greatest breadth, containing 12,000,000 square miles.

It has three principal ranges of mountains, and numerous extensive deserts.

The climate of most of Africa is exceedingly hot, and rain seldom falls. It is subject to scorching winds.

The well watered sections are exceedingly fertile, and yield the richest tropical products. The deserts are barren tracts of dry, burning sand.

It has rich mines of gold; and iron, copper and salt, are found in some parts.

Africa contains a great variety of wild animals. The principal are the lion, leopard, camelopard, elephant, rhinoceros, hippopotamus, panther, hyena, zebra, and antelope.

The most useful animals are the camel and the ass. The former requires little food, while it supplies the owner with milk.

There is a great variety of birds, of which the ostrich is the largest, and dwells in the deserts. The vulture is next in size and very ferocious.

Monkeys, insects, reptiles, and enormous serpents and alligators, are also very numerous.

Northern Africa is chiefly inhabited by Europeans, who are generally Mohammedans, and in various stages of civilization. Negroes inhabit the central and southern parts, most of whom are Pagans, and live in a barbarous state.

Africa contained in ancient times, many wealthy and enlightened nations, and is distinguished for its antiquities.

QUESTIONS. What is the position of Africa? What is said of its coast? What is the size of Africa? What is said of its mountains and deserts? Climate? Soil and productions? Minerals? Wild animals? Useful animals? Birds? Other animals? By whom is Africa inhabited? What did Africa formerly contain?

BARBARY STATES.

These states border on the Mediterranean Sea, and comprise the states of Morocco, Algiers, Tunis, Tripoli, and the districts of Barca and Beled-el-Jereed. They are traversed by the Atlas mountains, and contain elevated table lands.

The climate is warm, the soil fertile, and the productions resemble those of southern Europe.

Noxious animals and ferocious lions, panthers and hyenas, also serpents and scorpions of the most deadly venom, roam here.

Agriculture is not well understood, and manufactures and commerce are very limited.

The inhabitants are chiefly Moors, Jews, Berbers, and Arabs.

---

1. MOROCCO.

Square miles, 222,000. Population, 8,500,000.

Morocco, the ancient Mauritania, includes the kingdom of Morocco, Fez, and Tafilet. It yields an abundance of fruit and grain and is noted for the manufacture of morocco leather. Horses, cattle and sheep, are numerous. From the latter, wool of the finest quality is obtained in large quantities.

Morocco, the capital, is situated in a fertile plain, and is surrounded by a wall thirty feet in height. The streets are narrow, irregular and unpaved. It contains many elegant mosques.

Fez was formerly an important city, but is now much decayed. It has a variety of manufactures of the common articles of clothing. It contains upwards of two hundred mosques.

---

2. ALGIERS.

Square miles, 90,000. Population, 2,500,000.

Algiers, formerly called Numidia, is a mountainous country lying on the Mediterranean, east of Morocco.

A STREET IN ALGIERS.

It has a very variable though salubrious climate, and a soil which is rendered fertile by irrigation. The principal productions are figs, pomegranates, oranges, lemons, and dates.

It has extensive coral fisheries.

It is now a French colonial province, under the supreme power of a governor-general, appointed by the French Government.

ALGIERS, the capital, is strongly fortified, and has some commerce. It is rapidly improving in its appearance.

3. TUNIS.

Square miles, 70,000. Population, 2,500,000.

Tunis, the ancient Carthage, lies next east of Algiers, and is the most fertile and flourishing of the Barbary States.

Owing to the extortions of government, agriculture is very much neglected.

It is rich in mineral products.

The government is nominally tributary to the Turkish sultan.

TUNIS, the capital, is about twelve miles from the ruins of Carthage, and one of the finest cities in Africa. It has an extensive trade.

4. BELED EL JEREED.

Square miles, 140,000. Population, 500,000.

Beled el Jereed is a narrow but extensive tract of land, lying between the Atlas mountains and the Great Desert. The soil is generally sterile, but the country contains several oases fertile in dates. It is inhabited by nomadic tribes.

5. TRIPOLI.

Square miles, 105,000. Population, 1,500,000.

Tripoli is a barren and thinly populated state. Much of its surface is a desert, but some of its plains are very fertile. On these rich crops of wheat, barley, millet, and Indian corn, are grown.

The government is an unlimited and barbarous despotism.

TRIPOLI, the capital, is situated on the Mediterranean, and has a good harbor.

6. BARCA.

Square miles, 35,000. Population, 300,000.

Barca is a maritime country, east of Tripoli. It is fertile along the coast, but the interior and southern part is desert. It has no permanent rivers, but numerous mountain torrents.

It belongs to Tripoli. *Derne* is the capital.

QUESTIONS. Name the Barbary States. Give the square miles and population of each. What is said of their surface? Climate, soil and productions? Noxious animals? Agriculture, manufactures and commerce? Inhabitants?

Describe Morocco. Its productions and manufactures. Its animals. Its capital.

Describe Fez. Algiers. Its climate and soil. Productions. Government. Its capital.

Describe Tunis. Its agriculture. Minerals. Government. Its capital.

Describe Beled el Jereed.

Describe Tripoli. Its government. Its capital.

Describe Barca. Derne.

7. EGYPT.

Square miles, 180,000. Population, 2,890,000.

Egypt, a country in the north-eastern part of Africa, comprises the narrow valley of the Nile, with extensive deserts on either side. This valley, throughout its whole extent, is hemmed in on both sides by continuous chains of hills. Those on the east side approach more closely to the river.

The climate is remarkable for its uniformity. In the upper part, rain is hardly known, but the Nile overflows its banks, leaving behind a rich loam, that annually yields two or three crops.

Rice, cotton, wheat, maize, barley, durra, a kind of grain, and fruits, grow in great luxuriance.

Considerable attention is given to agriculture, though the system of husbandry is probably the same now that it was thousands of years ago.

THE SPHYNX AND PYRAMIDS.

Much trade is carried on by means of caravans. Canals have been constructed, and a railroad extends from Alexandria to Cairo.

Egypt is governed by a Pasha, subject to Turkey, who encourages education and the arts. The prevailing religion is the Mohammedan.

Egypt was anciently a wealthy and powerful kingdom. Many stupendous ruins of its former glory still remain. Pyramids, obelisks and catacombs are scattered over the country. The largest pyramid is near Cairo. It is 500 feet high and covers eleven acres. The ruins of Thebes extend several miles, and are among the most magnificent in the world.

CAIRO, the capital, is the largest city in Africa, and the center of trade with Europe and Asia. The streets are narrow, crooked, ill-paved and unfit for the passage of carriages.

Alexandria was once renowned in the arts and sciences. It is the principal seaport of Egypt and connected by means of steam vessels with the chief ports of the Mediterranean.

QUESTIONS. What is the extent of Egypt? Population? What does Egypt comprise? What is said of the valley of the Nile? What is said of the climate? Soil? Productions? Agriculture and trade? Government and religion? What was Egypt anciently? Describe the pyramid near Cairo. Ruins of Thebes. Cairo. Alexandria.

---

8. NUBIA.

Square miles, 300,000. Population, 500,000.

Nubia is situated south of Egypt, on the shore of the Red Sea.

It consists chiefly of mountains and sandy deserts. The cultivated portion occupies the narrow valley of the Nile, and yields cotton, barley, tobacco, and palm trees.

The climate is hot and dry, but healthful.

The Nubians belong to the Arabian and Ethiopian races. They are of a dark-brown complexion; bold, frank, cheerful, and simple in manners.

Nubia is divided into petty kingdoms, subject to the pasha of Egypt.

Magnificent ruins abound; the principal one of which is the temple of Ipsambul, which is cut out of a solid rock. It is supposed to be 2000 years old, but is in a state of complete preservation.

AFRICA.

TEMPLE OF IPSAMBUL.

NEW DONGOLA, the capital, is important as a military depot and place of trade.

KHARTOOM, the capital of a province of Nubia, is regularly built and very flourishing.

QUESTIONS. How many square miles has Nubia? What is its population? What is the surface of Nubia? Productions? Climate? Who inhabit it? How is it divided? What is said of its ruins? New Dongola? Khartoom?

9. ABYSSINIA.

Square miles, 250,000. Population, 280,000.

Abyssinia, comprised in the ancient Ethiopia, is a country of East Africa, south of Nubia. It is a mountainous country, with an agreeable climate and fertile soil.

Wheat, barley, oats, maize, rice, a small grain called teff, fruits, and honey, are the chief products. The minerals are iron ore, rock-salt and gold. Ivory and gold are the principal exports.

The inhabitants are Jews, Arabs and Negroes. Their religion is a curious mixture of the Jewish and Pagan religions.

The government is divided up among several petty states.

GONDAR, the capital city, is twenty miles from lake Dembea; it contains a ruined palace and was formerly a royal residence, but is now a meanly built town.

Massowah, the principal seaport town, is on a small island in the Red Sea.

QUESTIONS. What is the extent of Abyssinia? Population? How is Abyssinia situated? What is the surface? Climate and soil? What are the productions? Minerals? Exports? What is said of the inhabitants? The government? Gondar? Massowah?

EASTERN AFRICA.

EASTERN AFRICA comprises all the coast between Abyssinia and the Tropic of Capricorn. In consequence of the excessive heat, numerous wild animals, and ferocious natives, it has been little explored.

10. ADEL AND AJAN.

Adel and **Ajan** are noted for their gold, ivory, frankincense and myrrh.

Berbera is a seaport station on a bay of the gulf of Aden. An annual fair is held here from October till April, at which from ten to twenty thousand people assemble.

Zeyla stands on a low sandy cape on the straits of Bab-el-Mandeb.

11. ZANGUEBAR.

Zanguebar contains several independent states, and has a number of unimportant towns.

The trade is chiefly in the hands of the Arabs.

Magadoxo is a maritime town, enclosed by stone walls, and divided into two parts, one composed wholly of tombs.

12. MOZAMBIQUE.

Mozambique nominally belongs to the Portuguese. Its trade consists principally in gold and ivory.

MOZAMBIQUE, the residence of the Portuguese Governor, is situated on an island near the coast. It has a good anchorage for ships.

QUESTIONS. What does Eastern Africa comprise? what has prevented its being explored?

For what are Adel and Ajan noted? Describe Berbera. Zeyla.

Describe Zanguebar. What is said of the trade? Of Magadoxo?

What is said of Mozambique? Describe Mozambique.

SOUTHERN AFRICA.

SOUTHERN AFRICA includes Zooloo Country, Natal, Kaffraria, Bosjesman's Country, Cape Colony, and Hottentot Country.

13. ZOOLOO COUNTRY.

This is a small extent of territory, and lies south of Mozambique.

14. NATAL.

Natal, a colonial possession of Great Britain, lies south of Zooloo Country.

The surface is undulating, well watered, the soil generally fertile, and the climate healthy.

Cotton and indigo grow wild. The other productions are coffee, sugar, wheat, and tobacco.

Iron is abundant, and a superior kind of coal is found.

PIETERMARITZBURG, the capital, is fifty miles inland.

15. KAFFRARIA.

Kaffraria, a country in South-eastern Africa, is level near the coast; the western portion is varied. The soil is generally fertile. The principal productions are maize, millet, and melons.

The Kaffres are tall and well-formed. Their color is a dark gray. The men are chiefly engaged in war, and in the care of their cattle.

16. BOSJESMAN'S COUNTRY.

This country lies north-west of Natal and Kaffraria.

The inhabitants, a race of Hottentots, are of small stature and of a savage disposition.

17. CAPE COLONY.

Cape Colony, occupying the southern extremity of Africa, consists of several plateaus and mountain ranges, rising one above another.

The climate is changeable; the alternations of heat and cold being frequently great and sudden.

The soil is fertile on the coast, and produces an abundance of grain, fruits, and good pasturage. Large herds of cattle are kept by the farmers, or boors.

Cape Colony belongs to Great Britain, and is inhabited by English, Dutch, and Hottentots.

CAPE TOWN, the capital, is a fortified seaport, regularly laid out with broad streets lined with shade trees. It has a royal observatory and other public buildings, and is visited annually by a large number of vessels.

CAPE TOWN AND TABLE MOUNT.

18. HOTTENTOT COUNTRY.

The Hottentots are stupid and degraded. The wild Hottentots, called Bushmen, are a miserable race, living like wild beasts, and subsisting on roots, insects, and reptiles.

QUESTIONS. What does South Africa include?
What is said of the Zooloo Country.
What is said of Natal? Its surface, soil and climate? Productions? Minerals? Pietermaritzburg?
What is said of Kaffraria? The Kaffres?
What is said of Bosjesman's Country? The inhabitants?

What is said of Cape Colony? Its climate? Soil? Cattle? To whom does it belong? Describe Cape Town.

Describe the Hottentots.

WESTERN AFRICA.

WESTERN AFRICA embraces the coast from the Tropic of Capricorn to the Great Desert. It is remarkable for its fertility, luxuriant vegetation, and vast numbers of wild animals.

It is inhabited by degraded Negroes, many of whom worship reptiles. They are subject to vindictive chiefs.

Cimbebas, Lower and Upper Guinea, Liberia, Sierra Leone, and Senegambia, are its divisions.

19. CIMBEBAS.

Cimbebas lies north of Cape Colony, and is but little known. It is inhabited by an inoffensive farming community, who reside chiefly in the interior.

20. LOWER GUINEA.

This is a fertile and thickly populated country, embracing a number of different states.

The northern part is little known. The central and southern portions belong to the Portuguese.

The trade consists of ebony, palm-oil, and gold-dust.

Its principal divisions are Loango, Congo, Angola and Benguela. The palm tree is the most useful production.

AFRICA.

21. UPPER GUINEA.

This state is situated between the Kong Mountains and the Gulf of Guinea, and contains several native kingdoms.

It has a large trade in gold-dust and ivory.

Most of its inhabitants are deeply degraded and ferocious. Thousands of human beings are sometimes sacrificed at the death of a king.

The British, Dutch, and Danes, have several small garrisons on the coast.

22. LIBERIA.

Square miles, 25,000. Population, 250,000.

Liberia lies on the coast, west of Upper Guinea. It is well watered, and the soil is fertile, producing cotton, coffee, sugar-cane, dye-woods, and fruits.

It was established by the American Colonization Society in 1821, as a home for emancipated and free negroes.

It is a republic, the government consisting of a president, vice-president, senate, and a house of representatives.

MONROVIA is the capital and principal town, and has a number of schools, churches, and a public library.

23. SIERRA LEONE.

Square miles, 25,000. Population, 42,000.

This is a small British settlement, made in 1787, for the purpose of putting a stop to the slave trade, and civilizing Africa.

FREETOWN, the capital, is regularly built, and contains the government offices, barracks, and various schools.

24. SENEGAMBIA.

This extensive region in Western Africa, includes all the countries lying on the Senegal and Gambia rivers. The climate is extremely hot, and the soil well watered and fertile.

The principal productions are palm-oil, ivory, gold-dust and gums.

It is densely populated, and trades in ivory and gold-dust, with the English, French, and Portuguese, who have settlements on the coast.

25. FEZZAN.

Fezzan is a kingdom of Africa, bounded on all sides by the Sahara, or Great Desert, except on the north.

The northern part consists of ranges of mountains perfectly barren; in the south, sandy plains, destitute of vegetation, alternate with low hills and valleys, which contain all the cultivated soil in the country.

The principal products are dates, figs, pomegranates and garden vegetables.

It has considerable trade, carried on by caravans.

The country is governed by a chief with the rank of sultan.

QUESTIONS. What does Western Africa embrace? For what is it remarkable? By whom is it inhabited? What are its principal divisions?

Describe Cimbebas.

Describe Lower Guinea. To whom does it belong? What is said of its trade? What are its principal divisions.

Describe Upper Guinea. What is said of its trade? Inhabitants?

How is Liberia situated? What is said of its soil and productions? When was it colonized? What is its government? Describe Monrovia.

Describe Sierra Leone. Freetown.

What is said of Senegambia? Climate? Soil? Productions? Trade?

How is Fezzan situated? What is said of the surface and soil? Productions? Trade? How is it governed?

CENTRAL AFRICA.

This section includes all the interior of Africa south of the Great Desert, embracing Ethiopia and Soodan.

26. SOODAN.

Soodan has been only partially explored. It is a large, fertile and populous tract, embracing the valley of the Niger, and abounds with valuable tropical products.

It is divided into a large number of states, ruled by petty chiefs, called kings. The inhabitants are generally humane and industrious.

There are a number of large cities, of which Timbuctoo is the most important.

27. ETHIOPIA.

This is a vast country in Central Africa, lying south of the Mountains of the Moon.

It is for the most part an unexplored and unknown region. Recent travelers have represented the country as extremely populous, containing regularly organized governments.

QUESTIONS. What does Central Africa include? What is said of Soodan? How is it divided? What is said of the inhabitants? Cities? What is said of Ethiopia?

AFRICAN ISLANDS.
28. MADAGASCAR.

This island is in the Indian Ocean about one hundred miles from Africa. It is 1,000 miles in length with an average breadth of 240 miles, having an area a little larger than France.

It is low and level on the coast, and in the interior, mountainous. The heat in the low lands is often intense, and rains are nearly constant, rendering the climate of the coast very unhealthful, both to natives and Europeans. In the interior it is salubrious.

Its vegetable productions are rich and varied, containing many species of plants not found elsewhere. Cotton, sugar-cane, tobacco, hemp, and rice, are cultivated. Ginger, pepper, and indigo grow wild in the woods. It has also a variety of fruits, among which are the orange, peach, citron, and mulberry.

The population appears to have sprung from different races, but has a perfect unity of language. Though nearly in a barbarous condition, the people have manufactures of iron utensils and of cloths.

The government is a monarchical despotism. The religion is pagan.

TANANARIVOO, the capital, is near the center of the island. It is little known by Europeans, but is reported to be large, and to have manufactures of gold and silver chains, and of silk stuffs.

Bourbon and **Mauritius** are fertile islands. Coffee and sugar are the chief products. Bourbon has a volcano constantly burning.

Seychelles and **Amirante** Islands are dependencies of Mauritius. Both produce cotton and cocoa-nuts.

AFRICA.

Pemba, Zanzibar and **Monfia** are fertile islands belonging to Muscat.

Socotra, an island in the Indian ocean, one hundred and twenty miles from cape Guardafui, is inhabited principally by the Bedouins. It produces aloes of the finest quality. It belongs to the Sultan of Keshin.

The chief islands on the western coast, are the Azores, Madeira, Canary, and Cape Verde islands.

Excepting the Cape Verde islands, they have a mild healthful climate, a fertile soil, and produce wine and various kinds of grain and fruits in abundance.

The island of St. Helena is noted as the place of Napoleon's exile and death.

QUESTIONS. What is Madagascar? Its size? Surface? Climate? Productions? What is said of the population? Manufactures? Government? Religion? Tananarivoo?

What is said of Bourbon and Mauritius? Seychelles and Amirante? Pemba, Zanzibar and Monfia? Socotra? What are the principal islands on the western coast? What is said of their climate, soil, and productions? For what is St. Helena noted.

GENERAL QUESTIONS ON AFRICA.

How is Africa bounded? In which direction is it the longest? With what other grand division is it connected? What states lie north of the Sahara Desert? What states border on the Red Sea? What large state south of the Sahara Desert? What country occupies the greater part of Central Africa? What state extends farthest south? East? West?

Where are the Atlas Mountains? The Mountains of the Moon? Snow Mountains? Crystal Mountains? Where is the Sahara Desert? Libyan Desert? Nubian Desert?

What large river in Eastern Africa flowing north? Where is the Zambeze? Orange? Coanga? Congo? Niger? Senegal? Gambia? Where is Lake Tchad? Lake Dembea? Lake Nyassi? Lake Ngami?

Where is the Gulf of Sidra? Gulf of Aden? St. Helena Bay? Gulf of Guinea? Where is the Red Sea? Mozambique Channel?

Where is Socotra? Madagascar? Zanzibar? Mauritius? St. Helena? Ascension? Cape Verde Islands? Canary Islands? Azores? Cape Bon? Cape Guardafui? Cape Palmas? Cape Verde?

What is the latitude of Cape Bon? Cape of Good Hope? Straits of Bab el Mandeb? Between what meridians of longitude is Africa situated? In what zone is the greater part of Africa? What states in the North Temperate Zone? In the South Temperate Zone?

What is the climate of the Barbary States? Of Egypt? Of Nubia? Of Cape Colony? Of Madagascar? What fruits grow in Northern Africa? What grains? What are the productions of Egypt? Of Liberia? What animals are found in the Barbary States? For what are Adel and Ajan noted? What countries have a trade in ivory? In what countries is gold found? What other minerals in Africa?

What ruins in Egypt? In Nubia? Describe Cairo. Alexandria. Cape Town. Monrovia. What is the character of the inhabitants of Western Africa? What is the government of Egypt?

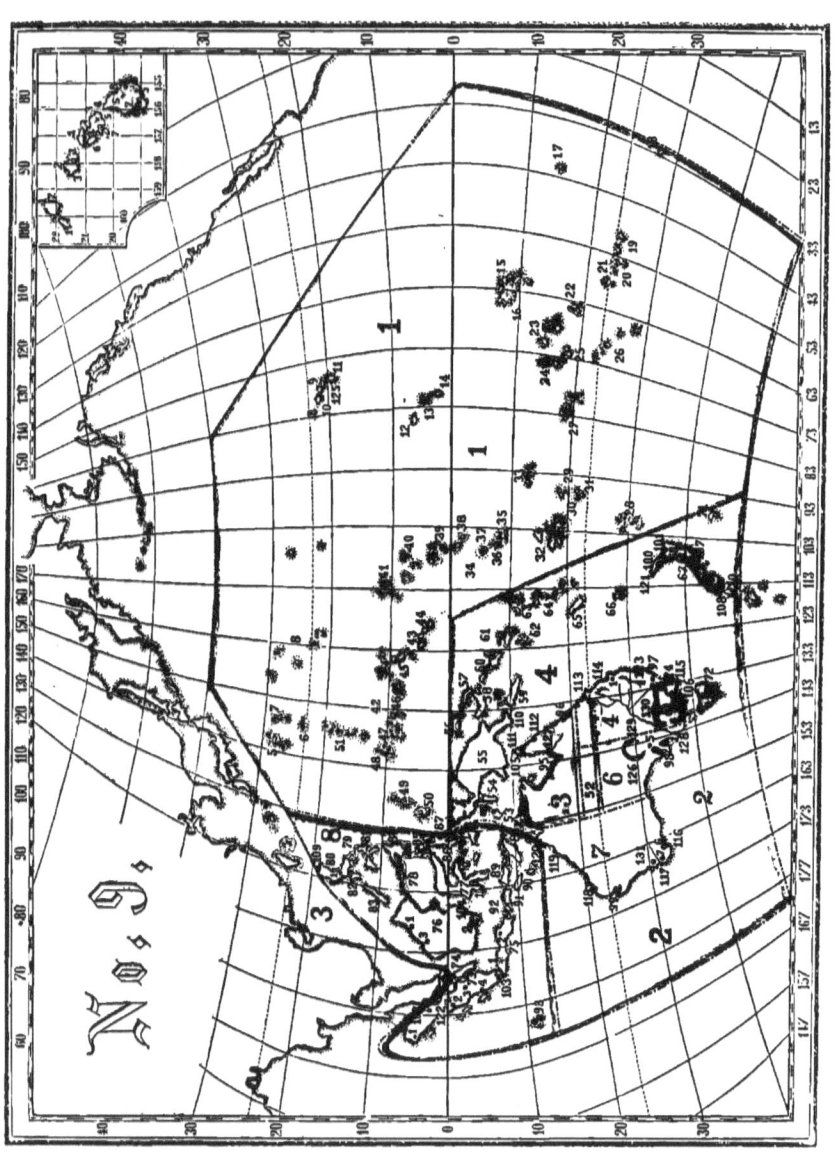

OCEANICA.

SQUARE MILES, 4,400,000.   POPULATION, 23,500,000.

KEY TO MAP NO. 9.

OCEANS AND SEAS.
1 Pacific Ocean,
2 Indian Ocean,
3 China Sea,
4 Coral Sea.

ISLANDS.

1 Polynesia.

5 Bonin Islands,
6 Magellan's Archipelago,
7   Guadalupe,
8 Anson's Archipelago,
9 Sandwich Islands,
10   Oahu,
11   Hawaii or Owhyhee,
12 Palmyras,
13 America Islands,
14 Christmas,
15 Marquesas Islands,
16   Nookaheeva,
17 St. Paul's,
18 Easter,
19 Ducie,
20 Pitcairn,
21 Gambier Islands,
22 Pearl Islands,
23 Palliser Islands,
24 Society Islands,
25   Tahiti,
26 Austral Islands,
27 Cook's Islands,
28 Kermadec Islands,
29 Friendly Islands,
30   Hapai Islands,
31   Tonga Islands,
32 Feejee Islands,

33 Navigator Islands,
34 Central Archipelago,
35   Mitchell's Islands,
36 De Peyster's Islands,
37   Tanwell's Islands,
38   Gilbert's Archipelago,
39   Scarborough's Range,
40   Mulgrave Islands,
41   Radack Islands,
42 Caroline Islands,
43   Ulalan,
44   Strong's,
45   Torre's,
46   Mortlock Islands,
47   Hall Islands,
48   Egoi Islands,
49   Pelew Islands,
50   St. Andrew's Islands,
51 Ladrone Islands.

2 Australasia.
    52 Australia.

3 North Australia.

4 New South Wales, 1 *Brisbane*, 2 Sydney.

5 Victoria, 3 Melbourne, 4 *Portland*.

6 South Australia, 5 Adelaide.

7 West Australia, 6 *Albany*, 7 *Freemantle*, 8 *Perth*.

    53 *Melville*,
    54 *Arroo Islands*,
    55 New Guinea,
    56 Admiralty Islands,
    57 New Ireland,
    58 New Britain,
    59 Louisiade,

OCEANICA.

60 NEW GEORGIA,
61 SOLOMON'S ARCHIPELAGO,
62 *Rennel Islands,*
63 *Egmont,*
64 NEW HEBRIDES,
65 NEW CALEDONIA,
66 NORFOLK,
67 NEW ZEALAND,
68   NEW ULSTER,
69   NEW MUNSTER,
70   NEW LEINSTER,
71 CHATHAM,
72 VAN DIEMEN'S LAND, 1 HOBART TOWN.

8 Malaysia.

73 SUMATRA,   1 ACHEEN, 2 *Padang,* 3 *Palembang,* 4 *Bencoolen.*
74 BANCA,
75 JAVA,   1 BATAVIA, 2 *Samarang.*
76 BORNEO,   1 BORNEO, 2 *Banjermassin,* 3 *Sarawak.*
77 CELEBES,   1 MACASSAR.
78 *Sooloo Islands,*
79 PHILIPPINE ISLANDS,
80   LUZON,   1 MANILLA.
81   SAMAR,
82   MINDORO,
83   PALAWAN,
84   MINDANAO,
85 *Sangir,*
86 SPICE ISLANDS,
87   GILOLO,
88 TIMOR,
89 FLORES,
90 *Sandalwood,*
91 SUMDAWA,
92 *Bally Islands,*
93 *Keeling.*

GULFS AND BAYS.

94 *Cambridge Gulf,*
95 GULF OF CARPENTARIA,
96 *Halifax Bay,*
97 *Botany Bay,*
98 SPENCER'S GULF,
99 *Shark's Bay,*
100 *Bay of Islands,*
101 *Bay of Plenty.*

STRAITS.

102 MALACCA,
103 SUNDA,
104 MACASSAR,
105 TORRES,
106 BASS,
107 COOK'S,
108 FOVEAUX.

CAPES.

109 *Engano,*
110 *Rodney,*
111 YORK,
112 *Flattery,*
113 *Townsend,*
114 *Sandy,*
115 HOWE,
116 CHATHAM,
117 LEEUWIN,
118 NORTH WEST,
119 *Leveque,*
120 *Bougainville,*
121 *Maria Van Diemen.*

MOUNTAINS.

122 *Mount Ophir,*
123 BLUE,
124 *Australian Alps,*
125 *Mount Kilauea.*

LAKE.

126 TORRENS.

RIVERS.

127 *Lynd,*
128 *Murray,*
129   *Darling,*
130   *Lachlan,*
131 *Swan.*

OCEANICA.

SANDWICH, OR HAWAIIAN ISLANDS.
1 Nihau.
2 Kauhai.
3 Oahu,   1 Honolulu.
4 Molokai.
5 Maui,   2 Lahaina, 3 Wairuku.
6 Lanai.
7 Kahoolawe.
8 Hawaii,   4 Hilo, 5 Kaaha, 6 Kealakeakua.

CAPES.
1 Koolau,
2 Kahaka,
3 Hana,
4 Upola.

MOUNTAINS.
5 Mauna Kea,
6 Kilauea,
7 Mauna Loa.

QUESTIONS ON THE MAP OF OCEANICA.

In what two oceans are the islands of Oceanica situated? Which are the three grand divisions of Oceanica? What part of Oceanica constitutes Malaysia? Australasia? Polynesia?

ISLANDS.

What are the principal islands in Polynesia? What archipelago is crossed by the equator? 34. What groups between the equator and ten degrees north latitude? 13, 39, 42. What two archipelagoes are crossed by the tropic of cancer? 6, 8. What are the principal groups in Polynesia south of the Equator? 15, 24, 27, 29, 32, 33.
Which is the largest island in Australasia? 52. What are the divisions of Australasia? What large island north of Australia? 55. What south? 72. South-east? 67. East? 65. What islands in Australasia east of New Guinea? 61.
What three large islands in Malaysia are crossed by the equator? 73, 76, 77. What group of islands north-east of Borneo? 79. East of Celebes? 86. What large island south-east of Sumatra? 75.

SEAS, GULFS, BAYS, AND STRAITS.

What sea west of the Philippine islands? 3. What sea east of Australia? 4.

What gulf north of Australia? 95. What gulf on the south? 98.
What two bays on the east of Australia? 96, 97. What bay on the west? 99. What bays on the north of New Zealand? 100, 101.
What strait north-east of Sumatra? 102. Between Sumatra and Java? 103. Between Australia and New Guinea? 105. Between Australia and Van Diemen's Land? 106. Between the islands of New Zealand? 107.

CAPES, MOUNTAINS AND RIVERS.

What cape north of the Philippine Islands? 109. What cape at the northern point of Australia? 111. What capes on the east? 112-114. Southwest? 116, 117. What cape west? 118.
What mountain in Sumatra? 122. What mountains in Australia? 123, 124.
What lake in Australia? 126.
What rivers in Australia? 127, 128, 131.

SANDWICH, OR HAWAIIAN ISLANDS.

Which is the largest of the Sandwich Islands? 8. What are the other principal islands? 1-7. Mention the principal towns of Hawaii. 4-6. Mountains. 5-7. What two towns in Maui? 2, 3. What town in Oahu? 1. Mention the principal capes of each of the four larger islands? 1-4.

OCEANICA.

SYDNEY.

DESCRIPTIVE GEOGRAPHY.

OCEANICA includes the islands lying in the Pacific and eastern portion of the Indian ocean, and is divided into Polynesia, Australasia and Malaysia.

QUESTIONS. What does Oceanica include, and how is it divided?

1. POLYNESIA.

Square miles, 151,000. Population, 445,000.

POLYNESIA includes a great number of islands in the Pacific ocean, lying on both sides of the equator. These islands are distributed into different groups, which are usually composed of one or more large islands and numerous smaller ones. They are all more or less of coral formation. The temperature, owing to the influence of the surrounding ocean, is mild and comparatively uniform. The climate is delightful and salubrious.

The soil is generally fertile, except on the mountains. The productions are breadfruit, cocoa, banana, yams, sweet potatoes, and cotton, besides various fruits. There are several species of timber trees, especially sandal wood, and a few spices.

The inhabitants consist of two races, one of Malay origin, and the other a variety of the negro race. A few years since they were all idolaters, and sunk in the lowest paganism. Through the efforts of missionaries many of them have received christianity and civilization.

OCEANICA.

The Sandwich Islands are the most important group of Polynesia, and form a kind of connecting link between America and China. The group consists of thirteen islands, seven of which are inhabited.

The surface is mountainous. The islands are of volcanic origin. Several active volcanoes still exist.

European manners and arts have been adopted by the people, and a regular government established. Churches and schools are common, and books and newspapers are printed in the language of the country.

Honolulu, the principal town and seaport of the Sandwich Islands, is on the south side of the island of Oahu. Its harbor, capable of containing between seventy and eighty ships, is often visited by British and American vessels.

QUESTIONS. What does Polynesia include? What is said of these islands? Climate? Soil? Productions? Trees? Inhabitants? Which is the most important group? What is said of the surface? Volcanoes? Arts and government? Churches and schools? Honolulu.

2. AUSTRALASIA.

Square miles, 3,500,000. Population, 1,500,000.

AUSTRALASIA embraces Australia, New Guinea, New Zealand, Van Dieman's Land, New Hebrides, and New Britain, with numerous smaller islands.

Australia is the largest island in the world, and on account of its vast extent is often called a continent. It lies between the Indian and Pacific oceans, south-east of Asia, and is about 2,400 miles in length from east to west, and nearly 2,000 in breadth from north to south.

It is traversed by several ranges of mountains, though it is mostly level.

It is subject to severe droughts of several months duration, which are sometimes followed by sudden and heavy rains. Notwithstanding these sudden changes, the climate, especially in the southern part, is salubrious.

The soil on the coast and in the lowlands is fertile.

Wheat, Indian corn, flax, indigo, and tobacco, are the principal productions. Oranges, lemons, figs, bananas, pine-apples, olives, and peaches, thrive well.

NATIVE NEW ZEALAND VILLAGE.

The chief mineral is gold which, since its discovery in 1850, has been exported in large quantities. There are also rich deposits of copper. Tin and iron are found to some extent.

The aboriginal inhabitants are usually small, very ignorant, and live in the lowest state of degradation.

The island is divided into New South Wales, North, West, and South Australia, and Victoria, and is claimed by Great Britain.

162   OCEANICA.

THE BAMBOO TREE.

The government consists of a legislative council, and a governor, appointed by the crown.

Melbourne and *Sydney* are the principal cities and seaports, and are rapidly increasing in population and importance.

Van Diemen's Land is directly south of Australia. The interior is rugged and mountainous. The climate and productions are similar to those of South Australia. This island was for a long time used by Great Britain as a penal colony.

Papua, or New Guinea, is a large island, north of Australia, lying immediately south of the equator. It is supposed to be mountainous in the interior. The coast is lined with coral reefs. Little is known of the climate and productions.

It is inhabited by negroes and Malays.

New Zealand consists of a group of islands in the south Pacific ocean, belonging to Great Britain. The two principal islands are New Ulster and New Munster.

The surface is mountainous, the climate remarkably healthful, and the soil fertile.

The native plants, like those of other islands in the South Pacific, differ from vegetable forms in other parts of the world. European fruits and plants are cultivated.

The inhabitants belong to the Malay race, and have been much improved, through the exertions of the missionaries laboring among them.

QUESTIONS. What does Australasia embrace? Describe Australia. Its situation and size. Its surface. Climate. Soil. Productions. Minerals. Inhabitants. How is the island divided? What is said of the government? Melbourne and Sydney?
How is Van Diemen's Land situated? Describe it. New Guinea. Of what does New Zealand consist? Describe its surface. Climate. Soil. Productions. Inhabitants.

---

3. MALAYSIA.

Square miles, 760,000. Population, 21,600,000.

MALAYSIA, or the Malay Archipelago, includes the most important and extensive group of islands on the globe, the largest of which are Borneo, Sumatra, Java and Celebes. Malaysia embraces also the Sunda, Philippine, and Spice Islands.

The surface is generally mountainous in the interior. The climate is for the most part warm, and in some portions delightful.

The soil is very fertile, and yields an abundance of spices, gums, and delicious fruits.

The interior of most of the islands is covered with thick jungles, containing forest trees of great variety and gigantic size. One of the most useful is the bamboo tree.

The principal minerals are gold, tin, silver, copper, iron, and coal.

The inhabitants are chiefly of the Malay race, and dwell principally upon the coast.

Their chief towns are in many instances built over the water.

The Philippines belong to Spain. Penang and a few other islands belong to Great Britain.

The north and north-west portions of Borneo and the Sooloo islands are under native rulers. The remainder of this vast Archipelago is under the control of the Dutch, and is frequently named the Dutch East Indies.

VILLAGE OF WAROU.

MANILLA, the capital of the Spanish possessions, and BATAVIA, the capital of the Dutch, are large and flourishing commercial cities.

QUESTIONS. What does Malaysia comprise? What can you say of the surface? Climate? Soil and productions? Forests? Minerals? Inhabitants? How are the towns built? To whom do the islands belong? Describe Manilla and Batavia.

GENERAL QUESTIONS ON OCEANICA.

Which division of Oceanica is nearest America? Nearest Asia? Which division contains the largest island?

On what island is Mount Ophir? Mount Kilauea? Where are the Blue Mountains?

Which is the largest river in Australia? What branches has it?

Where is the Gulf of Carpentaria? Halifax Bay? Botany Bay? Spencer's Gulf? Bay of Islands?

Where is the Strait of Malacca? Strait of Sunda? Strait of Macassar? Cook's Strait?

Where is New Guinea? Sumatra? Borneo? Java? Celebes? Where are the Philippine Isles? Sandwich Islands? Spice? New Zealand? Society Islands? Cook's? Friendly? Caroline? What islands are crossed by the Equator? What is the latitude of the Sandwich Islands? Longitude? In what zones is Oceanica?

What is the climate of Polynesia? What are the productions? Mention the principal town and seaport.

What is the climate of Australia? What minerals has it?

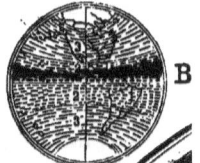

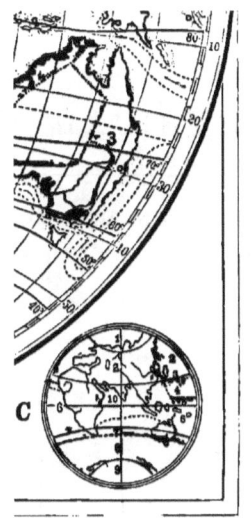

THE PHYSICAL WORLD.

KEY TO MAP NO. 10.

HYDROGRAPHIC BASINS.

1 Arctic,
2 Atlantic,
3 Pacific,
4 Indian,
5 Continental.

PRINCIPAL VOLCANOES.*

6 Hecla,
7 Vesuvius,
8 Stromboli,
9 Ætna,
10 Peak of Teneriffe,
11 Cotopaxi,
12 Jorullo, in Mexico.

OCEAN CURRENTS.

1 Arctic,
2 Gulf Stream,
3 Caribbean,
4 North Atlantic,
5 Guinea,
6 Equatorial,
7 Brazil,
8 South Atlantic,
9 Cape,
10 South Connecting,
11 Counter,
12 Mozambique,
13 Japan,
14 Antarctic,
15 Cape Horn,
16 Peruvian,

17 Mexican,
18 Sargossa Sea.

A GEOLOGY.

1 Granite, (*unstratified,*)
2 Primary, or Metamorphic,
3 Silurian,
4 Old Red Sandstone,
5 Carboniferous,
6 New Red Sandstone,
7 Oolite,
8 Cretaceous,
9 Tertiary,
10 Superficial.

B RAIN.

1 Constant Rain,
2 Periodical Rain,
3 Variable Rain,
4 Rainless District.

C WINDS AND CALMS.

1 North Polar Winds,
2 South-westerly Currents,
3 Calms of Cancer,
4 North-east Trade Winds,
5 Variable Winds and Calms,
6 South-east Trade Winds,
7 Calms of Capricorn,
8 North-westerly Currents,
9 South Polar Winds,
10 Monsoons.

Note. The Temperature is indicated by Isothermal Lines crossing the Map east and west.

* Volcanic regions are marked by small circles.

PHYSICAL GEOGRAPHY.

Physical Geography treats of the solid mass of the earth, of the waters that partly cover it, of the atmosphere that surrounds both, and of the vegetables and animals by which all these are inhabited.

Descriptive Geography has taught us that the surface of the earth is much diversified; that the land consists of continents and islands, mountains, plains and valleys; and the water of oceans, seas, lakes rivers, &c.

1. LAND.
GEOLOGY.

It has been found that there is an increase of heat as the earth is penetrated towards its center, and it is believed that the interior of the globe is in a fluid state, in consequence of the interior heat. It is also supposed that the solid land is only a crust formed by gradually cooling, and is less than a hundred miles in thickness.

Men have been able to penetrate this crust only a few thousand feet, but in consequence of the inclination of the layers of solid rock which compose it, they have been able to determine the composition and order of succession of the materials which compose the earth's crust for several miles in thickness.

There are in nature, about sixty simple substances or elements. The various minerals are composed of these elements alone or chemically combined. About four hundred mineral species are known, but many of these are quite rare.

The most common minerals are quartz, feldspar, mica, hornblende, talc, serpentine, and limestone. These, and many others, some of them metals, are mechanically combined into rocks and earths, and constitute the earth's crust.

The term *Rock*, in popular language, is applied only to the solid portions of the earth's crust, but in science, it extends to all the mineral portion of the earth.

All Rocks are either—
Stratified, or Unstratified.
Igneous, Aqueous, or Metamorphic.
Fossiliferous, or Non-fossiliferous.

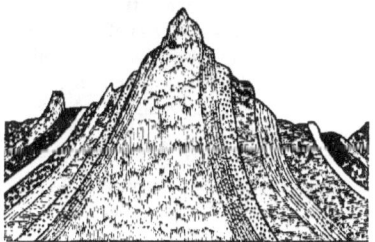

STRATIFIED.   UNSTRATIFIED.   STRATIFIED.

Stratified Rocks are such as are arranged in distinct layers or strata, as sandstone.

Unstratified Rocks are not arranged in layers, but are composed of minerals or broken pieces of other rocks in irregular masses, like granite.

Igneous Rocks are such as are supposed to owe their origin to intense heat. When formed by melted matter cooled at great depths, they are called *Plutonic Rocks*. When the products of volcanoes are cooled at the surface, they are called *Volcanic Rocks*.

Aqueous Rocks are made up of small particles deposited in water, and are usually stratified.

Metamorphic Rocks are Aqueous Rocks which have been changed in structure by heat, without being melted or entirely changed in form. They are usually found in connection with Igneous Rocks.

Fossiliferous Rocks are such as contain the remains of animals or plants, many of which are different from any that now exist. These fossils seem to indicate that the earth long ago was inhabited by families or races of the animal and vegetable kingdoms whose remains were deposited with the sediment which now composes the Stratified Rocks. Many of these species of animals and plants have become extinct.

Non-fossiliferous Rocks contain no fossils and are generally igneous and unstratified.

The lowest Rocks are the *Granite Rocks*, which are made up of quartz, feldspar and mica, mixed irregularly together, coarser or finer, as if the pieces had been broken up, half melted, and then cemented together under conditions of great heat and pressure. These are *Plutonic Rocks*, and are unstratified.

Above the Granite come many series of Stratified Rocks. Of these Rocks, the lowest is known as the *Primary* or *Metamorphic Formation*, consisting of gneiss, which resembles granite, except that it is stratified, mica slate, hornblende slate, and mountain limestone.

The *Silurian* series, which is the lowest of the Fossiliferous Rocks, follows, and above this series is the *Old Red Sandstone*, consisting of sandstone generally of a red color.

The next series is the *Carboniferous*, or *Coal-bearing*, which consists of carboniferous limestone, sandstone, and the coal measures, from which vast quantities of hard coal are obtained.

Over this lies the *New Red Sandstone*, then the *Oolite*, the *Cretaceous*, or *Chalky Formation*, and lastly, the *Tertiary*, or upper series, which is made up of the clays, marls, sand and drift that we now see on or near the surface of the earth.

Above these is the recent deposit of soil, or the *Alluvium*, which contains much decayed or decaying animal and vegetable matter.

In addition to the Granite Rocks which seem to form the basis of all the others, there are Granite Veins penetrating the Stratified Rocks.

There are also other Rocks of igneous origin found in connection with the Stratified Rocks. These are principally volcanic, and include Trap Rock, Basalt, Greenstone, the products of ancient volcanoes, and also the Lavas and other Rocks more recently ejected.

The presence or absence of certain Rocks gives general character to a country, affecting its configuration, and also contributing to the fertility or sterility of its soil. The crust of the earth is still undergoing important changes caused by igneous and aqueous forces.

QUESTIONS. Of what does Physical Geography treat? What has Descriptive Geography taught of the surface of the earth? What is said of the heat of the earth? In what state is the interior of the earth supposed to be? What is said of the crust? How far has the crust been penetrated? How much of its composition is known? How many simple elements are there? How many species of minerals are known? Which are the most common minerals? How are they combined? What is meant by the term Rock?

How are Rocks classified? What are Stratified Rocks? Unstratified Rocks? Igneous Rocks? Plutonic Rocks? Volcanic Rocks? Aqueous Rocks? Metamorphic Rocks? Fossiliferous Rocks? Non-fossiliferous Rocks? Describe the Granite Rocks. What are the lowest Stratified Rocks? Mention the succeeding series in their order. Describe Granite Veins. What other Unstratified Rocks occur? What is said of the effects of certain Rocks? Of changes now taking place?

CONTINENTS AND ISLANDS.

All the land on the globe is comprised in two great divisions, *Continents* and *Islands*.

There is far more land in the Northern than in the Southern Hemisphere. If a great circle be drawn through the south of Asia and the coast of Peru, nearly all the land surface of the globe will be on the upper or northern side of this line.

The land is arranged chiefly in two great masses called *Continents*. There is much doubt as to the mode by which these have arrived at their present form and condition. Many suppose there has been a succession of elevations and depressions, produced by the agency of the heat beneath. However this may be, they have undoubtedly passed through both sudden and gradual changes, with alternating periods of rest.

The Continents present several notable resemblances and differences.* Both have their great mountain ranges running in the same direction as the greatest length of land; both are broad at the north, and terminate at the south in tapering rocky points. With two exceptions, the important peninsulas of both point southward, and have to the eastward an island or groups of islands. A large member of each is nearly isolated, and has a deep bend of its western coast to the interior. They differ in the direction of the land,—that of the Western stretching from north to south, and that of the Eastern from east to west, giving to the former great variety of zone, hence of climate and production, and to the latter great extent in the same climatic belt.

The Western Continent is simple in its form, its edges mainly unindented by the sea, except on the eastern side, and its masses little broken by irregular or transverse mountains. The northern portion has more indentations than the southern. Its distinguishing characteristics are its lofty chain of mountains, uninterrupted from Behring's Strait to the Magellan, its vast plains, and its system of inland waters.

On the Eastern Continent, Africa is simple in its structure; but Europe is divided and re-divided by deep arms of the sea; and Asia, though so extensive as to keep a vast mass entire, still has in the east and south, a succession of land-locked seas and broad indenting bays. Each of these divisions is traversed by mountains, secondary to the main ranges, making comparatively small river basins. The marked feature of this Continent is its wide and elevated plateaus, which appear especially in Central Asia.

Islands are either *Continental*, having at one time formed part of the neighboring main land, as the British Isles; or are *Sandy* accumulations deposited by the waves, as along the east coast of North America; or are the products of *Volcanic action*, as the Azores; or are the work of the *Coral* insects, as many of those in the Pacific.

The Continental Islands usually resemble the adjacent portions of the Continents in formation.

* See Map No. 1.

A few Volcanic Islands have been formed by submarine volcanic action, since the christian era.

Coral Islands, which consist of a circular strip of coral enclosing a portion of shallow water, are called Atolls, and the water thus enclosed is called a Lagoon. Coral reefs, many miles in extent, are sometimes found surrounding Volcanic Islands.

QUESTIONS. How is the land on the globe divided? Which Hemisphere contains the most land? How is the land arranged? Describe the Continents. Which is the most simple in form? What are the characteristics of the Western Continent? Describe the Eastern Continent. What is its marked feature? How are Islands divided? What is said of the Continental Islands? Volcanic Islands? Coral Islands? Coral Reefs?

MOUNTAINS AND VOLCANOES.

Mountains sometimes occur singly, but they are usually found connected together, forming a *Chain or Range of Mountains.*

A number of Mountain chains nearly related to each other, extending in the same direction, constitutes a *Mountain System.*

The great Mountain Systems of the two Continents correspond to the general outline of the Continents. The principal Systems of the Western Continent extend north and south, while those of the Eastern Continent extend east and west.

On the Western Continent, the *Rocky Mountain System* in North America, and the *System of the Andes* in South America, constitute an almost uninterrupted succession of Mountain Chains extending from the Arctic Ocean to the southern point of the Continent.

The *California System* consists of several ranges in North America west of the Rocky Mountains.

The *Appalachian System* includes the Cumberland, Alleghany, Blue Ridge, Catskill, and other ranges extending from Alabama nearly to the Gulf of St. Lawrence, at a distance of from thirty to three hundred miles from the coast of the Atlantic Ocean.

In South America, the *Brazilian* and *Parima* are distinct Systems on the eastern coast, of less height and extent than the Andes, and nearly parallel to the Atlantic coast.

The *Great Eastern System*, consisting of nearly parallel ranges somewhat broken, extends nearly across the Eastern Continent, including the Cantabrian, Pyrenees, Alps and Balkan Mountains of Europe, and the Taurus, Elburg, Hindoo Koosh, Himalaya, Kuenlun, and Peling of Asia.

Another System, north of this, is composed of the Altai, Stanovoi and other ranges.

The *Scandinavian* and *Ural Mountains* are distinct Systems running in an oblique direction from the principal Systems, while the Appenines, Ghauts and other ranges, may be considered as spurs from the main System.

The principal mountain ranges of the Eastern Continent have a gradual slope to the north, and an abrupt descent to the south, while those of the Western Continent have the gradual slope to the east, and the abrupt descent on the west.

By *Volcanic action* is meant the influence exerted by the heated interior of the earth on its external covering. Its effects are known to us,—not only in the eruption of Volcanoes, but in Earthquakes, and all kindred phenomena, in emanations of gases and vapors from the earth, and in Geysers and Hot Springs.

A *Volcano*, properly so called, exists only where a permanent connection is established between the interior of the earth and the atmosphere. The number of active Volcanoes is estimated at about three hundred, of which two-thirds are found around the shores or on the islands of the Pacific Ocean.

THE CRATER OF ETNA.

There are five principal *Lines* of Volcanoes: one from Patagonia to Oregon, which is divided into several volcanic spaces, with intervals entirely free; one from the Aleutian Isles to Borneo; another in the East Indies, through Java and Sumatra; a fourth from Greece, through the Mediterranean, to the Azores; and the last from the West Indies, across Mexico, to the Sandwich Islands.

The vents of Iceland seem to form a short chain by themselves; and besides these, there are some isolated or grouped Volcanoes on land, and probably many in the bed of the ocean. Stromboli is noted for its constant activity,—Hecla, for its violent eruptions,—Cotopaxi, for its great height, and Jorullo, in Mexico, for having been thrown up from a plain within a few months.

Sudden and violent disturbances of the earth's crust are called *Earthquakes*, and occur usually within the region, though not in the immediate vicinity of Volcanoes. Some of the most destructive on record are those of Lisbon, in 1755, of Riobamba, in 1797, and those of Caracas and the Mississippi valley, in 1812.

QUESTIONS. How do Mountains occur? What is a Mountain System? To what do the Mountain Systems correspond? Describe the principal Systems of the Western Continent. Of the Eastern Continent. What is peculiar to the Mountains of each Continent? What is meant by Volcanic action? How many Volcanoes are now active? Describe the principal Volcanic regions. For what is Stromboli noted? Hecla? Cotopaxi? Jorullo? What are Earthquakes? Mention some of the most destructive.

PLATEAUS AND PLAINS.

Plateaus are extensive elevated tracts of land with a surface generally level, though they may sometimes contain hills or mountain ridges.

Plains are low tracts of land nearly level. The two Continents are not only characterized by their Mountain Systems, but by their Plateaus and Plains. While each Continent contains both Plateaus and Plains, the Western Continent may be distinguished for its Plains, while the Eastern is distinguished for its Plateaus.

On the Western Continent, a Plateau extends along the base of the Rocky Mountains from the southern part of British America to the Isthmus of Panama. It includes the Utah basin, and the great

Mexican Plateau, on which the city of Mexico is situated.

In South America there are several elevated Plains connected with the Andes, the principal of which, the *Plateau of Lake Titicaca*, is one of the highest Plateaus in America. The city of Potosi is situated on the southern end of this Plateau.

The greater part of Central and Western Asia is one vast Plateau traversed by Mountain Chains. This great Plateau includes the great *Desert of Cobi*, and is also the source of most of the Asiatic Rivers. The southern portion of Hindostan contains the *Plateau of the Deccan*, which is often the resort of the Europeans of Hindostan in the hot season. By ascending this Plateau, they may enjoy a temperate climate in the torrid zone. The principal Plateau of Europe is that of Spain.

North America has a *Great Central Plain* extending from the Arctic Ocean to the Gulf of Mexico. The northern part is drained by the waters which flow into Hudson's Bay and the Arctic Ocean, and the southern part includes the great valley of the Mississippi and the basin of the Gulf of Mexico. There is also a narrow plain east of the Alleghany Mountains extending from Maryland to Florida. The lower part of this is swampy.

In South America a great Plain east of the Andes extends through nearly the whole length of this division. It branches off into the *Plain of the Orinoco* on the north-east, and the *Plain of the La Plata* in the southern part.

A large part of the South American Plains are covered with grass, which grows luxuriantly during the rainy seasons affording pasturage to vast herds of cattle.

The principal Plains of the Eastern Continent are the great *Northern European Plains*, which extend from the Bay of Biscay through the northern part of central Europe to the Ural Mountains, and the *Northern Asiatic Plain* which extends from the Ural Mountains to Behring's Strait. The European Plain has, most of it, a deep fertile soil, very productive. A part of it is still covered with extensive forests. The northern part of the Asiatic Plain is frozen to a great depth.

The smaller Plains of Europe are found in northern Italy, Austria and Turkey. Plains of limited extent skirt the eastern and south-eastern shores of Asia and the lower part of the principal river basins.

The principal Plains of Africa are the great *Desert of Sahara*, the narrow *Plain of Egypt*, known as the valley of the Nile, and the *Plain of Central and Southern Africa*, which has not yet been thoroughly explored.

QUESTIONS. What are Plateaus? Plains? Which Continent is distinguished for its Plains? Its Plateaus? Describe the Plateaus of North America. South America. Asia. Describe the Plains of North America. South America. The Plains of Europe and Asia. Of Africa.

2. WATER.
SPRINGS, LAKES, AND RIVERS.

The Waters of the land are found in the form of *Springs*, *Lakes*, and *Rivers*.

Springs are Hot or Cold, according to the depth of the reservoirs by which they are supplied. If these are above the stratum of invariable temperature, the heat of the water will only vary with the seasons; if the water come from this stratum itself, it will be invariable; if from below it, its

PHYSICAL GEOGRAPHY. 173

temperature will be proportionate to the depth.

Hot and Boiling Springs are very constant in their heat, and are more frequent in volcanic regions, though there are many examples of them remote from such places. Many mineral substances are dissolved by both Hot and Cold Springs, whence the medicinal properties of their waters; especially are they often highly impregnated with common salt.

The principal *Mineral Springs* in the United States are the Salt Springs of Syracuse and Salina in New York, and those on the Kanawha river in Virginia; also the Medicinal Springs of Saratoga, New York; and the Sulphur Springs of Virginia.

Lakes are of four kinds; those having inlets and outlets, as the great American Lakes; those having neither inlets nor outlets, found among mountains and fed by Springs, and in which the evaporation equals the supply; those having outlets but no inlets, which are fed by Springs, and are the sources of Rivers; and those having inlets but no outlets, as the Caspian, Aral, and Dead Seas in Asia; Titicaca and the great Salt Lake, in America. These last, with their tributaries, form Continental Systems of Rivers, and their basins cover a vast extent of territory.

Rivers are streams of water flowing over the land to some other body of water. They have their origin in Springs, Lakes, and in ice-covered mountains. The basin of a River is the entire country drained by it and its tributaries, and the elevation, whether great or small, which separates one such basin from another, is their watershed. The velocity of a River depends on the form and slope of its bed, and the volume and pressure of water in the upper part of its course. The Danube, Tigris and Indus are the most rapid of the large Rivers.

Owing to the structure of the highland and mountain chains, most of the important Rivers flow in an easterly direction, and the next in size towards the south and north, while those flowing west are generally small.

DELTA.

The soil borne down by streams is deposited as their velocity diminishes, and if the lower courses be through a flat country, subject to inundation, Deltas are formed at their mouths, as in the Mississippi and Nile.

QUESTIONS. How are the waters of the land found? Describe Springs. Hot and Boiling Springs. Mention the principal Mineral Springs of the United States. Describe Lakes. Rivers. What is meant by the basin of a River? Upon what does the velocity of a River depend? In what direction do the largest Rivers flow? How are Deltas formed?

THE OCEAN.

The great mass of Waters, covering two-thirds of the earth's surface, receives the general name of *Ocean*. This contains from three to four per cent. of salts, is of a dark blue or green color, and of great depth. Of the five Oceans, the *Pacific* is the largest, and is remarkable for its calm waters and many islands. The *Indian*, really a branch of this, is noted for its periodical and violent winds. The *Atlantic* occupies a long and narrow trough between the two continents; it is deep, almost unbroken by islands, traversed by well defined currents, and extends through all zones of climate. The *Northern* and *Southern* Oceans are within the Polar Circles, and are alike remarkable for their masses of ice and the icebergs which they send off to the warmer seas.

The Basin of an Ocean includes not only the space actually occupied by its waters, but all the land drained by Rivers flowing into it. The Atlantic receives the waters of Western Europe, Northern and Western Africa, and of the greater part of America; the Northern Ocean, those of the great northern slope of the Eastern Continent, and the vast upper plain of North America; the Indian, those of Southern Asia and Eastern Africa; and the Pacific those of Eastern Asia and of America west of the mountains.

The Ocean is characterized by three great movements, *Waves, Tides,* and *Currents.*

Waves are the alternate elevations and depressions of the surface of a body of water, produced by a force acting unequally on that surface. There is no real onward motion, except in case of violent winds and over shoals.

Tides are alternate risings and fallings of the water of the Ocean, occurring twice in twenty-four hours, and are owing to the united attraction of the sun and moon. The influence affects the whole mass of the water, and is thought to originate in the unbroken expanse of water about the Antarctic Circle, and to spread thence to all the Seas having ready communication with each other. In the open Ocean the rise of the Tide is small, being only two or three feet; it varies on various shores, and when it enters narrow bays, or is forced around a head land, it sometimes rises to the hight of forty, fifty, and even seventy feet, as in Bristol, England,—St. Malo, France,—and in the Bay of Fundy.

The Tidal Wave occupies about a day and a half in traveling from its great southern reservoir to the British Isles. It moves rapidly through deep Seas, and slowly through shallows, as in the Pacific, where its influence is hardly perceptible.

Currents are like Rivers in the Ocean, effecting an interchange of the waters of one latitude with those of another. Temporary Currents are produced by violent winds or by Tides, as Hurlgate, in East River, near New York. Periodical Currents are owing to periodical winds, as the Monsoons of the Indian Ocean.

Constant Currents are the result of constant forces, of which the principal are, the heat of the sun, the salts of the sea, and the rotation of the earth. Direction is often given to them by the configuration of the land, and together they constitute a great system of Oceanic circulation. They seem, like the Tides, to have their source in the Southern Ocean; a great stream known as the *Antarctic Current*, flowing thence northward toward South America, where it is divided; a small part goes east, around Cape Horn, while the rest flows north along the western coast, and turning suddenly to the west, is lost in the *Equatorial Current of the Pacific.* This flows westward until it meets China, India, and the East India

Islands; a part makes its way among these and joins the *Equatorial Current of the Indian Ocean*. Passing between Madagascar and the main land, it rounds Cape of Good Hope and turns northward along the coast of Africa, until off Guinea it flows westward in the *Atlantic Equatorial*. This, reaching Brazil, is divided; one branch flowing south, then eastward to the Indian Ocean, is known as the *Southern Connecting Current;* the other and principal branch goes round the point of Brazil, through the Caribbean Sea, sweeps round the Gulf of Mexico, and appears off the peninsula of Florida as the *Gulf Stream*. This great current flows along the United States coast, toward Newfoundland, where, spreading, it goes eastward, mingling with and warming the waters west of Europe. The British Isles divide it, a part of it going north to the Polar Sea, and a part, turning south, seems to appear again on the coast of Africa in the *North African and Guinea Current*, which completes the circuit of the North Atlantic by mingling with the Equatorial Current. Within this circuit of waters is an area matted over with gulf weed, known as the *Sargossa Sea*.

A stream originates in the ice masses around the North Pole, and coming southward past Labrador, divides, sending one Current inside the Gulf Stream to the Gulf of Mexico, and another, as an Under Current, to the Caribbean. On the eastern coast of Asia is the *Japan Current*, in many respects closely resembling the Gulf Stream of the Atlantic. Like that, it has a Cold Counter Current near the coast, and also sends a Return Current along the shores of California and Mexico, to mingle with the Pacific Equatorial.

QUESTIONS. What is the Ocean? Describe the Pacific Ocean. Indian. Atlantic. Northern. Southern. What is meant by the Basin of an Ocean? Describe the Hydrographic Systems of each Ocean. By what is the Ocean characterized? Describe Waves. Tides. Currents. The Antarctic Current. Equatorial Currents. Southern Connecting Current. The Gulf Stream. Guinea Current. Sargossa Sea. Japan Current.

3. ATMOSPHERE.
TEMPERATURE AND WINDS.

The Atmosphere is the fluid which we breathe, and which surrounds the earth to a height, probably of forty or fifty miles. It has weight and great elasticity, and is nearly colorless.

The quantity of sensible Heat, as indicated by the thermometer, is called *Temperature*. The depth to which the solid earth is affected by Heat or Cold varies with the latitude; at the equator it is about one foot; in the temperate zones, fifty or sixty feet; in the Polar regions, 300 or 400 feet. Below this the Heat increases regularly. In the ocean there is also a line of Invariable Temperature, (39°.5,) found at the equator at a depth of 7,200 feet, in lat. 56°, at the surface, and in lat. 70°, 4,500 feet below it. The Temperature of water is far more equable than that of the land. The Atmosphere receives its Sensible Heat chiefly by radiation from the earth. The Temperature of any place depends principally on its latitude, its elevation, the vicinity of the sea, and prevailing winds.

Wind is air in motion. Whenever the equilibrium of the atmosphere is, for any cause, disturbed, there follows an exchange of place among its particles, until this equilibrium is restored. The Heat of the earth in the equatorial regions causes the rarefied air to rise, to supply the place of which other air rushes in from the north and south, the air which ascends flowing off to the Poles again, thus completing the circuit of the globe. The revolution of the earth on its axis gives a westward direction to the air from the Poles, and an eastward one to the returning currents. The force and constancy of these are greatly modified by the alternating land and water over which they flow.

WATER SPOUTS.

Within the Tropics, gentle winds blow constantly from the east, called the *Trade* Winds. These are in two bands or zones, between which is a zone of calms that is near but north of the equator, and shifts its position with the change of seasons. Outside of these *Trades* are narrow belts of calms, north of the northern and south of the southern, of which the prevailing direction of the winds is found to be from the west, as far as 60° or 70° of latitude, beyond which limits the courses of the winds are not accurately known.

The westerly winds of the temperate zone are called the *Return Trades*. They are by no means constant, and their prevalence is determined only by careful and continued observation.

There are certain *Periodical* Winds, such as the *Morning* and *Evening Breezes* on the sea-coast; the *Monsoons* of the Indian Ocean, changing their course with the seasons; the *Etesian* Winds, blowing from the north in the Mediterranean in summer; and the cold *Northers* of Texas and Mexico.

Winds are hot or cold, moist or dry, taking these characters from the countries over which they pass. Among the noted Hot Winds are the *Simoon*, of Arabia, Syria, and Nubia, and the *Sirocco*, of the Sahara Desert.

Whirlwinds are produced by currents meeting each other obliquely. *Hurricanes*, are violent revolving Winds, which occur chiefly in the West Indies, the Indian Ocean, and Chinese waters. They spring up suddenly, move rapidly over wide areas, and are more frequent in the Autumn. *Waterspouts*, caused by Whirlwinds near the surface of the water, are very common in the Mediterranean.

QUESTIONS. What is the Atmosphere? What is Temperature? Upon what does the Temperature of a place depend? What causes Wind? What are the principal prevailing Winds? The most noted Hot Winds? What are Whirlwinds? Hurricanes? Waterspouts?

MOISTURE AND CLIMATE.

The Atmosphere is constantly receiving Moisture from the earth, by means of evaporation. The capacity of the Air for containing this moisture depends on its temperature. It is said to be *saturated*, or at the Dew point, when it contains all its temperature will allow it to receive, and any above this quantity will be condensed and precipitated. It is often deposited, during still nights, on bodies which are cooler than the Dew point of Atmosphere at the time, and in this form is called *Dew*. *Hoar-frost* is frozen Dew.

Mists and *Fogs* are masses of vapor near the earth, sufficiently condensed to be visible, differing from *Clouds* only in position. When Clouds come in contact with air or vapor cooler than themselves, their moisture is condensed and falls to the earth in the form of *Rain*. *Hail* is frozen Rain, and *Snow* is frozen vapor.

Rain is very unequally distributed; it is found that it decreases in quantity from the Equator to the Poles, and from the coasts to the interior of a continent; that the greatest number of rainy days occur in the temperate zones; that more Rain falls in mountainous than level districts, and more in the Northern than in the Southern Hemisphere; and the same is true of the western coasts of the continents in the temperate zones, because the moisture is brought by westerly winds, which lose it before they reach the eastern shores.

Rains are *Periodical* within the Tropics and wherever periodical winds prevail; and are *Frequent* beyond the Tropics, where it may rain on any day of the year. Large *Rainless Districts* occur in Peru, Central America, and Mexico, and in Central Asia; the moisture brought from the sea by the winds being condensed by mountain ranges before they arrive at these districts. The annual fall of rain is estimated at 8.5 feet in the Torrid Zone, at 3.05 feet in the Temperate, and in the Frigid at 1.25 feet.

By the *Snow Line* is meant the limit on mountains above which the snow is perpetual. At and below this limit the snow and ice are melted or softened by the heat of summer, and here it is that *Glaciers* have their origin. These are large masses of ice and snow, which, becoming attached, are in time consolidated, and, increasing from year to year by additions from above, move slowly down valleys and gorges, until, reaching a milder temperature, they dissolve and form the sources of rivers.

By *Climate* is meant the condition of the Atmosphere with reference to heat and cold, moisture and dryness, healthiness and unhealthiness. It is affected, in all these particulars, by the form and elevation of the land, the nature of the soil, and the neighborhood of bodies of water, and is by no means the same in similar latitudes. Lines passing through places which have the same mean temperature, are called *Isothermal Lines*. By tracing any one of these throughout its course, it will be found to pass over widely differing latitudes. Especially is this the case with those Isotherms which cross North America and the Atlantic Ocean.

QUESTIONS. What is Dew? Frost? What are Mists and Fogs? What is said of Rain? Hail and Snow? Where are Rains Periodical? Frequent? Where are the Rainless Districts? What is the annual fall of Rain? What is meant by the Snow Line? What are Glaciers? What is Climate? What are Isothermal Lines?

4. GEOGRAPHICAL DISTRIBUTION OF PLANTS.

The whole number of species of Plants on the globe is estimated at 130,000.

They appear to have originally had their native regions adapted by soil and climate for their growth and perfection, and to which they were principally confined. Natural means and artificial agencies have distributed many Plants over a large extent of country, and to a great distance from their native soil.

The most important influences affecting vegetation are heat, light, and moisture.

The most constant heat and the greatest amount of rain, we have already noticed, are found in the Torrid Zone.

TORRID ZONE.

In this zone vegetation exists in its greatest variety and luxuriance. The most gorgeous flowers, the most luscious fruits, and the hardest and heaviest timber are found in the Torrid Zone.

In the Temperate Zones, the most important grains are found; such as wheat, rye, maize, barley, oats; also the common grasses, and fruits, such as apples, pears, grapes and berries, and plants for clothing, as flax, hemp and cotton.

This zone also contains majestic forests of the oak, hickory, chestnut, maple, pine, fir, and cedar.

In the Frigid Zones vegetation is scanty, and, in some parts of these zones, ceases to exist. Barley and oats are produced on the borders of the Temperate Zone, but the principal Plants of the Frigid Zones are mosses, lichens, dwarf trees and shrubs.

Besides the limitation of Plants by climate, there are also local and restricted regions with plants peculiar to the locality. Thus Australia constitutes a botanical region differing from all others. Countries in the same latitude differ essentially in their species of vegetation, but the most important productions of each zone are most widely distributed.

QUESTIONS. What is the estimated number of species of Plants on the globe? What is said of the native regions of Plants? Of the distribution of Plants? What are most important influences affecting vegetation? What is said of the vegetation of the Torrid Zone? Of the Temperate Zone? Of the Frigid Zone? Of local and restricted botanical regions?

5. GEOGRAPHICAL DISTRIBUTION OF ANIMALS.

Animals are adapted to different climates and diverse circumstances, by variety in clothing and physical structure. In the Torrid Zone, quadrupeds are usually nearly naked, or furnished with a coat of short and thin hair; in the Temperate Zone, they are covered with thick hair, or with wool; while in the Frigid Zone, they are supplied with thick fur.

It is in the Torrid Zone that Animal life is most abundantly developed. This zone contains the greatest variety of insects, reptiles and birds, as well as the largest quadrupeds, such as the elephant, rhinoceros, camel, camelopard, tapir and hippopotamus.

The most poisonous reptiles and insects, and the most savage beasts of prey are found in this zone. Among these may be mentioned the lion, tiger, elephant, puma, and hyena.

Birds of the largest size and most beautiful plumage are found in this zone, such as the bird of paradise, the parrot tribe and the ostrich.

The coral forming tribes are found chiefly in this zone. Here are also the largest monkeys.

The Temperate Zones contain the greatest number of useful and domestic animals, such as the horse, ox, sheep and deer tribes. The chief beasts of prey are the lynx, wild cat, wolf, bear, fox, and weasel. The animals of the Temperate Zones are, many of them, gregarious, or accustomed to collect in flocks or herds. Many of the birds are migratory, passing the summer in the north, and returning to warmer climes on the approach of winter.

The Frigid Zone contains few species of animals, and those the most hardy, such as the white bear, moose, reindeer, Arctic fox, seals, whales, and walruses. There are a few species of birds, such as eagles, gulls, cormorants, and petrels.

Some Animals, like some species of plants, are confined to particular regions. The giraffe, gorilla, and some varieties of baboons and monkeys, are found only in Africa. The island of Madagascar has a large number of species peculiar to itself. Australia and many of the East Indian Islands have species found no where else. Australia is distinguished for its marsupial quadrupeds.

In North America, the grizzly bear and the American buffalo are found in large numbers, and in South America, the sloth, armadillo, vampire, and a species of monkey peculiar to this continent.

QUESTIONS. How are Animals adapted to different climates? What is said of the clothing of Animals in different zones? What Animals does the Torrid Zone contain? What kind of birds? Where are the coral tribes found? What class of Animals does the Temperate Zone contain? Mention the chief beasts of prey in the Temperate Zone? What is said of the Animals in the Frigid Zone? Of Animals peculiar to particular regions? Mention some of these Animals and their locality.

GENERAL QUESTIONS ON PHYSICAL GEOGRAPHY.

What is Physical Geography? Of what is the earth's crust composed? Mention the different kinds of Rocks. How are Igneous Rocks formed? Aqueous Rocks? What are the principal Stratified Rocks?

Which Continent contains the most land? Give the principal characteristics of each Continent. What are the different kinds of Islands? What are the principal Mountain Systems of the Western Continent? Of the Eastern Continent? Where are the principal Volcanoes found? Where is Hecla? Vesuvius? Etna? Peak of Teneriffe? Cotopaxi? Describe the Plateaus of the Western Continent. Of the Eastern Continent. What are the most noted Plains of the Western Continent? Of the Eastern?

What are the principal River Systems of the Western Continent? Of the Eastern Continent? What is meant by a Delta? Point out on the map the different Hydrographic Basins. What are Ocean Currents? Point out the Equatorial Currents. Describe the Gulf Stream. Sargossa Sea. Japan Current. Brazil Current. Mozambique Current. Cape Horn Current. What is the direction of the Peruvian Current?

Where are the Trade Winds found? Monsoons? What are the most noted Hot Winds? Where do Hurricanes occur? Where are the principal rainless districts? Through what countries does the north Isotherm of 70 degrees pass? Of 50 degrees? Of 32 degrees?

How many species of Plants are supposed to exist on the globe? What kinds of Plants are found in the Torrid Zone? Temperate Zones? Frigid Zones? What can you say of the characteristics of the Animals of the Torrid Zone? Of the Temperate Zones? Of the Frigid Zones?

PRONOUNCING VOCABULARY AND TABLES.

NOTE. The following Pronouncing Vocabulary contains the names of the countries, states, cities, towns, oceans, gulfs, bays, seas, islands, peninsulas, capes, mountains, deserts, lakes, and rivers, found on the Outline Maps, or mentioned in the Geography. Lippincott's Pronouncing Gazetteer of the World, a work prepared with great care and accuracy, has been adopted as the standard of pronunciation.

The extent of countries, the population of cities and towns, the length of rivers, and the height of mountains, have been given wherever authority could be found for the same. In the population of cities and towns, the latest census taken has been followed.

KEY TO THE PRONUNCIATION OF VOWELS.

Fàte, fär, fåll, făt,—mòte, mŏt, hĕr,—pīne, pĭt,—nòte, nŏt,—tùbe, tŭb, fůll. Vowels not marked, (excepting final e,) when ending a syllable that is accented, are long; when followed by a final consonant, they are short or obscure.

I. STATES AND COUNTRIES.

North America.

AMERICA, BRITISH,	brit'-ish.
AMERICA, RUSSIAN,	roo'-shun.
AMERICA, CENTRAL,	sen'-tral.
BALIZE,	bå-leź'.
CANADA,	kan'-a-da.
GREENLAND,	green'-land.
LABRADOR,	lab'-ra-dor.
MEXICO,	mex'-e-ko.
STATES OF,	
CHIAPAS,	che-ă'-pås.
CHIHUAHUA,	che-wå'-wå.
CINALOA,	sin-å-lo'-å.
COAHUILA,	ko-å-we'-lå.
COLIMA,	ko-le'-må.
DURANGO,	doo-răn'-go.
GUANAJUATO,	gwå-nå-hwå'to
GUERRERO,	gher-ra'-ro.
JALISCO,	hå-lis'ko.
MICHOACAN,	me-cho'-å-căn.
NEW LEON,	nu le'-on.
OAJACA,	wå-hå'-kå.
PUEBLA,	pwŏb'-lå.
QUERETARO,	ka-ra'-tå-ro.
SAN LUIS POTOSI,	sån loo'-is po-to'-se.
SONORA,	so-no'-rå.
TABASCO,	tå-bås'-ko.
TAMAULIPAS,	tå-maw'-le-pås.
TEHUANTEPEC,	ta-wån-tå-pĕk'.
VERA CRUZ,	vå'-rå kroos.
YUCATAN,	yoo-kå-tån'.
ZACATECAS,	zåk-a-ta'-kas.
NEW BRUNSWICK,	nu bruns'-wik.
NOVA SCOTIA,	no'-va sko-she-a.

UNITED STATES,	u-nī'-ted states
STATES AND TERRITORIES,	
CAROLINA,	kar-o-li'-na.
COLUMBIA, DISTRICT OF,	ko-lum'-be-a.
ALABAMA,	al-a-bå'-ma.
ARKANSAS,	ar-kan'-sas.
CALIFORNIA,	kal-e-for'-ne-a.
CONNECTICUT,	kou-net'-e-kut.
DELAWARE,	del'-a-wår.
FLORIDA,	flor'-e-da.
GEORGIA,	jor'-je-a.
ILLINOIS,	il-lin-oi'.
INDIANA,	in-de-an'-a.
INDIAN,	in'-de-an.
IOWA,	i'-o-wa.
KANSAS,	kan'-sas.
KENTUCKY,	ken-tuk'-e.
LOUISIANA,	loo-e-ze-å'-na.
MAINE,	måne.
MARYLAND,	ma'-re-land.
MASSACHUSETTS,	mas'-sa-chu'-setts.
MICHIGAN,	mish'-e-gan.
MINNESOTA,	min'-ne-so'-ta.
MISSISSIPPI,	mis-sis-sip'-pe.
MISSOURI,	mis-soo'-re.
NEBRASKA,	ne-bras'-ka.
NEW HAMPSHIRE,	nu hamp'-shir.
NEW JERSEY,	nu jer'-ze.
NEW YORK,	nu york.
OHIO,	o-hī'-o.
OREGON,	or'-e-gon.
PENNSYLVANIA,	pen-sil-va'-ne-a
RHODE ISLAND,	rŏd i'-land.
TENNESSEE,	ten-nes-se'.
TEXAS,	tex'-as.
UTAH,	yoo'-tå.

VERMONT,	ver-mont'.
VIRGINIA,	ver-jin'-e-a.
WASHINGTON,	wåsh'-ing-tun.
WISCONSIN,	wis-kon'-sin.

South America.

ARGENTINE REPUBLIC,	ar'-jen-teen
BOLIVIA,	bo-le'-ve-a.
BRAZIL,	brå-zil'.
CHILI,	chil'-le.
ECUADOR,	ek-wå-dôr'.
GUIANA,	ghe-å'-nå.
NEW GRANADA,	grå-nå'-då.
PARAGUAY,	på-rå-gwå'.
PATAGONIA,	på-tå-gō'-ne-a.
PERU,	pe-roo'.
URUGUAY,	oo-roo-gwå'.
VENEZUELA,	ven-ez-wo'-la.

Europe.

AUSTRIA,	ås'-tre-a.
BADEN,	bå'-den.
BAVARIA,	bå-vå'-re-a.
BELGIUM,	bel'-je-um.
DENMARK,	den'-mark.
ENGLAND,	ing'-gland.
FRANCE,	fråns.
GERMANY,	jer'-ma-ne.
GREECE,	grēs.
HANOVER,	han'-o-ver.
HOLLAND,	hol'-land.
IRELAND,	ire'-land.
ITALY,	it'-a-le.
LAPLAND,	lap'-land.
MECKLENBURG,	mek'-len-burg.

PRONOUNCING VOCABULARY.

Modena,	mod'-ĕn-ȧ.	Corea,	ko-re'-a.	Bosjesman's,	bos'-yes-mȧuz'
Naples,	nā'-pl'z.	Farther India,	in'-de-a.	Cape Colony,	kāp kol'-o-ne.
Norway,	nor'-wā.	Georgia,	jor'-jē-a.	Cimberas,	sim-bā'-bas.
Parma,	pär'-ma.	Hindostan,	hin-doo-stăn'.	Egypt,	e'-jipt.
Poland,	po'-land.	Japan,	jȧ-păn'.	Essawahil,	es-sȧ'-wȧ-heel.
Portugal,	pŏr'-tu-gal.	Malacca,	mȧ-lak'-ka.	Ethiopia,	e-the-o'-pe-a.
Prussia,	proo'-she-a.	Mantchooria,	man-choo'-re-a	Fezzan,	fŏz-zăn'.
Russia,	roo'-she-a.	Mongolia,	mon-go'-le-a.	Guinea,	ghin'-ne.
Sardinia,	sȧr-din'-e-a.	Persia,	per'-she-a.	Hottentot,	hot'-ten-tot.
Saxony,	sax'-ŏ-ne.	Siam,	si-am'.	Kaffraria,	kāf-frā'-re-a.
Scotland,	skot'-land.	Siberia,	si-be'-re-a.	Liberia,	li-be'-re-a.
Spain,	spane.	Soongaria,	soong-gȧ'-re-a.	Madagascar,	mad-a-gas'-kar.
Sweden,	swe'-den.	Syria,	sĭr'-e-a.	Morocco,	mo-rok'ko.
Switzerland,	swit'-zer-land.	Tenasserim,	ten-as'-se-rim.	Mozambique,	mo-zam-beek'.
Turkey,	tur'-ke.	Thibet,	tib'-et.	Natal,	nȧ-tȧl'.
Tuscany,	tus'-kȧ-ne.	Tooreistan, Independent,		Nubia,	nu'-be-a.
Venice,	ven'-is.		toor-kis-tȧn'.	Senegambia,	sĕn-e-gam'be-a.
Wales,	wālz.	Turkey,	tur'-ke.	Sierra Leone,	se-er'-rȧ le-ŏn'.
Wurtemburg,	wur'-tem-berg.				

Asia.

Afganistan,	ȧf-găn'-is-tăn'.	Abyssinia,	ab-is-sin'-e-a.	Australasia,	aus-tral-a'she-a.
Anam,	ȧ-năm'.	Adel,	ȧ-dĕl'.	Australia,	aws-tra'-le-a.
Arabia,	a-rā'-be-a.	Ajan,	ȧ-zhan'.	Malaysia,	ma-la'-she-a.
Beloochistan,	bel-oo-kis-tȧn'.	Algiers,	ȧl-jeerz'.	New South Wales,	nu south wālz.
Burmah,	bur'-ma.	Barca,	bȧr'-ka.	Polynesia,	pol-e-ne'she-a.
China,	chī'-na.	Beled-el-Jereed,	be-lĕd'-el-jer-eed'.	Victoria,	vik-to'-re-a.
Chinese Tartary,	tar'-ta-re.				

Africa.

Oceanica.

II. CITIES AND TOWNS.

North America.

			Burlington, Iowa,	bur'-ling-tun,	6,700
			Cairo,	kī'-ro,	
Abbeville,	ab'-be-vil,		Camden,	kam'den,	14,300
Acapulco,	ȧ-kȧ-pool'-ko,	5,000	Campeachy,	kam-pe'-che,	19,000
Adrian,	a'dre-an,	6,210	Cape Mattier,	ha'-te-en,	12,000
Alton,	ȧl'-tun,	6,300	Carlisle,	kar-lil',	5,000
Albany,	āl'-ba-ne,	62,300	Charleston,	chȧrlz'-tun,	40,500
Annapolis,	an-nap'o-lis,	4,500	Chicago,	she-kā'-go,	137,000
Ann Arbor,	an ȧr'-bor,	5,000	Chihuahua,	che-wȧ'-wȧ,	15,000
Appalachicola,	ap-pe-lȧ-che-ko'-la,	1,000	Chillicothe,	chil-li-kŏth'-e,	7,600
Arispe,	ȧ-ris'-pȧ,	7,000	Cincinnati,	sin'-sin-nȧ'-te,	161,000
Astoria,	as-to'-re-a,		Ciudad Real,	se-oo-dȧd' re-ȧl',	
Atlanta,	at-lan'-ta,	9,500	Cleveland,	kleve'-land,	43,400
Augusta, Me.,	au-gus'-ta,	7,600	Coburg,	ko'-burg,	4,500
Augusta, Ga.,	au-gus'-ta,	12,400	Colima,	ko-le'-ma,	
Austin,	ȧs'-tin,	3,000	Collingwood,	kol'-ling-wood,	
Balize,	ba-leez',	3,000	Columbia, S. C.,	ko-lum'-be-a,	8,000
Baltimore,	bȧl'-te-mŏr,	212,400	Columbia, Tenn.,	ko-lum'-be-a,	2,500
Bangor,	ban'-gor,	16,400	Columbus, Ga.,	ko-lum'-bus,	9,600
Batesville,	bates'-vil,	1,700	Columbus, O.,	ko-lum'-bus,	18,500
Baton Rouge,	bȧ'-ton roozh,	5,400	Columbus, Miss.,	ko-lum'-bus,	3,300
Bath,	bȧth,	8,000	Concord,	kon'-kord,	10,800
Bathurst,	bȧth'-urst,	2,000	Corpus Christi,	kor'-pus kris'-te,	1,200
Beaufort,	bu'-fort,	2,000	Council Bluff,	koun'-sil bluf,	5,000
Benecia,	be-nish'-e-a,	2,000	Culiacan,	koo-le-ȧ-kȧn',	7,000
Boston,	bos'-tun,	177,800	Cumberland,	kum'-ber-land,	8,400
Bowling Green,	bŏ'-ling green,	3,000	Darien,	dȧ'-re-en,	500
Brantford,	brant'-ford,	4,000	Dayton,	dȧ'-tun,	20,400
Brattleboro,	brat'-t'l-bur-ro,	4,000	Des Moines,	de moin',	3,500
Brockville,	brok'-vil,	3,000	Davenport,	dav'-en-port,	11,000
Brooklyn,	brook'-lin,	266,600	Detroit,	de-troit',	45,600
Buffalo,	buf'-fa-lo,	81,100	Dorchester,	dor'-ches-ter,	
Burlington, Vt.,	bur'-ling-tun,	7,700	Dover,	do'-ver,	4,000

182 PRONOUNCING VOCABULARY.

Name	Pronunciation	Pop.	Name	Pronunciation	Pop.
Dubuque,	du-book',	13,000	Liverpool,	liv'-er-pool,	
Dunkirk,	dun'-kirk,	4,400	London,	lun'-dun,	6,000
Durango,	doo-rang'-go,	22,000	Loreto,	lo-ra'-to,	
Easton, Pa.,	ês'-ton,	8,900	Louisville,	loo'-is-vil,	69,700
Easton, Md.,	ês'-ton,	1,500	Lowell,	lo'-el,	36,800
Eastport,	êst'-port,	4,200	Lunenburg,	lu'-nen-burg,	
Edenton,	ê'-den-tun,	1,600	Lynchburg,	linch'-burg,	6,800
Elmira,	el-mi'-ra,	8,600	Macon,	ma'-kon,	8,200
Erie,	ê'-re,	9,400	Madison, Ind.,	mad'-i-sun,	8,100
Evansville,	ev'-ans-vil,	11,400	Madison City, Wis.,	mad'-i-sun,	6,600
Fayetteville,	fa'-et-vil,	4,800	Manchester,	man'-ches-ter,	20,000
Fillmore City,	fil'-môr sit'-e,		Marshall,	mar'-shal,	4,000
Fond du Lac,	fond du lak',	5,400	Marysville,	ma'-riz-vil,	9,000
Fort Vancouver,	van-koo'-ver,		Matagorda,	mâ-ta-gor'-da,	1,200
Frankfort,	frank'-fort,	5,000	Matamoras,	mâ-ta-mo'-ras,	20,000
Fredericksburg,	fred'-er-iks-burg,	5,000	Matanzas,	mâ-tan'-zas,	46,000
Frederickton,	fred'-er-ik-tun,	5,000	Maysville,	mâz'-vil,	7,000
Galena,	ga-le'-na,	8,100	Mazatlan,	mâz-ât-lan',	11,000
Galveston,	gal'-ves-tun,	7,300	Memphis,	mem'-fis,	22,600
Georgetown, S. C.,	jorj'-town,	1,600	Merida,	mêr'-e-dâ,	40,000
Georgetown, Ky.,	jorj'-town,	2,000	Mexico,	mex'-i-kô,	180,000
Goliad,	go'-le-ad,		Michigan City,	mish'-e-gan,	2,400
Grand Haven,	grand hâ'-ven,	800	Milledgeville,	mil'-ej-vil,	3,500
Grand Rapids,	grand râ'-pids,	8,000	Milwaukee,	mil-wâ'-ke,	45,200
Green Bay,	green bay,	2,500	Mobile,	mo-beel',	29,200
Guadalajara,	gwâ-dâ-lâ-hâ'-râ,	70,000	Monroe,	mon-ro',	3,500
Guanajuato,	gwâ-nâ-hwâ'-to,	63,000	Monterey, Mex.,	mon-tâ-râ',	12,000
Halifax,	hal'-e-fax,	28,000	Monterey, Cal.,	mon-tâ-râ',	2,000
Hamilton, U. C.,	ham'-il-tun,	20,000	Montgomery,	mont-gom'-er-e,	35,900
Harper's Ferry,	hâr'-per's fer'-re,	2,000	Montpelier,	mont-peel'-yer,	2,400
Harrisburg,	har'-ris-burg,	13,400	Montreal,	mont-re-âl',	77,400
Hartford,	hârt'-ford,	29,100	Murfreesboro',	mur'-frcs-bur-o,	2,000
Havana,	ha-van'-a,	200,000	Muscatine,	mus'-ka-teen',	5,300
Helena,	hel-ê'-nu,		Nashua,	nash'-yu-a,	10,000
Holsteinburg,	hol'-stin-burg,		Nashville,	nash'-vil,	16,900
Houston,	hu'-ston,	5,000	Nassau,	nas'-sâ,	7,000
Huntsville,	hunts'-vil,	4,000	Natchez,	natch'-ez,	6,600
Iowa City,	I'-o-wa sit'-e,	5,200	Natchitoches,	natch-i-totch'-iz,	1,300
Independence,	in-de-pen'-dens,	3,000	New Albany,	âl'-ba-ne,	12,400
Indianapolis,	in-de-an-ap'-o-lis,	18,000	Newark,	nu'-ark,	71,900
Jackson, Miss.,	jak'-sun,	3,500	New Bedford,	nu bed'-ford,	22,300
Jackson, Tenn.,	jak'-sun,	2,500	Newbern,	nu'-bern,	5,400
Jackson, Mich.,	jak'-sun,	4,500	New Guatemala,	gwâ-te-mâ'-lâ,	50,000
Janesville,	jâns'-vil,	7,700	New Haven,	nu ha'-ven,	39,200
Jalapa,	hâ-lâ'-pâ,	10,000	New Hernnutt,	nu heru'-hut,	
Jefferson City,	jef-fer-sun sit'-e,	2,500	New London,	lun'-dun,	10,100
Julianshaab,	yoo'-le-âns-hâb',		New Orleans,	or'-leanz,	168,600
Kalamazoo,	kal-a-ma-zoo',	6,000	Newport,	nu'-pôrt,	10,500
Key West,	ke west',	2,800	New York,	nu york',	813,600
Kingston, U. C.,	kingz'-tun,	16,000	Niagara,	ni-ag'-a-ra,	4,500
Kingston, W. I.,	kingz'-tun,	35,000	Norfolk,	nor'-folk,	15,600
Knoxville,	nox'-vil,	5,000	Oajaca,	wâ-hâ'-kâ,	2,500
La Crosse,	la kros',	2,000	Ogdensburg,	og'-dens-burg,	7,400
Lafayette,	lâf-â-yet',	9,400	Old Guatemala,	gwâ-te-mâ'-lâ,	
Lancaster,	lan'-kas-tur,	17,000	Olympia,	o-lim'-pe-a,	1,200
Lansing,	lan'-sing,	3,000	Omaha,	o-mâ'-ha,	1,800
La Paz,	la paz',		Oswego,	os-we'-go,	16,800
Lawrence,	lâ-rens,	17,600	Ottawa,	ot'-ta-wa,	8,000
Leavenworth,	lev'-en-wurth,		Pacific City,	pa-sif'-ik sit'-e,	
Lecompton,	le-komp'-tun,		Paducah,	pa-du'-ka,	3,000
Lewistown,	lu'-is-town,	3,000	Paterson,	pat'-er-sun,	19,500
Lexington, Ky.,	lex'-ing-tun,	9,300	Pensacola,	pen-sa-ko'-la,	3,600
Lexington, Mo.,	lex'-ing-tun,	4,000	Peoria,	pe-o'-re-a,	14,400
Lichtenau,	lik'-teh-naw,		Petersburg,	pe'-terz'-burg,	18,200
Lichtenfels,	lik'-ten-fêls,		Philadelphia,	fil-a-del'-fe-a,	565,500
Little Rock,	lit'-tle rok,	3,800	Picton,	pik'-tun,	1,500

PRONOUNCING VOCABULARY. 183

Place	Pronunciation	Population
Pittsburg,	pits'-burg,	40,200
Placer City,	pla'-ser sit'-e,	6,000
Plattsburg,	plats'-burg,	6,600
Port au Prince,	port o prins,	20,000
Portland, Me.,	pòrt'-land,	26,300
Portland, Oregon,	pòrt'-land,	
Portsmouth, N. H.,	pòrts'-muth,	9,800
Portsmouth, Ohio,	pòrts'-muth,	6,200
Potosi,	po-to'-se,	500
Pottsville,	pots'-vil,	9,400
Prairie du Chien,	pra'-re du sheen,	2,000
Providence,	prov'-i-dens,	50,600
Puebla,	pweb'-la,	70,000
Puerto Principe,	pwer'-to preen'-se-pâ,	45,000
Quebec,	kwe-bĕk',	42,000
Queretaro,	kâ-râ-tâ'-ro,	30,000
Quincy,	quin'-se,	13,700
Racine,	râs-seen',	7,800
Raleigh,	râ'-le,	4,700
Reading,	rĕd'-ing,	23,100
Richmond,	rich'-mund,	37,900
Rio Grande City	re'-o grând,	1,000
Rochester,	roch'-es-ter,	48,200
Rock Island,	ĭ'-land,	5,100
Sacramento,	sak-ra-men'-to,	13,700
Salem, Oregon,	sa'-lem,	1,000
Saltillo,	sal-tĕl'-yo,	20,000
Salt Lake City,	salt lăk sit'-e,	8,200
San Diego,	sân de-a'-go,	2,000
Sandusky,	sau-dus'-ke,	8,400
San Francisco,	sân frân-sis'-ko,	56,800
San Jose,	sân ho-sâ',	18,000
San Luis Potosi,	sân loo'-is po-to'-se,	40,000
San Salvador,	sân sâl-vâ-dòr',	18,000
Santa Fe,	sân-tâ fâ',	4,600
Santiago,	sân-te-â'-go,	26,000
Sault St. Marie,	soo sânt mâ'-re	1,000
Savannah,	sa-van'-na,	22,200
Shelburne,	shel'-burn,	20,000
Sherbrooke,	sher'-brook,	1,500
Shreveport,	shreve'-port,	3,000
Sitka,	sit'-ka,	1,000
Socorro,	so-kor'ro,	
Somerset,	sum'-er-set,	4,000
Sonora,	so-no'-ra,	3,000
South Bend,	south bend,	2,000
Spanish Town,	span'-ish town,	6,000
Springfield, Mass.,	spring'-fĕld,	15,200
Springfield, Ill.,	spring'-fĕld,	6,500
St. Andrews,	sânt au'-drewz,	8,000
St. Anthony,	sânt au'-to-ne,	3,500
St. Augustine,	sânt â-gus-teen',	2,000
St. Charles,	sânt charlz',	
St. Domingo,	sânt do-ming'-go,	15,000
St. Hyacinthe,	sânt hĭ'-a-sinth,	4,500
St. John's, N. B.,	sânt jonz',	22,000
St. John's, L. C.,	sânt jonz',	2,500
St. John's, Newfoundland,	sânt jonz',	25,000
St. Louis,	sânt loo'-is,	160,700
St. Paul,	sânt paul',	10,400
Steubenville,	stu'-beu-vil,	6,100
Stockton,	stok'-tun,	10,000
Sukkertop,	suk'-ker-top,	
Sydney,	sĭd'-ne,	700
Syracuse,	sĕr'-a-kŭs,	28,100
Tabasco,	tâ-bâs'-ko,	
Tallahassee,	tal-la-has'-se,	1,000
Taos,	tâ'-os,	9,500
Tehuantepec,	tâ-wân-tâ-pŏk',	8,000
Terre Haute,	tĕr'-re hòt,	8,500
Three Rivers,	thre riv'-erz,	6,600
Toledo,	to-le'-do,	13,700
Topeka,	to-pe'-ka,	
Toronto,	to-ron'-to,	50,000
Trenton,	tren'-tun,	17,200
Troy,	troi,	39,200
Tuscaloosa,	tus-ka-loo'-sa,	3,900
Upernavik,	oo-per-nâ'-vik,	
Utica,	u'-te-ka,	22,500
Valladolid,	vâl-yâ-do-lēd',	18,000
Van Buren,	vân bu'-ren,	1,800
Vera Cruz,	va'-ra krooz,	8,200
Vicksburg,	viks'-burg,	4,500
Victoria,	vik-to'-re-a,	
Vincennes,	vin-senz',	2,200
Wabounse,	wâ-bouns',	
Washington,	wâsh'-ing-tun,	61,100
Wetumpka,	we-tump'-ka,	3,500
Wheeling,	wheel'-ing,	14,100
Whitehall,	white'-hâll,	5,000
Wilmington, Del.,	wil'-ming-tun,	21,200
Wilmington, N. C.	wil'-ming-tun,	9,000
Wilkesbarre,	wilks'-bar-re,	5,800
Worcester,	woos'-ter,	24,900
Yarmouth,	yar'-muth,	13,500
Zacatecas,	zâk-a-tâ-kas,	25,000
Zanesville,	zâuz'-vil,	9,200

South America.

Place	Pronunciation	Population
Aracati,	â-râ-kâ-te',	5,000
Arequipa,	â-râ-ke'-pâ,	35,000
Arica,	ê-ro'-kâ,	9,500
Aspinwall,	as'-pin-wâl,	3,000
Assumption,	as-sump'-shun,	12,000
Bahia,	bâ-e'-â,	100,000
Barra,	bâr'-ra,	6,000
Bogota,	bo-go-tâ',	48,000
Bolivar City,	bol'-e-var sit'-e,	8,500
Buenos Ayres,	bů'-nos â'-riz,	120,000
Callao,	kâl-lâ'-o,	15,000
Caracas,	kâ-râ'-kâs,	40,000
Cartagena,	kâr-tâ-je'-nâ,	18,000
Castro,	kâs'-tro,	3,500
Catamarca,	kâ-tâ-mar'-kâ,	4,000
Caxamarca,	kâ-hâ-mâr'-ka,	8,000
Cayenne,	kī-en',	6,000
Cerro Pasco,	ser'-ro pâs'-ko,	16,000
Chuquisaca,	choo-ke-sâ'-kâ,	20,000
Codija,	ko-be'-hâ,	800
Cochabamba,	ko-châ-bam'-ba,	30,000
Concepcion, Paraguay,	kon-sĕp-se-on',	10,000
Concepcion, Chili,	kon-sĕp-se-on',	7,000
Copiapo,	kô-pe-â-po',	4,000
Coquimbo,	ko-keem'-bo,	7,000
Cordova,	kor'-do-va,	14,000
Coro,	ko'-ro,	4,000
Corrientes,	kor-re-en'-tez,	20,000
Cuenca,	kwen'-ka,	20,000
Cumana,	koo-mâ-nâ',	8,000
Curucuaty,	koo-roo-gwâ-te',	
Cuyaba,	koo-yâ'-ba,	3,000

PRONOUNCING VOCABULARY.

Cuzco,	kuz'-ko,	30,000	Antwerp,	ant'-werp,	90,000
Diamantina,	de-á-mån-te'-nå,	4,500	Archangel,	årk-ån'-gel,	25,000
Espirito San	ès-pǐr'-e-to sån'-to,	1,000	Arta,	år'-tå,	5,000
Georgetown,	jorj'-town,	23,000	Astrakan,	ås-trå-kån',	46,000
Guayaquil,	gwǐ'-a-keel,	25,000	Athens,	ath'-enz,	30,000
Honda,	hon'-då,	5,000	Augsburg,	augs'-burg,	38,000
Humanga,	wå-mång'-gå,	26,000	Badajos,	bad-a-hòs',	12,000
Huasco,	wås'-ko,		Barcelona,	bår-så-lo'-nå,	132,000
Ibarra,	e-bår'-rå,	12,000	Bari,	bå'-re,	27,300
La Guayra,	lå gwǐ'-rå,	8,000	Basel,	ba'-zel,	27,300
La Paz,	lå påz,	20,000	Bastia,	bås-te'-å,	12,600
Lima,	le'-må,	100,000	Bayonne,	bå-yòn',	18,900
Loja,	lo'-hå,	16,300	Belfast,	bel-fåst',	120,000
Macapa,	må-kå-på',	6,000	Belgrade,	bel-grade',	30,000
Maldonado,	mål-do-nå'-do,	2,000	Bergen,	ber'-ghen,	25,600
Maracaybo,	må-rå-kǐ'-bo,	9,000	Berlin,	ber-lin',	548,000
Maranham,	må-ran-åm',	30,000	Berne,	bern,	28,000
Matto Grosso,	måt-to' gros'-so,	14,000	Bilbao,	bil-bå'-o,	11,900
Mendoza,	men-do'-za,	12,000	Birmingham,	bir'-ming-ham,	296,000
Mompox,	mom'-po,	10,000	Bochnia,	bok'-ne-a,	5,300
Montevideo,	mon-te-vid'-e-o,	15,000	Bologna,	bo-lòn'-yå,	75,000
Nkembucu,	nå-èm-boo'-koo,		Bordeaux,	bor-do',	163,000
New Amsterdam,	nu am'-ster-dam,	5,000	Bosna Serai,	bos'-nå ser-ǐ',	60,000
Panama,	pån-å-må',	6,000	Braga,	brå'-gå,	17,000
Para,	på-rå',	10,000	Brahilov,	brå-he-lov',	6,000
Paramaribo,	pår-a-mar'-e-bo,	20,000	Bremen,	brěm'-en,	74,000
Parnahiba,	pår-nå-e'-bå,	10,000	Breslau,	brěs'-lo,	146,200
Payta,	pǐ'tå,	5,000	Brest,	brěst,	61,000
Pernambuco,	pěr-nåm-boo'-ko,	24,000	Bristol,	bris'-tol,	154,000
Popayan,	po-på-yån',	20,000	Brunn,	brůn,	45,000
Porto Alegre,	por'-to å'-lå-grå,	4,000	Brussels,	bru-sel',	263,400
Potosi,	po-to'-se,	17,000	Bucharest,	bu-kå-rěst',	60,800
Puno,	poo'-no,	9,000	Buda,	bu'-da,	40,500
Quillota,	keel-yo'-tå,	10,000	Burgos,	boor'-gos,	15,500
Quito,	ke'-to,	50,000	Cadiz,	kå'-diz,	54,000
Riobamba,	re-o-båm'-ba,	16,000	Caen,	kòn,	45,500
Rio Grande,	re'-o grånd,	3,600	Cagliari,	kal'-yå-re,	30,000
Rioja,	re-o'-hå,	4,000	Calais,	kal'-is,	100,000
Rio Janeiro,	rǐ'-o ja-ne'-ro,	170,000	Cambridge,	kåm'-brij,	28,000
San Paulo,	san pow'-lo,	22,000	Cardigan,	går'-de-gan,	3,000
Santa Marta,	sån'-ta mår'-ta,	8,000	Carlscrona,	kårls-kroo'-na,	12,000
Santarem,	sån-tå-rem',	10,000	Carlshrue,	kårls' roo,	25,700
Santiago, A. R.,	sån-te-å'-go,	48,000	Caernarvon,	ker-når'-von,	9,000
Santiago, Chili,	sån-te-å'-go,	80,000	Cartagena,	går-ta-je'-na,	28,000
Socorro,	so-kor'-ro,	12,000	Catania,	kå-tå'-ne-å,	54,000
Trujillo, Peru,	troo-heel'-yo,	8,000	Cattaro,	kåt-tå'-ro,	4,000
Trujillo, Ven.,	troo-heel'-yo,	4,000	Cherbourg,	sher'-burg,	28,000
Tucuman,	too-koo-mån',	9,000	Christiania,	kris-te-å'-ne-a,	26,000
Valdivia,	vål-de'-ve-a,		Coimbra,	ko-eem'-brn,	15,000
Valencia,	vå-len'-she-å,	17,000	Colberg,	kol'-burg,	7,600
Valparaiso,	vål-på-rǐ'-zo,	50,000	Cologne,	ko-lòn',	120,500
Villa Rica,	veel'-ya re'-kå,	8,000	Compostela,	kom-pos-ta'-lå,	29,000
			Constantinople,	kon-stan-te-no'-p'l,	187,000
	Europe.		Copenhagen,	ko-pen-hå'-gen,	133,000
			Cordova,	kor'-do-va,	42,000
Aberdeen,	ab-er-děn',	72,000	Corinth,	kor'-inth,	2,000
Abo,	å-bo',	15,000	Cork,	kork,	78,800
Adrianople,	ad-re-an-o'-pel,	160,000	Corunna,	ko-run'-na,	19,000
Agram,	ǒg-rǒm',	14,800	Cracow,	krå'-kò,	43,000
Aix la Chapelle,	åks lå shå-pel',	45,600	Cronstadt, Aus.,	kròn'-stått,	36,000
Ajaccio,	å-yåt'cho,	12,000	Cronstadt, Russia,	kròn'-stått,	40,000
Alicante,	å-le-kån'-tå,	19,000	Dantzic,	dant'-zik,	58,000
Amiens,	am'-l-enz,	52,200	Debreczin,	då-brět'-siu,	63,000
Amsterdam,	åm-ster-dåm',	248,700	Dijon,	de-zhon',	32,500
Ancona,	an'-ko-nå,	36,000	Dover,	do'-ver,	22,000
Angers,	an'-jerz,	46,600	Dresden,	drěz'-den,	104,500

PRONOUNCING VOCABULARY. 185

Drontheim,	drŏnt'-him,	13,800	Madrid,	må-drid',	260,000
Dublin,	dub'-lin,	250,000	Magdeburg,	mag'-de-burg,	68,000
Dundee,	dun-dê',	79,000	Malaga,	mal'-a-ga,	68,500
Edinburgh,	ĕd'-in-bŭr-rŭh,	160,000	Manchester,	man'-ches-ter,	338,000
Elberfeld,	ŏl'-ber-fĕlt,	35,000	Mannheim,	măn'-hīm,	23,500
Elsinore,	ĕl'-sin-òr,	8,000	Mantua,	man'-tu-a,	31,000
Elvas,	el'-vas,	16,500	Marino,	mȧ-re'-no,	5,100
Evora,	ev'-o-ra,	15,000	Marseilles,	mar-sålz',	261,000
Falun,	fȧ'-loon,	4,500	Memel,	mĕm'-el, or mȧ'-mel,	9,900
Ferrol,	fĕr-rol',	16,600	Merthyr Tydvil,	mer'-ther tid'-vil,	63,100
Flensborg,	flens'-borg,	16,500	Messina,	mes-se'-na,	97,000
Florence,	flor'-ens,	111,000	Metz,	mĕts,	43,500
Frankfort,	frank'-fŭrt,	62,500	Milan,	mil'-an,	162,000
Gallipoli,	gȧl-lip'-o-le,	17,000	Minsk,	minsk,	23,600
Galway,	gȧl'-wȧ,	24,700	Modena,	mod'-ȧ-nȧ,	27,500
Gefle,	yĕv'-la,	8,100	Montpelier,	mont-pĕl'-yer,	38,000
Geneva,	jen-e'-va,	29,000	Moscow,	mos'-ko,	386,000
Genoa,	jen'-o-a,	125,000	Munich,	mu'-nik,	120,000
Ghent,	ghĕnt,	112,500	Murcia,	mŭr'-she-a,	55,000
Gibraltar,	je-brȧl'-ter,	17,000	Nancy,	nan'-se,	45,100
Gijon,	he-hŏn',	6,500	Nantes,	nants,	113,600
Glasgow,	glas'-go,	350,000	Naples,	na'-ples,	416,000
Gothenburg,	got'-en-burg,	29,000	Nauplia,	naw'-ple-a,	14,000
Gottingen,	gĕt'-ing-en,	10,700	Newcastle,	nû-kas'-sel,	109,000
Granada,	grȧ-nȧ'-dȧ,	61,600	Nice,	nees,	25,000
Gratz,	grĕts,	50,000	Norwich,	nor'-rij,	74,400
Groningen,	gron'-ing-en,	33,700	Novgorod,	nov-go-rod',	32,000
Hague,	haig,	72,500	Nuremburg,	nu'-rem-burg,	45,400
Halle,	hȧl'-le,	20,800	Odessa,	o-des'-sa,	104,000
Hamburg,	ham'-burg,	161,400	Olmutz,	ol'-mutz,	12,600
Hanover,	han'-o-ver,	42,500	Oporto,	o-por'-to,	80,000
Havre,	hȧv'-r,	74,000	Orel,	o-rĕl',	25,700
Hermanstadt,	hĕr'-mȧn-stȧtt,	21,000	Orleans,	or'-le-anz,	47,400
Hull,	hull,	99,000	Padua,	pad'-u-a,	60,000
Inverness,	in-ver-nes',	12,700	Paisley,	pȧz'-le,	48,000
Ismail,	is-mȧ-ĕl',	21,700	Palermo,	pȧ-ler'-mo,	167,000
Jassy,	jas'-se,	20,000	Paris,	par'-is,	1,696,000
Kalmar,	kȧl'-mar,	6,000	Parma,	pȧr'-ma,	40,000
Kalooga,	kȧ-loo'-gȧ,	30,000	Patras,	pȧ-trȧs',	8,000
Kazan,	kȧ-zȧn',	41,300	Perth,	perth,	24,000
Kherson,	ker-sŏn',	24,400	Pesth,	pĕst,	132,000
Kiev,	ke-ĕv',	60,600	Plymouth,	plim'-uth,	52,200
Kola,	ko'-lȧ,	1,000	Portsmouth,	pŏrts'-muth,	94,500
Konigsberg,	kongs'-berg,	4,000	Posen,	po'-zen,	32,000
Konigsberg,	kĕn'-igz-berg,	94,000	Potsdam,	pots'-dam,	38,000
Larissa,	la-ris'-sa,	20,000	Prague,	praig,	142,700
Laybach,	lī'-bȧk,	17,400	Presburg,	pres'-burg,	38,000
Leeds,	leeds,	207,000	Ragusa,	rȧ-goo'-sȧ,	6,000
Leghorn,	lĕg'-horn, or lĕg-horu',	80,000	Reggio,	rĕd'-jo,	18,500
Leipsic,	līp'-sik,	66,000	Rennes,	renn,	39,500
Lemberg,	lem'-burg,	71,000	Revel,	rĕv'-el,	25,000
Leon,	le'-on,	7,100	Rheims,	reemz,	45,800
Leige,	leej,	66,500	Riga,	re'-gȧ,	72,000
Liegnitz,	leeg'-nits,	14,000	Rome,	rŏm,	176,000
Lille,	leel,	132,000	Rotterdam,	rot'-ter-dam,	89,000
Limerick,	lim'-er-ik,	44,000	Rouen,	roo-en',	102,000
Limoges,	le-moj',	27,000	Salamanca,	sȧ-lȧ-mȧng'-kȧ,	14,000
Lintz,	lints,	31,000	Salerno,	sȧ-ler'-no,	19,000
Lisbon,	liz'-bon,	280,000	Salonica,	sȧ-lo-ne'-kȧ,	75,000
Liverpool,	liv'-er-pool,	444,000	San Marino,	sȧn mȧ-re'-no,	7,600
London,	lŭn'-dŭn,	2,803,000	Saragossa,	sȧ-rȧ-gos'-sȧ,	30,000
Londonderry,	lŭn'-dŭn-der'-re,	20,000	Saratov,	sȧ-rȧ-tov',	61,000
L'Orient,	lo-re-ŏn',	26,000	Sassari,	sȧs'-sȧ-re,	24,500
Lubeck,	lu'-bĕk,	27,000	Schwerin,	shwa-reen',	17,400
Lublin,	loo'-blin,	16,000	Scutari,	skoo'-tȧ-re,	40,000
Lyons,	lī'-onz, or le-ong',	319,000	Seres,	sĕr'-es,	30,000

PRONOUNCING VOCABULARY.

Setubal,	så-too'-bål,	15,000	Bassorah,	bås'-so-rå,	60,000
Sevastopol,	sèv'-as-to'-pol,	40,000	Benares,	ben-å'-rèz,	580,000
Seville,	sev'-il, or se-vill',	85,000	Beyroot,	bå'-root',	30,000
Sheffield,	shef'-fèld,	185,000	Bokhara,	bo-kå'-rå,	100,000
Shoomla,	shoom'-lå,	21,000	Bombay,	bom-ba',	500,000
Silistria,	se-lis'-tre-å,	20,000	Brusa,	broo'-så,	60,000
Sleswick,	sles'-wik,	12,000	Cabool,	kåb-ool',	60,000
Sligo,	sli'-go,	11,000	Calcutta,	kal-kut'-ta,	300,000
Smolensk,	smo-lensk',	13,000	Canton,	kan'-tun,	1,000,000
Sophia,	so-fe'-å,	50,000	Cashmere,	kash-meer',	200,000
Southampton,	suth-hamp'-tun,	35,500	Chinyang,	shin-yang',	120,000
St. Etienne,	sånt a-te-èn',	92,000	Colombo,	ko-lum'-bo,	32,000
Stettin,	stèt-teen',	47,000	Dacca,	dak'-ka,	200,000
St. Petersburg,	pe'-ters-burg,	520,000	Damascus,	da-mas'-kus,	112,000
Stockholm,	stòk'-hòm,	93,000	Delhi,	del'-le,	250,000
Strasburg,	stràs'-burg,	82,000	Derayeh,	da-ri'-eh,	15,000
Stuttgart,	stoot'-gårt,	30,000	Diarbekir,	de'-ar-be-keer',	40,000
Syracuse,	sir'-a-kùz,	11,000	Eeleg,	e'-le,	75,000
Taranto,	tå'-rån-to,	15,000	Erzroom,	erz-room',	50,000
Temesvar,	tem-esh-var',	19,000	Hangchowfoo,	hång'-chow'-foo',	
Thorn,	tòrn,	12,700	Herat,	her-åt',	30,000
Toledo,	to-le'-do,	13,000	Hue,	hoo'-å,	60,000
Tornea,	tor'-ne-a,	700	Hyderabad,	hi'-der-a-båd',	200,000
Tortosa,	tor-to'-sa,	20,600	Hydrabad,	hi-drå-båd',	20,000
Toulon,	too'-lòn',	85,000	Irkootsk,	ir-kootsk',	120,000
Toulouse,	too'-looz',	113,000	Ispahan,	is-pa-hån',	150,000
Tours,	toor,	35,000	Jerusalem,	je-ru'-sa-lem,	20,000
Trapani,	trå'-på-ne,	25,000	Jiga Gounggar,	jo'-gå goong'-gar',	100,000
Trieste,	tre-èst',	105,000	Kars,	kårs,	12,000
Tripolitza,	tre-po-lit'-zå,	10,000	Kashgar,	kash'-går',	16,000
Troyes,	troi,	27,500	Kelat,	ke-låt',	12,000
Turin,	tu'-rin,	143,000	Ketcho,	ketch'-o,	100,000
Tver,	tvèr,	24,000	Khiva,	ke'-vå,	10,000
Ulm,	ùlm,	13,500	Khokan,	ko'-kån',	80,000
Upsal,	ùp'-sal,	5,000	Kiakhta,	ke-åk'-tå,	5,000
Valencia,	vå-lèn'-she-a,	76,000	Kingkitao,	king-ke-tå'-e,	
Valladolid,	val-la-do-lèd',	30,000	Lahore,	lå-hòr',	20,000
Varna,	vår'-nå,	14,000	Lassa,	las'-sa,	50,000
Venice,	vèn'-is,	118,000	Lucknow,	luck'-now',	300,000
Verona,	va-ro'-nå,	48,000	Macao,	må-kow',	40,000
Vienna,	ve-en'-nå,	476,000	Madras,	ma-dras',	720,000
Vilna,	vil'-nå,	52,500	Maimatchin,	mi-mi-chin',	1,500
Warsaw,	wår'-saw,	164,000	Malacca,	må-lac'-ca,	12,000
Waterford,	wå'-ter-ford,	25,000	Mecca,	mek'-ka,	30,000
Wick,	wik,	11,800	Medina,	me-de'-nå,	20,000
Widin,	vid'-din,	25,000	Meshed,	mesh'-ed,	45,000
Wielicska,	ve-litch'-ka,	4,500	Miako,	me-å'-ko,	500,000
Yanina,	yån'-ne-nå,	36,000	Mocha,	mo'-kå,	7,000
Yaroslav,	yå-ro-slåv',	35,000	Monchoboo,	mon-cho-boo',	4,000
York,	york,	40,000	Mosul,	mo'-sùl,	40,000
Zurich,	zu'-rik,	17,400	Muscat,	mus-kat',	40,000
			Nagpoor,	någ-poor',	115,000
	Asia.		Nanking,	nån-king',	400,000
			Okhotsk,	o-kotsk',	800
Aden,	å'-den,	20,000	Omsk,	omsk,	11,500
Ahmedabad,	å-med-å-bad',	100,000	Oojein,	oo-jån',	
Aleppo,	a-lep'-po,	75,000	Osaka,	o-så'-kå,	800,000
Amarapoora,	åm-å-ra-poo'-rå,		Patna,	pat'-na,	284,000
Amherst,	am'-erst,	5,000	Peking,	pe'-king',	1,500,000
Amoy,	å-moi',	300,000	Peshawer,	pèsh-ow'-er,	50,000
Amritseer,	åm-rit-seer',	115,000	Petra,	po'-tra,	
Ava,	å'-va,	25,000	Petropualovski,	på-tro-pow-lov'-ske,	900
Bagdad,	båg-dåd',	65,000	Poonah,	poo'-na,	90,000
Bangkok,	ban-kok',	60,000	Rangoon,	rång'-goon',	20,000
Barnaul,	bar-nowl',	10,000	Resht,	resht,	50,000
Baroda,	bå-ro'-da,	100,000	Saghalien,	så-gå-le'-en,	

PRONOUNCING VOCABULARY.

Place	Pronunciation	Population
Saigon,	si-gon',	180,000
Samarcand,	să-măr-kănd',	10,000
Sana,	să-uă',	40,000
Shanghai,	shaug'-hī',	190,000
Shieraz,	she-raz',	30,000
Singapore,	sing'-gă-pore',	50,000
Smyrna,	smyr'-na,	150,000
Surat,	soo'-răt',	157,000
Taureez,	tă'-breez',	60,000
Tashkend,	tăsh-kend',	40,000
Teentsin,	teent'-seen',	
Teheran,	teh'-her-ăn',	60,000
Tiflis,	tif'-lis,	50,000
Tobolsk,	to-bolsk',	20,000
Tomsk,	tomsk,	24,000
Trebizond,	treb'-e-zond',	40,000
Yakootsk,	yă'-kootsk',	7,000
Yarkand,	yăr'-kănd',	100,000
Yeddo,	yěd'-do,	1,500,000
Yekaterinboorg,	yă-kă-tă-riu-boorg',	15,000

Africa.

Place	Pronunciation	Population
Abbeokoota,	ab-be-o-koo'-tă,	50,000
Adomet,	ab'-o-mă',	20,000
Alexandria,	al-ex-an'-dre-a,	60,000
Algiers,	ăl-jeerz',	93,000
Angornou,	ăn-gor-noo',	30,000
Antalo,	ăn-tă'-lo,	8,000
Bathurst,	bath'-urst,	3,000
Bengazi,	bĕn-gă'-ze,	5,000
Benin,	ben-een',	15,000
Berbera,	ber'-be-ra,	15,000
Bona,	ko'-nă,	10,000
Booda,	boo'-da,	
Cairo,	kī'-ro,	250,000
Cape Town,	kăp town,	23,000
Constantine,	kou'-stăn teen',	20,000
Coomassie,	koo-măs'-se,	18,000
Damietta,	dam-e-ĕt'-ta,	28,000
Derne,	der'-něh,	6,000
Fez,	fez,	90,000
Freetown,	fre'-town,	18,000
Georgetown,	jorj'-town,	
Gondar,	gon'-dar,	6,000
Graham's Town,	gra'-hamz town,	6,000
Kairwan,	kir'-wan,	50,000
Kano,	kă'-no,	30,000
Katunga,	kă-tŭng'-gă,	18,000)
Kemmoo,	kem'-moo,	
Khartoom,	kar-toom',	18,000
Konbe,	kob'-be,	6,000
Kurricane,	kur-re-kă'-na,	16,000
Lattakoo,	lăt-ta-koo',	
Loango,	lo-ang'-go,	20,000
Magadoxo,	mag-a-dox'-o,	4,000
Mananzary,	mă-năn-ză'-re',	
Massowah,	măs'-so-wă,	4,000
Mequinez,	měk'-e-něz',	50,000
Mesurata,	mes-oo-ră'-tă,	
Mombas,	mom'-băs,	2,000
Monrovia,	mou-ro'-ve-a,	2,000
Moorzook,	moor-zook',	3,500
Morocco,	mo-rok'-ko,	100,000
Mozambique,	mo-zam-beek',	4,000
New Benguela,	new bĕn-gă'-lă,	
New Dongola,	new dong-go-lă,	4,000
Obeid,	o-băd',	30,000
Oran,	o-ran',	24,000
Pietermaritzburg,	pe'-ter-mă-ritz-burg,	2,000
Quilimane,	ke-le-mă'-nă,	2,000
Rabatt,	ră'-băt',	27,000
Rosetta,	ro-zet'-tă,	4,000
Saccatoo,	săk-kă-too',	40,000
San Salvador,	săn săl-va-dŏr',	20,000
Sego,	se'-go,	30,000
Sennaar,	sĕn-năr',	4,000
Sioot,	se-oot',	20,000
Sofala,	so-fă'-lă,	
St. Louis,	sănt loo'-is,	12,000
St. Paul de Loanda,	dă lo-an'-dă,	
Tamatav,	tă-mă-tăv',	
Tananarivoo,	tă-nă-nă'-re-voo',	12,000
Teemboo,	teem'-boo,	16,000
Timbuctoo,	teem-buk'-too,	12,000
Touggoort,	toog-goort',	
Tripoli,	trip'-o-le,	15,000
Tunis,	tu'-nis,	130,000
Zeyla,	ză'-lă,	500
Zueela,	zoo-e'-la.	

Oceanica.

Place	Pronunciation	Population
Acheen,	at-cheen',	40,000
Adelaide,	ad'-e-lăd,	20,000
Albany,	ăl'-ba-ne,	
Banjermassin,	băn-yer-măs-sin',	1,500
Batavia,	ba-ta'-ve-a,	120,000
Bencoolen,	běn-koo'-len,	6,000
Borneo,	bor'-ne-o,	22,000
Brisbane,	briz'-băn,	1,000
Freemantle,	fre'-man-tl,	
Hilo,	hī'-lo,	
Hobart Town,	ho'-bart-town,	25,000
Honolulu,	hon'-o-loo'-loo,	6,000
Kaaha,	kă-ă-hă',	
Kealakeakua,	kă-lă-kă-ă-koo'-ă,	
Lahaina,	la-hī'-nă,	
Macassar,	mă-kăs'-sar,	20,000
Manilla,	mă-ne'-la,	140,000
Melbourne,	mel'-burn,	60,000
Padang,	pă-dăng',	22,000
Palembang,	pă'-lĕm-băng',	25,000
Perth,	perth,	
Portland,	pŏrt'-land,	
Samarang,	să-mă-răng',	50,000
Sarawak,	să-ră'-wăk',	12,000
Sydney,	sid'-ne,	100,000
Wairuku,	wa-ru'-ku,	

III. OCEANS, SEAS, GULFS AND BAYS.

Aden,	à'-děn, or à'-dŏn.	Cruz,	krooz.	Notre Dame,	nŏt'-r dàm.
Adriatic,	ad-re-at'-ik.	Cutch,	kătch.	Obi,	o'-be.
Ægean,	e-je'-an.	Darien,	da-ri-en'.	Okhotsk,	o'-kotsk.
Albemarle,	al'-be-marl.	Dead,	děd.	Onega,	o-ne'-ga.
Algoa,	a'-go'-à.	Delagoa,	del-a-go'-a.	Ormus,	or'-mus.
All Saints,	all sànts.	Delaware,	děl'-a-wâr.	Pacific,	pa-sif'-ik.
Anadir,	à-nà-deer'.	Disco,	dis'-ko.	Pamlico,	pam'-le-ko.
Antarctic,	ant-ârk'-tik.	Donegal,	don'-e-gal.	Panama,	pàn-a-mà'.
Antongil,	àn-ton-zheel'.	Eastern,	ěst'-ern.	Paranagua,	pà-rà-nà'-guà.
Appalachee,	ap-pa-là'-che.	English,	ing'-lish.	Paria,	pà'-re-à.
Arabian,	ar-a'-be-an.	Faxe,	faks'-à.	Passamaquoddy,	pas-sa-ma-quod'-de.
Aral,	ar'-al.	Finland,	fin'-land.		
Archipelago,	ar-ke-pel'-a-go.	Forth,	fôrth.	Pecheelee,	pà-che-le'.
Arctic,	ârk'-tik.	Fundy,	fun'-de.	Penas,	pěn'-yàs.
Atlantic,	at-lan'-tik.	Galveston,	gal'-ves-tun.	Penjinsk,	pěn-jinsk'.
Azof,	a'-zof.	Galway,	gàl'-wa.	Penobscot,	pe-nob'-skot.
Baffin's,	baf'-finz.	Genoa,	jen'-o-a.	Pensacola,	pen-sa-ko'-la.
Baltic,	bàl'-tik.	Georgia,	jor'-je-a.	Persian,	per'-shan.
Bengal,	ben-gàl'.	Great Fish,	grāt fish.	Pinzon,	pin-zòn'.
Benin,	ben-een'.	Guatamala,	gwà-te-mà'-là.	Placentia,	pla-sen'-shà.
Bembatooka,	bem-ba-too'-ka.	Guataquil,	gwí-à-keel'.	Plenty,	plen'-te.
Biafra,	be-af'-ra.	Guattecas,	gwí-ta'-kàs.	Prince of Wales,	prins of wàlz.
Biscay,	bis'-ka.	Guinea,	ghin'-ne.	Queen Adelaide's,	ad'-e-làd.
Black,	blàk.	Halifax,	hal'-e-fax.	Red,	red.
Blanco,	blàn'-ko.	Honduras,	hon-doo'-ras.	Riga,	rē'-ga.
Bonavista,	bo-na-vis'-ta.	Hudson,	hud'-sun.	San Diego,	sàn de-à'-go.
Boothia,	boo'-the-à.	Humboldt,	hum'-bolt.	San Francisco,	sàn fràn-sis'-ko.
Botany,	bot'-a-ne.	Indian,	in'-de-an.	Shark's,	sharkz.
Bothnia,	both'-ne-à.	Irish,	l'-rish.	Siam,	sī'-am.
Brede,	bra'-dà.	Islands, Bay of,	i'-lands.	Sidra,	sid'-ra.
Bristol,	bris'-tol.	James's,	jàmz'-ez.	Spencer,	spen'-ser.
Burgas,	boor-gàs'.	Japan,	jà-pan'.	St. George's,	jor'-jes.
Cades,	kàb'-es.	Jijiginsk,	je-je-ghinsk'.	St. Helena,	hel-e'-na.
California,	kal-e-for'-ne-a.	Kamtchatka,	kàm-chàt'-ka.	St. Lawrence,	sànt law'-rens.
Cambay,	kam-bà'.	Kara,	kà'-rà.	St. Matthias,	sànt mat-thī'-as.
Cambridge,	kàm'-brij.	Lena,	là'-nà.	Tampa,	tam'-pa.
Campeachy,	kam-pe'-che.	Lyons,	lī'-onz.	Taranto,	tà'-ràn to.
Carpentaria,	kàr-pen-tà'-re-a.	Madre de Dios,	mà'-drà dà do'-òs.	Teheekata,	ches-ki-a.
Caribbean,	kàr-rib-be'an.	Maracaybo,	mà-rà-kī'-bo.	Tehuantepec,	tà wàn-tà-pek'.
Caspian,	kàs'-pe-an.	Marmora,	màr'-mo-ra.	Tomsk,	tòmsk.
Chalkur,	shà-loor'.	Martaban,	màr'-ta-ban'.	Tonquin,	ton-keen'.
Charlotte,	shar'-lot.	Massachusetts,	mas-sa-chu'-sets.	Ungava,	ŭn-gà'-va.
Chatham,	chat'-am.	Matagorda,	mat-a-gor'-da.	Venezuela,	věn-ěz-we'-la.
Chesapeake,	ches'-a-peek.	Mediterranean,	med-i-ter-ra'-	Victoria,	vik-to'-re-a.
China,	chi'-na.	Manaar,	ma-na'. ne-an.	Walvisch,	wàl'-vish.
Choco,	cho'-ko.	Melville,	měl'-vil.	White,	white.
Chonos,	ko'-nos.	Mexico,	měx'-i-co.	Yenno,	yed'-do.
Concepcion,	kon-sěp-se-òn'.	Mobile,	mo-beel'.	Yellow,	yel'-low.
Coral,	kor'-al.	Monterey,	mon-ta-rà'.	Yenisee,	yěn-e-sà'-e.
Corea,	ko-re'-a.	Murray,	mur'-re.	Yesso,	yes'-so.
Coronation,	kor-o-na'-shun.	Narragansett,	nar-ra-gan'-set.	Zuyder Zee,	zī-der-zo'.
Corpus Christi,	kor'-pus kris'-te.	North,	north.		

IV. STRAITS AND CHANNELS.

Babel Mandeb,	bàb-ěl-man'-deb.	Bristol,	bris'-tol.	Dardanelles,	dar-dà-nělz'.
Bank,	bànk.	Canadian,	ka-na'-de-an.	Davis,	da'-vis.
Barrow,	bar'-row.	Canso,	kan'-so.	Dover,	do'-ver.
Bass,	bàs.	Cattegat,	kat'-te-gat.	English,	ing'-lish.
Behrings,	be'-ringz.	Charlotte,	shàr'-lot.	Florida,	flor'-e-da.
Bellisle,	běl-ile'.	Cook,	kook.	Formosa,	for-mo'-sa.
Bonifacio,	bo-ne-fà'-cho.	Corea,	ko-re'-a.	Foveaux,	fo-vo'.
Bosporus,	bos'-po-rus.	Cumberland,	kum'-ber-land.	Frobisher,	frob'-ish-er.

PRONOUNCING VOCABULARY. 189

GIBRALTAR,	je-brål'-ter.	MOZAMBIQUE,	mo-zam-beek'.	SMITH,	smith.
HUDSON'S,	hud'-sunz.	NORTH,	north.	THE SOUND,	sound.
JUAN DE FUCA,	ju'-an da fŭ'-kå.	NORTHUMBERLAND,	north-um'-ber-land.	ST. MARY'S,	sånt ma'-riz.
LANCASTER,	lan'-kas-ter.			SUNDA,	sun'-da.
LE MAIRE,	le mår.	NORTON,	nor'-tun.	TARTARY,	tår'-tår-re.
LONG ISLAND,	long ĭ'-land.	ORMUS,	or'-mus.	TORRES,	tor'-res.
MACASSAR,	må-kås'-sar.	OTRANTO,	o-trån'-to.	VICTORIA,	vik-to'-re-a.
MAGELLAN,	må-jel'-lan.	PALK'S,	pawks.	WELLINGTON,	wel'-ling-tun.
MALACCA,	må-lak'-ka.	PEROUSE,	pe-rooz'.	YENIKALE,	yěn-e-kå'-la.
MANAAR,	må-når'.	PRINCE REGENT'S,	prins re'-gents.	YESSO,	yes'-so.
MELVILLE,	mel'-vil.	PRINCE WILLIAM,	prins wil'-yum.	YUCATAN,	yu-kå-tån'.
MESSINA,	mes-se'-nå.	SKAGER RACK,	skag'-er rak.		

V. ISLANDS.

		SHOOMAGINS,	shoo-må'-gins.	BORNHOLM,	born'-holm.
North America.		SITKA,	sit'-ka.	CANDIA,	kan'-de-å.
ANTICOSTI,	an-te-kos'-te.	SOUTHAMPTON,	south-amp'-tun.	CEPHALONIA,	sĕf-å-lo'-ne-å.
ANTILLES,	an-teel'.	THE THREE MARIAS,	ma-rī'-as.	CERIGO,	chĕr'-e-go.
BAHAMA,	ba-hå'-ma.	TIBURN,	tī'-burn.	CORFU,	kor'-fu.
BARING,	ba'-ring.	TORTUGAS,	tor-too'-gas.	CORSICA,	kor'-se-ka.
BERMUDAS,	ber-moo'-da.	VANCOUVER'S,	van-koo'-verz.	CYCLADES,	sik'-la-dēz.
BOOTHIA,	boo'-the-a.	VICTORIA,	vik-to'-re-a.	CYPRUS,	sī'-prus.
CAPE BRETON,	kåp brit'-un.			DAGO,	då'-go.
CARIBBEES,	kar'-re-bēz.	**South America.**		ELBA,	el'-ba.
CARMEN,	kår'-men.	ABROLHOS,	å-bròl'-yòse.	FALSTER,	fål'-ster.
CERROS,	ser'-ros.	BALLENY,	bal'-le-ne.	FAROE,	få'-ro.
COZUMEL,	ko-zoo-mel'.	BARBADOES,	bår-bå'-doz.	FUNEN,	fu'-nen.
CUBA,	ku'-ba.	BUEN AYRE,	bwen īr'-a.	GOTHLAND,	gŏth'-land.
CUMBERLAND,	kum'-ber-land.	CANANEA,	kå-nå-nå'-å.	GREAT BRITAIN,	gråt brit'-un.
DISCO,	dis'-ko.	CHILOE,	cheel-o-å'.	GUERNSEY,	ghurn'-ze.
ESPIRITU SANTO,	ĕs-pĭr'-e-too sån'-to.	CURACOA,	ku-ra-so'-a.	HEBRIDES,	hĕb'-rid-ez.
FLORIDA KEYS,	flor'-e-da keez.	FALKLAND,	fålk'-land.	ICELAND,	ise'-land.
GREENLAND,	green'-land.	GALLIPAGOS,	gal-li-på'-gòs.	IONIAN,	ī-o'-ne-an.
GEORGIAN,	jor'-je-an.	GRAHAM'S LAND,	gra'-amz land.	IRELAND,	īre'-land.
GREAT MANITOULINE,	man-e-too'-lin.	GRENADA,	gren-å'-da.	IVICA,	e-ve'-ka.
GUAHHANI,	gwå-nå-hå'-ne.	HERMIT,	hor'-mit.	JERSEY,	jer'-ze.
HAYTI,	hå'-te.	ITAMARACA,	e-tå-må-rå'-ca.	LAALAND,	lå'-land.
ICELAND,	ise'-land.	JOANNES,	jo-ån'-nĕs.	LIPARI,	lip-a'-re, or le'-på-re.
JAMAICA,	ja-må'-ka.	JUAN FERNANDEZ,	ju'-an fer-nan'-dez.	LOFFODEN,	lof'-fo-den.
KODIAK,	ko'-de-ak.			MAGEROE,	maj'-er-o.
LONG,	long.	LOBOS,	lo'-bos.	MAJORCA,	ma-jor'-kå.
MAGDALEN,	mag'-da-len.	MARGARITA,	mar-ga-re'-ta.	MALTA,	mål'-tå.
MANITOULINE,	man-e-too'-lin.	PUNA,	poo'-nå.	MAN,	man.
MANSFIELD,	mans'-fēld.	QUIBO,	ke'-bo.	MINORCA,	min-or'-kå.
MARGARITA,	mår-ga-re'-ta.	SOUTH GEORGIAN,	jor'-je-an.	MITYLENE,	mit-e-le'-ne.
MARTHA'S VINEYARD,	mar'-thaz vin'-yard.	STATEN LAND,	ståt'-en land.	NEGROPONT,	neg'-ro-pont.
		ST. ANNE,	sånt an.	OESEL,	e'-sel.
MELVILLE,	mel'-vil.	ST. CATHARINA,	sånt kå-tå-re'-na.	OLAND,	o'-land.
NANTUCKET,	nan-tuk'-et.	ST. FELIX,	sånt fe'-lix.	ORKNEY,	ork'-ne.
NEWFOUNDLAND,	nu'-fund-land.	ST. SEBASTIAN,	sånt se-bast'-yan.	RHODES,	rōdz.
NORTH DEVON,	north dev'-on.	ST. VINCENT,	sånt vin'-sent.	RUGEN,	ru'-ghen.
NUNNIVAK,	noo-ne-våk'.	TERRA DEL FUEGO,	tĕr'-rå del fwå'-go	SAMOS,	så'-mos.
ORLEANS,	or'-le-anz.	TOBAGO,	to-ba'-go.	SARDINIA,	sår-din'-e-a.
PORTO RICO,	pōr'-to re'-ko.	TRINIDAD,	trin-i-dad'.	SCARPANTO,	skår-pan'-to.
PINES, ISLE OF,	pines.	WELLINGTON,	wel'-ling-tun.	SCILLY,	sil'-le.
PRINCE EDWARD,	prins ed'-ward.			SONOR,	so'-ro.
PRINCE WILLIAM,	prins wil'-yum.	**Europe.**		SPITZBERGEN,	spitz-berj'-en.
QUEEN CHARLOTTE,	shar'-lot.	ALAND,	å'-land.	STALIMNI,	stå-lim'-ne.
REVILLAGIGEDO,	rå-veel'-yå-he-hå'-do.	ANGLESEA,	ang'-g'l-se.	WIGHT,	wīt.
		AZORES,	az'-ōrs.	ZANTE,	zån'-te.
SANTA BARBARA,	sån'-tå bår'-bå-rå			ZEALAND,	ze'-land.

Asia.

ANDAMAN,	an-da-man'.
BAHREIN,	bå-råne'.
BEHRINGS,	be'-ringz.
CEYLON,	se'-lon.
CORALLINE,	kor'-al-lin.
CYPRUS,	sī'-prus.
FADIEVSKOI,	få-de-ĕv'-skoi.
FORMOSA,	for-mo'-sa.
HAINAN,	hī-nån.'
HONG KONG,	hong kong'.
JUNK CEYLON,	junk se'-lon.
KIOOSIOO,	ke-oo'-se-oo'.
KISHM,	kish'-em.
KOURILE,	koo'-ril.
KOTELNOI,	ko-tel-noi'.
LACCADIVE,	lăk'-ka-dīv.
LIAGHOFF,	le-åg'-hof.
LOO CHOO,	loo choo'.
MALDIVE,	mal'-dīv.
NEW SIBERIA,	nu sī-be'-re-a.
NICOBAR,	nik'-o-bar.
NIPHON,	nī-fon'.
NOVA ZEMBLA,	no'-va zem'-bla.
PENANG,	pe-nang'.
QUELPAERT,	kwĕl'-part.
SAGHALIEN,	så-gå-le'-en.
SIKOKF,	se-kof'.
SINGAPORE,	sing-ga-pore'.
SOCOTRA,	sok-o'-trå.
STATEN,	stat'-en.
SUMATRA,	soo-må'-trå.
TCHANTAR,	chån'-tå.
YESSO,	yes'-so.

Africa.

ADD EL CURIA,	åbd ĕl koo-re'-å.
AMIRANTE,	am-e-rant'.
ANNOBON,	ån-no-bon'.
ASCENSION,	as-sen'-shun.
AZORES,	az'-ôrz.
BOURBON,	boor-bon'.
CANARY,	ka-na'-re.
CAPE VERDE,	kåp verd'.
COMORO,	kom'-o-ro.
ENDERBY,	en'-der-be.
FERNANDO PO,	fer-nån'-do po'.
KERGUELEN,	kerg-e-len'.
MADAGASCAR,	mad-a-gas'-kar.
MADEIRA,	må-de'-rå.
MASCARENTIA,	mas-ka-ren'-she-a
MAURITIUS,	mau-rish'-e-us.
MONFIA,	mon-fe'-a.
PEMBA,	pem'-ba.
PRINCE'S,	prins'-ez.
SEYCHELLES,	sa-shel'.
SOCOTRA,	sok-o'-trå.
ST. HELENA,	sånt hel-ĕ'-na.
ST. THOMAS,	sånt tom'-as.
ZANZIBAR,	zån'-ze-bar.

Oceanica.

ADMIRALTY,	ad'-mi-ral'-te.
AMERICA,	a-mer'-e-ka.
ANSON'S,	an'-sunz.
ARROO,	ar-roo'.
AUSTRAL,	aws'-tral.
AUSTRALASIA,	aws-tral-a'-she-a.
AUSTRALIA,	aws-trå'-le-a.
BALLY,	bal'-le.
BANCA,	bånk'-å.
BONIN,	bo-neen'.
BORNEO,	bor'-ne-o.
CAROLINE,	kar'-o-lin.
CELEBES,	sĕl'-e-bĕs.
CENTRAL,	sen'-tral.
CHATHAM,	chat'-am.
CHRISTMAS,	krist'-mas.
COOK'S,	kooks.
DE PEYSTER,	de pī'-ster.
DUCIE,	du'-se.
EASTER,	ĕs'-ter.
EGMONT,	eg'-mont.
EGOI,	e-goi'.
FRIENDLY,	frend'-le.
FEEJEE,	fe'-je.
FLORES,	flo'-res.
GAMBIER,	gam'-be-er.
GILBERTS,	gil'-bertz.
GILOLO,	je-lo'-lo.
GUADALUPE,	gwå-då-loo'-på.
HALL,	hål.
HAPAI,	hå'-pī.
HAWAII,	hå-wa'-e.
JAVA,	jå'-vå.
KAHOOLAWE,	kå-hoo-lå'-we.
KAUHAI,	kow'-hī.
KEELING,	keel'-ing.
KERMADEC,	ker-ma-dek'.
LADRONES,	låd-rōnz'.
LANAI,	lå'-nī.
LOUISIADE,	loo-e-ze-åd'.
LUZON,	loo-zon'.
MAGELLAN'S,	ma-jel'-lanz.
MALAYSIA,	mal-å'-she-a.
MARQUESAS,	mår-kå'-sås.
MAUI,	mow'-e.
MELVILLE,	mel'-vil.
MINDANAO,	min-då-nå'-o.
MINDORO,	min-do'-ro.
MITCHELL'S,	mitch'-elz.
MOLOKAI,	mo-lo-kī'.
MORTLOCK,	mort'-lok.
MULGRAVE,	mul'-gråv.
NAVIGATOR,	nav'-i-ga-tor.
NEW BRITAIN,	nu brit'-en.
NEW CALEDONIA,	nu kal-e-do'-ne-a.
NEW GEORGIA,	nu jor'-je-å.
NEW GUINEA,	nu ghin'-e.
NEW HEBRIDES,	nu heb'-re-dez.
NEW IRELAND,	nu īre'-land.
NEW LEINSTER,	nu lin'-ster.
NEW MUNSTER,	nu mun'-ster.
NEW ULSTER,	nu ul'-ster.
NEW ZEALAND,	nu ze'-land.
NIHAU,	ne-how'.
NOOKAHEEVA,	noo-kå-he'-vå.
NORFOLK,	nor'-fåk.
OAHU,	wå'-hoo.
OWHYHE,	o-wī'-he.
PALAWAN,	på-lå-wån'.
PALLISER,	pal-lī'-ser.
PALMYRAS,	pal-mī'-ras.
PEARL,	purl.
PELEW,	pe-lew'.
PHILIPPINE,	fil'-ip-pin.
PITCAIRN,	pit'-kirn.
RADACK,	rå-dåk'.
RENNELL,	ren-nel'.
SANDALWOOD,	san'-dal-wood.
SANDWICH,	saud'-wich.
SANGIR,	sån-gheer'.
SAMAR,	så-mår'.
SCARBOROUGH,	skår'-bur-ro.
SOCIETY,	so-sī'-e-te.
SOLOMAN'S,	sol'-o-munz.
SOOLOO,	soo-loo'.
SPICE,	spīs.
ST. ANDREW'S,	sånt an'-drews.
ST. PAUL'S,	sånt pawlz'.
STRONG'S,	strongs.
SUMATRA,	soo-må'-tra.
SUMDAWA,	soom-baw'-wa.
TAHITI,	ta-he'-te.
TASWELL'S,	tas'-wels.
TIMOR,	te'-môr.
TONGA,	ton'-ga.
TORRES,	tor'-res.
ULALAN,	oo-la'-lan.
VAN DIEMAN'S LAND,	vån de'-manz land.

VI. PENINSULAS, ISTHMUSES, AND CAPES.

North America.

ALASKA,	ål-ås'-kå.
ANN,	an.
BARROW,	bår'-ro.
BATHURST,	bath'-urst.
BAULD,	bawld.
BREWSTER,	bru'-ster.
CALIFORNIA,	kal-e-for'-ne-a.
CANAVERAL,	kan-av'-e-ral.
CANSO,	kan'-so.
CATOCHE,	kå-to'-che.
CHARLES,	chårlz.
CHUDLEIGH,	chud'-le.
COD,	kod.
CONCEPTION,	kon-sep'-shun.
CORRIENTES,	kor-re-en'-tes.
DARIEN,	da-re'-en'.

PRONOUNCING VOCABULARY.

Des Montes,	da mon'-ta.	Gallinas,	gal-ye'-nas.	Rasalhad,	rås-al-håd'.
Desconocida,	da'-kon-o-se'-da.	Horn,	hôrn.	Romania,	ro-må'-ne-a.
Elizabeth,	e-liz'-a-beth.	North,	nôrth.	St. Thaddeus,	sånt thad'-de-us.
Farewell,	fare-wel'.	Orange,	or'-anj.	Suez,	soo-ěz'.
Fear,	fear.	Pillar,	pil'-lar.	Zelania,	ze-lå'-ne-a.
Flattery,	flat'-ter-re.	San Francisco,	från-sis'-ko.		
Florida,	flor'-e-da.	San Lorenzo,	lo-ren'-zo.	**Africa.**	
Gracias á Dios,	grå'-se-ås å de'-ŏs.	St. Antonio,	ån-to'-ne-o.		
Hatteras,	hat'-ter-as.	St. Roque,	rŏk.	Ambro,	am'-bro.
Henlopen,	hen-lo'-pen.			Agulhas,	å-gool'yas.
Henry,	hen'-ry.	**Europe.**		Bassas,	bas'-sas.
Icy,	i'-se.			Bon,	bŏn.
Labrador,	lab'-ra-dŏr.	Clear,	klèr.	Bojador,	boj-a-dor'.
Lookout,	look-out'.	Corso,	kor'-so.	Blanco,	blan'-ko.
Malabar,	mal'a-bår.	Crimea,	krim'-e-a.	Corrientes,	kor-re-en'-tĕs.
May,	må.	Finisterre,	fin-is-tair'.	Cross,	krŏs.
Mendocino,	měn-do-se'-no.	Gata,	gå'-tå.	Delgado,	děl-gå'-do.
Morro Hermoso,	mor'-ro her-mo'-so.	La Hogue,	la hôg'.	Frio,	free'-o.
North,	north.	Land's End,	landz end'.	Guardafui,	gwår-då-fwe'.
Nova Scotia,	no-va sko'-she-a.	Matapan,	måt-å-pån'.	Good Hope,	good hôp'.
Orford,	or'-ford.	Naze,	nåz.	Noon,	noon.
Palma,	pal'-ma.	North,	north.	Orfui,	or'-fwe.
Prince of Wales,	prins of wålz.	Ortegal,	or-tå-gål'.	Palmas,	pal'-mas.
Race,	rås.	Palos,	på'-lŏs.	St. Mary,	sånt ma'-re.
Ray,	rå.	Passaro,	pås-sa'-ro.	Suez,	soo-ěz'.
Roman,	ro'-man.	San Martin,	sån mår'-tin.	Verde,	věrd.
Romanzoff,	ro-man-zof'.	Spartivento,	spar-te-ven'-to.		
Roxo,	roks'-o.	St. Vincent,	sånt vin'-sent.	**Oceanica.**	
Sable,	sa'-bl.	Sviatoi,	sve'å-toi.		
San Antonio,	sån åu-to'-ne-o.	Teulada,	tě-oo-lå'-då.	Bougainville,	boo-gan-vil'.
San Blas,	sån blås'.	Trafalgar,	traf-al-går'.	Chatham,	chat'-am.
San Lazaro,	sån låz'-a-ro.	Wrath,	råth.	Engano,	ěn-gå'-no.
St. Lucas,	sånt loo'-kas.			Flattery,	flat'-ter-re.
St. Mary,	sånt ma'-re.	**Asia.**		Howe,	how.
St. Lewis,	sånt lu'-is.			Hana,	hå'-nå.
Walsingham,	wal'-sing-ham.	Cambodia,	kam-bo'-de-a.	Kauaka,	kå-hå'-kå.
Whittle,	whit'-tle.	Chelagsnoi,	che låg sloi'.	Koolau,	koo'-lau.
Yucatan,	yoo-kå-tån'.	Corea,	ko-re'-a.	Lekuwin,	le'-win, or lå'win.
		Cornorin,	kom'o-rin.	Leveque,	lå-vǎk'.
South America.		East,	ěst.	Maria Van Dieman,	do'-man.
		Isolette,	e-so-let'.	Northwest,	nôrth-west'.
Blanco,	blån'-ko.	Kamtchatka,	kåm-chåt'-ka.	Rodney,	rod'-ne.
Corrientes,	kor-re-en'-tes.	Kraw,	kraw.	Sandy,	san'-de.
Darien,	då-re-en'.	Lopatka,	lo-pat'-ka.	Townsend,	town'-send.
Frio,	fre'-o.	Negrais,	ne-grise'.	Upola,	oo-pa'-lå.
		Northeast,	nôrth-ěst'.	York,	york.

VII. MOUNTAINS.

North America.

		HEIGHT IN FEET.			
			Green,	green,	4,360
			Katahdin,	ka-tå'-din,	5,380
Alleghany,	al-le-ga'-ne,	4,200	Ozark,	o'-zark.	
Arctic Highlands,	ark'-tik high'-lands.		Popocatapetl,	po-po-kåt-a-pet'-l,	17,720
Black Hills,	blåk hilz.		Rocky,	rok'-c.	
Blue Ridge,	blu'-rij,	6,470	Mt. Brown,	brown,	16,000
Cascade,	kas'-kåd.		Fremont's Peak,	fre-montz',	13,500
Mt. Hood,	hood,	14,000	Mt. Hooker,	hook'-er,	15,700
Mt. St. Helens,	sånt hel'-enz.		Long's Peak,	longz,	12,000
Mt. Ranier,	ra'-neer.		Pike's Peak,	pikz,	11,500
Catskill,	kats'-kil,	3,800	Spanish Peak,	span'-ish.	
Coast,	kŏst.		Sierra Madre,	se-er'-rå må'-dra.	
Cosigcina,	ko-se-ghe'-nå.		Sierra Nevada,	se-er'-rå nå-vå'-då.	
Cumberland,	kum'-ber-land.		Mt. St. Elias,	sånt e-li'-as,	17,900
Mt. Fairweather,	får'-weth-er,	14,000	White,	white,	6,230

PRONOUNCING VOCABULARY.

South America.

ACARAY,	ak-a-rå'.	
ANDES,	an'-dez.	
ACONCAGUA,	å-kon-kå'-gwå,	23,900
CHIMBORAZO,	chim-bo-rå'-zo,	21,425
CHUQUIBAMBA,	choo-ke-båm'-bå,	21,000
COTOPAXI,	ko-to-pax'-e,	18,870
GUALATEIRI,	gwå'-lå-tå-e-re'.	
ILLIMANI,	cel'-yn-må'-nc,	21,150
SORATA,	so-rå'-tå,	21,280
BRAZILIAN,	bra-zeel'-yan.	
GERAL,	zha'-rål.	
PACARAIMA,	på-kå-rī'-må.	

Europe.

ALPS,		
MONT BLANC,	blank,	15,800
APENNINES,	ap'-en-nīnz.	
MT. VESUVIUS,	ve-soo'-ve-us,	3,950
AUVERGNE,	o-vårn',	6,221
BALKAN,	bål'-kån,	10,000
CANTABRIAN,	kan-tå'-bre-ån,	11,000
CARPATHIAN,	kår-på'-the-an,	8,675
CAUCASUS,	kaw'-kå-sus,	18,000
CEVENNES,	så-venn',	5,820
MT. ETNA,	et'-na,	10,885
GRAMPIAN,	gram'-pe-an,	4,370
MT. HECLA,	hek'-la,	5,210
MONTSERRAT.	mont-ser-rat',	3,300
PYRENEES,	pīr'-en-eez,	11,425
SCANDINAVIAN,	skan-de-na'-ve-an.	8,720
SIERRA MORENA,	se êr'-ra mo-rå'-nå,	4,000
SIERRA NEVADA,	se-êr'-rå nå-vå'-då,	11,657
URAL,	yoo'-ral,	5,300

Asia.

ALDAN,	ål-dån',	4,260
ALTAI,	ål-tī',	12,210
ARARAT,	å'-ra-rat,	17,000
BELOOR,	be-loor',	20,000

CAUCASUS,	kaw'-kå-sus,	18,493
DEMAVEND,	dem-å-vend',	14,700
ELBROOZ,	êl'-brooz.	
KONJAKOFSKI,	kon-ja-kof'-ski.	
GHAUTS,	gawts,	8,000
HIMALAYA,	him-a-lī'-a.	
EVERETT,	ev'-er-et.	
KUNCHINGINGA,	koon-chin-jing'-gå,	28,177
HINDOO KOOSH,	hin'-do koosh.	
KHINGAN,	king-gan'.	
KUENLUN,	kwen-loon',	14,700
MELING,	ma-ling'.	
PELING,	pa-ling'.	
RAMLEAH,	ram'-le-a.	
SINAI,	sī'-nå, or sī'-nå-I,	7,500
STANOVOI,	stå'-no-voi'.	
TAURUS,	tå'-rus,	13,100
THIAN SHAN,	te'-åu shån.	

Africa.

ABDA YARET,	åb'-bå yå'-ret,	15,000
ATLAS,	at'-las.	
MT. MILTSEEN,	milt-seen',	11,400
CAMEROONS,	kam-er-oons',	13,000
CRYSTAL,	krist'-al.	
KONG,	kong,	4,000
LUPATA,	loo-på'-tå.	
MOON,	moon.	
KENIA,	ke'-ne-a,	20,000
KILIMANDJARO,	kil'-e-mån'-jå-ro',	20,000
RADAMA,	rå'-då-må'.	
RED,	rêd.	
SNOW,	sno.	

Oceanica.

AUSTRALIAN ALPS,	ôs-trå'-le-an,	12,000
BLUE,	blů,	3,360
KILAUEA,	ke-lau'-e-a.	
MAUNA KEA,	mau'-na ke'-a.	
MAUNA LOA,	mau'-na lo'-a.	
OPHIR,	o'-fur.	

VIII. DESERTS AND OASES.

South America.

ATACAMA,	å-tå-kå'-må.

Asia.

AKHAF,	åk'-håf.
COBI,	ko'-be.

GREAT SALT,	grât sâlt.
SANDY,	san'-de.

Africa.

AGADEZ,	å'-gå-dez.
BILMAH,	bil'-må.

CHALLEHENGA,	chål'-le-hen-gå.
LIBYAN,	lib'-e-an.
NUBIAN,	nu'-be-an.
SAHARA,	så-hå'-rå.
SEEWAH,	se'-wå.
TIBESTI,	te'-bes-te'.
TUAT,	too-at'.

IX. LAKES.

North America.

ABBITIBBEE,	ab-be-tib'-e.
ATHABASCA,	ath-a-bas'-ka.
CANIAPUSCAW,	kan'-e-ap'-us-kaw.

CHAMPLAIN,	sham-plån'.
CHAPALA,	chå-på'-lå.
CHESUNCOOK,	che-sun'-kook.
DEER,	deer.
ERIE,	e'-re.
GEORGIAN,	jor'-jo-an.

GRAND,	grånd.
GREAT BEAR,	bår.
GREAT SALT,	sålt.
GREAT SLAVE,	slåv.
GREEN,	grên.
HURON,	hu'-run.

PRONOUNCING VOCABULARY.

KLAMATH,	klåm'-åt, or klå-måth'.	**South America.**		**Asia.**	
LITTLE SLAVE,	slåv.	BEVEDERO,	bå-vå-då'-ro.	BAIKAL,	bī'-kal.
MANITOBA,	man'-e-to'-ba.	COLUGUAPE,	ko-loo-gwå'-på.	BALKASH,	bål-kåsh'.
MICHIGAN,	mish'-e-gån.	IBERA,	e-bå'-rå.	KOKO NOR,	kō-kō nōr'.
MISTISSINNY,	mis'-tis-sin'-ny.	MARACAYDO,	mår-å-kī'-bo.	LOP NOR,	lŏp nōr'.
MOOSEHEAD,	moose'-head.	MIRIM,	me-reeng'.	OOROOMEEYAH,	oo-roo-me'-yå.
NICARAGUA,	nik-ar-å'-gwå.	PATOS,	på'-tōs.	POYANG,	po-yång'.
NICOLLET,	nik-o-lå'.	PORONGOS,	po-rŏn'-gōs.	TCHANY,	chå'-ne.
NIPISSING,	nip'-is-sing.	REYES,	rå'-yōs.	TONTINGHOO,	ton'-ting-hoo.
NITCHEGUON,	nitch'-e-gwon'.	TITICACA,	te-te-kå'-kå.	ZAIZAN,	zī-zån'.
OKECHOBEE,	o'-ke-cho'-be.			ZURRAH,	zur'-ra.
ONTARIO,	on-ta'-re-o.	**Europe.**			
PONTCHARTRAIN,	pŏn-char-trån'.			**Africa.**	
PYRAMID,	pir'-a-mid.	CONSTANCE,	kon'-stanz.	DEDO,	då'-bo.
RAINY,	ra'-ne.	GENEVA,	jeu-e'-va.	DEMBEA,	dem'-be-a.
RED,	red.	ILMEN,	il-men', or il'-men	FITTRE,	fit'-trå.
SAGINAW,	sag'-e-nå.	LADOGA,	la-do'-gå.	MARAVI,	må-rå'-ve.
SIMCOE,	sim'-ko.	MAELAR,	må'-lar.	MELGIG,	měl-ghig'.
ST. CLAIR,	sånt klår'.	ONEGA,	o-ne'-ga.	NGAMI,	n'gå'-me.
ST. JOHN,	sånt jon'.	PEIPUS,	på'-e-poos.	NYASSI,	ne-ås'se.
SUPERIOR,	su-pe'-re-ur.	PLATTEN SEE,	plåt'-ten så.	SINKAU,	sib'-ka.
TERMINOS,	ter'-me-nŏs.	PURUS,	poo'-roos.	TCHAD,	chåd.
TULE,	too'-le, or too'-lå.	SEGO,	så'-go.	UKEREWE,	u-ke-ra'-we.
UTAH,	yoo'-tå.	VIGO,	ve'-go.		
WINNIPEG,	win'-e-peg.	WENER,	wå'-ner.	**Oceanica.**	
WINNIPEGOOS,	win'-e-pe-goos.	WETTER,	wet'-ter.		
WOODS,	woodz.			TORRENS,	tor'-renz.

X. RIVERS.

North America.		LENGTH IN MILES.		FEATHER,	feth'-er.	
				FLINT,	flint,	300
ABBITIBBEE,	ab-be-tib'-e,	250		GALLATIN,	gal'-la-tin,	150
ALABAMA,	al-a-båm'-a,	380		GATINEAU,	gå-te-no',	400
ALBANY,	ål'-ba-ne,	340		GILA,	heel'-å,	450
ALLEGHANY,	al-le-ga'-ne,	400		GRAND, Mich.,	grand,	270
ALTAMAHAW,	ål'-ta-ma-haw',	140		GRANDE, Mex.,	grand,	300
ANDROSCOGGIN,	an-dros-kog'-in,	140		GREAT FISH,	gråt fish.	
APPALACHICOLA,	ap'-pa-lah-che-ko'-la,	100		GREAT WHALE,	gråt whål.	
ARKANSAS,	år-kan'-sas,	2,000		GREAT PEDEE,	gråt pŏ'-dē,	300
ATHABASCA,	ath-å-bas'-ka,	500		GREEN, Ky.,	green,	300
BALSAS,	bal'-sas.			HARRICANAW,	har-re-kn'-nå,	270
BEAR,	bare,	400		HUDSON,	hud'-sun,	300
BIG HORN,	big horn,	400		HUMBOLDT,	hum'-bōlt,	350
BIG SANDY,	big san'-dy,	80		ILLINOIS,	il'-lin-oi',	400
BRAZOS,	brå'-zos,	900		IOWA,	ī'-o-wa,	300
CANADIAN,	ka-na'-de-an,	900		JAMES,	jåmz,	500
CAPE FEAR,	kåp fēr,	300		JEFFERSON,	jef'-fer-sun.	
CHATTEHOOCHE,	chat-ta-hoo'-che,	550		KANAWHA,	kå-naw'-wa,	400
CHOWAN,	cho-wån',	50		KANSAS,	kan'-sas,	1,000
CHURCHILL,	church'-il,	700		KASKASKIA,	kas-kas'-ke-a,	300
CLARKE'S,	klarkz,	650		KENNEDEC,	ken-ne-bek',	200
COLORADO, Texas,	kol-o-rå'-do,	900		KENTUCKY,	ken-tuk'-e,	260
COLORADO, Cal.,	kol-o-rå'-do,	*1,200		KLAMATH,	klå'-math,	250
COLUMBIA,	ko-lum'-be-a,	1,000		KOKSAK,	kok'-sak.	
CONNECTICUT,	kon-net'-i-kut,	400		LEWIS,	lu'-is,	900
CUMBERLAND,	kum'-ber-land,	600		MACKENZIE,	mak-kĕn'-ze,	900
DELAWARE,	del'-a-ware,	300		MADAWASKA,	mad-a-was'-ka,	210
DES MOINES,	de moin',	400		MADISON,	mad'-i-sun.	
DETROIT,	de-troit',	25		MAUMEE,	må-mē',	100
EAST MAIN,	ŏst mane',	400		MERRIMAC,	mer'-ri-mak,	110
				MIAMI,	mi-å'-me,	150
* Including the Green.				MINNESOTA,	min-ne-so'-ta,	450

11

PRONOUNCING VOCABULARY.

Miramichi,	mir'-a-me'-she',	75
Mississippi,	mis-sis-sip'-pe,	3,160
Missouri,	mis-soo'-re,	3,100
Mobile,	mo-beel',	50
Mohawk,	mo'-båk,	160
Monongahela,	mo-non-ga-hê'-la,	250
Moose,	moos,	250
Muskingum,	mus-king'-gum,	110
Nebraska,	ne-bras'-ka,	400
Neches,	netch'-ez,	150
Nelson,	nel'-sun,	300
Neuse,	nuse,	300
Niagara,	ni-åg'-a-ra,	34
Nicollet,	nik'-o-lå'.	
North Fork,	north fork,	800
Nueces,	nwå'-ses,	350
Ocmulgee,	ok'-mul-ge,	300
Oconee,	ô-ko'-ne,	250
Ohio,	o-hi'-o,	950
Osage,	o'-såj,	200
Ottawa,	ot'-ta-wå,	800
Pascagoula,	pas'-ka-goo'-la,	100
Peace,	pês,	800
Pearl,	perl,	250
Pecos,	pa'-kôs,	700
Penobscot,	pê-nob'-skot,	800
Potomac,	po-to'-mak,	400
Rappahannock,	rap-pa-han'-nok,	125
Red,	red,	1,200
Republican Fork,	re-pub'-le-kan fork,	400
Rio Grande, Mex.,	ri'-o grand',	1,800
Rio Virgen,	re'-o vêr'-hen.	
Roanoke,	ro-an-ôk',	450
Rock,	rok,	330
Rupert,	roo'-pert,	300
Sabine,	sa-been',	500
Saco,	saw'-ko,	150
Sacramento,	sak-ra-men'-to,	370
Saguenay,	såg-a-nå',	100
Salmon,	sal'-mun.	
San Joaquin,	sån-ho'-å-keen',	350
Santander,	sån-tan'-der,	110
Santee,	sån-tô',	150
Saskatchewan,	sås-kåtch'-e-won,	1,300
Savannah,	sa-van'-na,	450
Scioto,	si-o'-to,	200
Severn,	sev'-urn,	350
Slave,	slåv,	300
Smoky Hill,	smo'-ke hill',	800
Sorel, or Richelieu,	so'-rel',	80
South Fork,	south fork'.	
St. Clair,	sånt klår',	40
St. Croix,	kroi,	75
St. Francis,	fran'-sis.	
St. Francis, Miss.	fran'-sis,	450
St. John's, Flor.,	jonz,	250
St. John,	jon,	450
St. Joseph's,	jo'-zefs,	250
St. Lawrence,	lå'-rens,	750
St. Mary's,	ma'-riz,	100
St. Maurice,	sånt må'-ris,	400
Susquehanna,	sus-kwe-han'-na,	400
Scwanee,	su-wå'-ne.	
Tar,	tar.	
Tennessee,	ten-nes-se',	800
Tombigbee,	tom-big'-be,	450
Trinity,	trin'-e-te,	550
Tula,	too'-la,	200
Uscmasinta,	oo-soo-må-sin'-tå,	400
Wabash,	wå'-bash,	550
Washitaw,	wåsh'-e-taw,	500
Wateree,	wå-ter-e',	200
White, Ind.,	whit,	50
White, Ark.,	whit,	800
Willamette,	wil-lå-met',	150
Wisconsin,	wis-kon'-sin,	600
Yaqui,	yå-ke',	400
Yazoo,	yå-zoo',	290
Yellow Stone,	yel'-low stôn,	1,000

South America.

Amazon,	am'-a-zon,	4,000
Aniba,	å-ne-bå'.	
Apure,	å-poo'-rå.	
Araguay,	år-å-gwi',	1,000
Arinos,	å-re'-nôs,	700
Beni,	bå-ne',	1,000
Biobio,	be'-o-be'-o,	200
Berbice,	ber-bees',	200
Branco,	brån'-ko,	120
Camarones,	kam-a-ro'-nez.	
Caqueta, or Japura,	kå-kå'-tå,	1,200
Caroni,	kå-ro-ne',	400
Cauca,	kow'-kå,	600
Chico,	che'-ko,	
Colorado,	kol'-o-rå'-do,	800
Cosiquare, or Cassiquiare,	ko-se-kå'-re, kås-se-ke-å'-ra.	150
Cuyaba,	koo-yå'-bå.	
Demerara,	dêm'-er-å'-rå,	180
Desaguadero,	dês'-å-gwå-då'-ro,	180
Dulce,	dool'-så.	
Essequibo,	ês-se-ke'-bo,	450
Guapai,	gwå-pi',	550
Guapore,	gwå-po'-rå,	400
Guaviare,	gwå-ve-å'-rå,	450
Gurapy, or Gurupi,	goo-roo-pe',	250
Huallaga,	hwål-yå'-gå,	500
Javary,	hå-vå-re',	450
Jurua,	hoo-roo'-å.	
Jutay,	hoo-ti',	
Madeira,	må-då'-rå,	*1,800
Magdalena,	mag-da-le'-na,	900
Mamore,	må-mo-rå',	500
Maranham, or Miarim,	mar'-an-håm',	350
Marowyne,	må'-ro-win',	400
Meta,	må'-tå,	500
Napo,	nå'-po,	500
Negro,	nå'-gro,	1,000
Orinoco,	o-re-no'-ko,	1,600
Otapok,	o'-yå-pok',	180
Para,	på-rå',	200
Paraguay,	på-rå-gwå', or på-rå-gwi',	1,000
Parahiba,	på-rå-e'-bå,	300
Parana,	på-rå-nå',	2,000
Paranaiba,	på-rå-nå-e'-bå,	500
Parima,	på-re'-må.	
Parnahiba,	pår-nå-e'-bå,	750
Pilcomayo,	pil-ko-mi'-o,	1,000

* Including the Mamore.

Port Desire,	port de-sīr',	200		Neva,	nä'-vä,	40
Purus,	poo'-roos,	500		Niemen,	ne'-men,	400
Putumayo,	poo-too-mī'-o,	700		Oder,	o'-der,	550
Rio de la Plata,	re'-o dä lä plä'-tä,	*2,500		Oka,	o'-kä,	650
Rio das Mortes,	re'-o däs mor'-tes.			Onega,	o-nä'-gä,	250
Rio Negro, Pat.,	re'-o nä'-gro,	600		Oosa,	oo'-sä,	200
Salado, (148,)	sä-lä'-do,	1,000		Petchora,	petch'-o-rä,	900
Salado, (150,)	sä-lä'-do,	400		Po,	po,	340
Santa Cruz,	sän'-tä kroos,	200		Pripets,	prip'-ěts,	350
St. Francisco,	fran-sis'-ko,	1,250		Pruth,	prüth,	360
Surinam,	soo-rin-am',	300		Rhine,	rīn,	950
Tacuari,	tä-ku'-ä-re.			Rhone,	rōn,	540
Tapajos,	tä-pä'-zhos,	500		Samara,	sä-mä-rä',	280
Tercero,	ter-sä'-ro.			Saone,	sōn,	320
Tiete,	te-ä'-tä,	500		Save,	säv, or säv,	550
Tocantins,	to-kän-tōns',	1,000		Seine,	sän, or sěn,	500
Tres Barras,	trěs bär'-ras.			Severn,	sev'-ern,	210
Trombetas,	trom-ba'-täs.			Shannon,	shan'-nun,	220
Uaupes,	wow'-pes.			Skelleftea,	skěl-lef'-te-a,	120
Ucayale,	oo-kī-ä'-la,	500		Sookhona,	soo-ko'-nä,	250
Uruguay,	oo'-roo-gwä,	800		Sura,	soo'-rä,	400
Vermejo,	věr-mä'-ho,	780		Sveer,	svěr,	130
Xingu,	shin-goo',	1,300		Tagus,	ta'-gus,	540
				Terek,	tä-rěk',	350
	Europe.			Thames,	těmz,	220
				Theiss,	tīs,	500
Bielaia,	be-ä'-lī'-ä,	500		Tiber,	tī'-ber,	185
Bog,	bog,	340		Tornea,	tor'-ne-a,	230
Bug,	bug,	300		Umea,	oo'-me-a,	250
Danube,	dan'-ube,	1,800		Ural,	yoo'-ral,	1,800
Dahl,	däl.			Viatka,	ve-ät'-kä,	500
Desna,	děs'-nä,	500		Vistula,	vis'-tu-la,	530
Dnieper,	ne'-per,	1,230		Vitchegda,	ve-chěg'-dä,	380
Dniester,	nees'-ter,	500		Volga,	vol'-gä,	2,500
Don,	don,	1,000		Volkhov,	vol-kov',	130
Donets,	do-nŏts',	400		Wartha,	war'-tä,	450
Dordogne,	dor-dōn',	220		Weser,	we'-ser,	230
Douro,	doo'-ro,	400				
Drammen,	dräm'-men.				Asia.	
Drave,	dräv,	360				
Duna,	du'-nä,	400		Aldan,	äl-dän',	300
Dwina,	dwī'-na,	330		Amga,	äm'-gä,	460
Ebro,	e'-bro,	340		Amoo,	ä-moo',	1,300
Elbe,	ělb,	550		Amoor,	ä-moor',	2,200
Garonne,	gä-ron',	380		Anabara,	ä-nä'-bä-rä',	400
Glommen,	glom'-men,	260		Anadir,	ä-nä-deer',	450
Guadalquiver,	gaw-dal-kwiv'-er,	280		Angara,	äng-gä-rä',	1,000
Guadiana,	gwä-de-ä'-nä,	380		Argoon,	ar'-goon'.	
Humber,	hum'-ber,	40		Attruck,	at'-truk.	
Indal,	in'-dal,	60		Brahmapootra,	brah'-ma-poo'-tra,	1,500
Kama,	kä'-mä,	1,400		Cambodia,	kam-bo'-de-a,	1,800
Kem,	kem,	100		Chenaud,	che-naub',	700
Keni,	ke'-ni.			Euphrates,	u-frā'-těz,	1,800
Khoper,	ko'-per,	250		Ganges,	gan'-jěz,	1,960
Klar,	klär,	200		Godavery,	go-dä'-ver-e,	700
Kooban,	koo'-bän,	380		Helmund,	hěl-mŭnd',	650
Kooma,	koo'-mä,	300		Hoang Ho,	ho-ang' ho,	2,000
Loire,	lwär,	640		Hoang Kiang,	ho-ang' ke-äng,	800
Lulea,	loo'-le-a,	200		Indighirka,	in'-de-ghir'-kä,	750
Manitch,	mä-neetch',	300		Indus,	in'-dŭs,	1,650
Maritza,	mä-rit'-zä,	260		Irrawaddy,	ir'-ra-wä'-de,	1,200
Meuse,	muz,	430		Irtish,	ir'-tish,	1,700
Mezene,	měz-än',	450		Ishim,	ish'-im,	700
Minho,	meen'-yo,	180		Khatanga,	kä-tän'-gä,	650
				Kolyma,	ko-le-mä',	700
	* Including the Paraguay.			Koor,	koor,	520

Kistnah,	kist'-na,	600	Chadda,	chad'-da.	
Lena,	le'-na,	2,400	Coanza,	ko-ăn'-za,	500
Mahanuddy,	mă-ha-nud'-de,	250	Congo,	kong'-go,	240
Menam,	mă'-nam',	800	Gambia,	găm'-be-a,	1,000
Nerbudda,	ner-bŭd'-dă,	620	Gojeb,	go'-jeb'.	
Obi,	o'-be,	2,000	Haines,	hănz.	
Olenek,	o-lă-něk',	800	Juda,	zhoo'-bă.	
Oosuori,	oo'-soo-re',	340	Matoni,	mă-to'-ni.	
Pei Ho,	pa hŏ,	170	Misskład,	mis-se-lăd'.	
Piasina,	pe-ă-se'-nă,	250	Niger,	ni'-jer,	2,500
Salwin,	săl'-win.		Nile,	nil,	1,800
Selenga,	să-lĕng'-ga,	500	Orange,	or'-inj,	1,000
Shilka,	shil'-kă.		Ozi,	o'-ze.	
Sihon,	si-hon',	900	Rio Grande,	re'-o grănd'.	
Soongari,	soon-gă'-re, or soon-		Sadaki,	să-bă'-ke.	
	gă-re',	800	Senegal,	sen'-e-găl,	1,000
Sutlej,	sŭt'-lej,	950	Shary,	shă'-re.	
Chikiri,	che-ke'-re',	450	St. Paul,	sănt păl,	300
Tigris,	ti'-gris,	1,150	Tacazze,	tă-kăt'-să.	
Tobol,	to-bol',	500	Umbre,	oom'-bră.	
Toongooska,	toong-goos'-kă.		Vaal,	văl.	
Ural,	yoo'-ral,	1,800	Volta,	vol'-tă,	360
Vitim,	vit'-im,	900	White,	whit,	1,200
Yana,	yă'-nă,	600	Ykoo,	yă-oo',	300
Yangtse Kiang,	yăng'-tse ke-ang',	2,500	Zambeze,	zam-ba'-ze.	
Yarkand,	yar'-kand',	500			
Yenisei,	yĕn'-e-să'-e,	2,500	**Australia.**		
Africa.			Darling,	dar'-ling,	1,000
			Lachlan,	lak'-lăn,	400
Ambriz,	am'-briz.		Lynd,	lind.	
Bembarooghe,	bem-ba-rooj'.		Murray,	mur'-ra,	1,400
Blue,	blu,	800	Swan,	swan.	

STATISTICAL TABLES.

RAILROADS IN THE UNITED STATES.

STATES.	Total length of lines.	Miles in operation.	Actual length in state.	STATES.	Total length of lines.	Miles in operation.	Actual length in state.
Alabama,	1,822.4	798.6	628.9	Mississippi,	445.1	365.4	691.1
Arkansas,	701.3	38.5	38.5	Missouri,	1,337.3	723.2	723.2
California,	308.8	22.5	22.5	New Hampshire,	599.9	565.2	561.7
Connecticut,	520.7	665.6	599.3	New Jersey,	658.9	556.4	556.4
Delaware,	117.9	117.9	127.1	New York,	3,610.6	2,756.4	2,779.8
Florida,	730.5	289.8	289.8	North Carolina,	1,020.2	770.2	703.2
Georgia,	1,617.2	1,241.7	1,234.5	Ohio,	4,084.7	3,008.2	3,016.7
Illinois,	3,500.7	2,752.7	2,727.7	Oregon,	300.0		
Indiana,	1,839.0	1,327.9	2,005.4	Pennsylvania,	3,995.1	3,081.1	2,787.1
Iowa,	1,806.8	395.3	395.3	Rhode Island,	86.9	63.6	100.9
Kentucky,	698.4	458.5	510.5	South Carolina,	1,136.0	607.3	900.3
Louisiana,	1,160.0	419.0	294.0	Tennessee,	1,434.4	1,062.3	977.5
Maine,	618.1	544.6	476.4	Texas,	2,667.0	284.5	284.5
Maryland & Dist. Col.,	889.3	833.3	478.1	Vermont,	588.5	537.9	561.1
Massachusetts,	1,507.3	1,428.3	1,391.1	Virginia,	2,058.5	1,525.7	1,755.7
Michigan,	1,747.8	1,132.8	796.9	Wisconsin,	2,224.3	826.0	876.0
Minnesota,	1,167.5						

POPULATION OF THE UNITED STATES, FOR EVERY TWENTY YEARS, FROM 1800 TO 1860.

STATES.	1800.	1820.	1840.	1860.	STATES.	1800.	1820.	1840.	1860.
ALABAMA,		127,901	590,756	964,296	MINNESOTA,				162,022
ARKANSAS,		14,273	97,574	435,427	MISSISSIPPI,	8,850	75,448	375,651	791,395
CALIFORNIA,				380,015	MISSOURI,		66,586	383,702	1,173,317
CONNECTICUT,	251,002	275,202	309,076	460,151	NEW HAMPSHIRE,	183,762	244,161	284,574	326,072
DELAWARE,	64,273	72,749	78,085	112,218	NEW JERSEY,	211,949	277,575	373,306	672,031
FLORIDA,			54,477	140,439	NEW YORK,	586,756	1,372,812	2,428,921	3,887,542
GEORGIA,	162,101	340,987	691,392	1,057,327	NORTH CAROLINA,	478,103	638,829	753,419	992,667
ILLINOIS,		55,211	476,183	1,711,753	OHIO,	45,365	581,434	1,519,467	2,339,599
INDIANA,	4,875	147,178	685,866	1,350,479	OREGON,				52,464
IOWA,			43,112	674,948	PENNSYLVANIA,	602,365	1,049,458	1,724,033	2,906,370
KANSAS,				107,110	RHODE ISLAND,	69,122	83,059	108,830	174,621
KENTUCKY,	220,955	564,317	779,828	1,155,713	SOUTH CAROLINA,	345,591	502,741	594,398	703,312
LOUISIANA,		153,407	352,411	709,433	TENNESSEE,	105,602	422,813	829,210	1,100,847
MAINE,	151,719	298,335	501,793	628,276	TEXAS,				601,039
MARYLAND,	341,548	407,350	470,019	687,034	VERMONT,	154,465	235,764	291,948	315,116
MASSACHUSETTS,	423,245	523,287	737,699	1,231,065	VIRGINIA,	880,200	1,065,379	1,239,797	1,596,083
MICHIGAN,		8,896	212,267	749,112	WISCONSIN,			30,945	775,873

HISTORICAL TABLE OF THE UNITED STATES.

STATES AND TERRITORIES.	When settled.	Where settled.	By whom settled.	When admitted into the Union.	
VIRGINIA,	1607	Jamestown,	English,	June 26th,	1788
NEW YORK,	1614	Albany,	Dutch,	July 26th,	1788
MASSACHUSETTS,	1620	Plymouth,	English,	February 6th,	1788
NEW HAMPSHIRE,	1624	Dover,	English,	June 21st,	1788
NEW JERSEY,	1624	Bergen,	Dutch and Danes,	December 18th,	1787
DELAWARE,	1627	Cape Henlopen,	Swedes and Finns,	December 7th,	1787
CONNECTICUT,	1633	Windsor,	Emigrants from Massachusetts,	January 9th,	1788
MARYLAND,	1624	St. Mary's,	English,	April 28th,	1788
RHODE ISLAND,	1636	Providence,	Roger Williams,	May 29th,	1790
NORTH CAROLINA,	1663	Albemarle,	English,	November 21st,	1789
SOUTH CAROLINA,	1670	Port Royal,	English,	May 23d,	1788
PENNSYLVANIA,	1682	Philadelphia,	English,	December 12th,	1787
GEORGIA,	1733	Savannah,	English,	January 2d,	1788
FLORIDA,	1565	St. Augustine,	Spanish,	March 3d,	1845
MAINE,	1625	Bristol,	English,	March 5th,	1820
WISCONSIN,	1669	Green Bay,	French,	May 29th,	1848
MICHIGAN,	1670	Detroit,	French,	January 26th,	1837
ARKANSAS,	1685	Arkansas Post,	French,	June 15th,	1836
TEXAS,	1690	San Antonio,	Spanish,	December 29th,	1845
INDIANA,	1690	Vincennes,	French,	December 11th,	1816
LOUISIANA,	1699	Abbeville,	French,	April 6th,	1812
ALABAMA,	1711	Mobile,	French,	December 14th,	1819
MISSISSIPPI,	1716	Natchez,	French,	December 10th,	1817
ILLINOIS,	1720	Kaskaskia,	French,	December 3d,	1818
VERMONT,	1725	Fort Dummer,	Emigrants from Massachusetts,	March 4th,	1791
TENNESSEE,	1757	Fort London,	Emigrants from North Carolina,	June 1st,	1796
MISSOURI,	1764	St. Louis,	French,	August 10th,	1821
CALIFORNIA,	1769	San Diego,	Spanish,	September 9th,	1850
KENTUCKY,	1775	Boonesboro',	Daniel Boone,	June 1st,	1792
OHIO,	1788	Marietta,	Emigrants from New England,	November 29th,	1832
IOWA,	1833	Burlington,	Emigrants from New England,	March 3d,	1845
MINNESOTA,	1865	St. Paul,	Emigrants from the East,	May 11th,	1858
OREGON,	1839	Astoria,	Emigrants from the East,	February 14th,	1859
KANSAS,			Emigrants from the East,		1861

COLLEGES AND PROFESSIONAL SCHOOLS OF THE UNITED STATES.

Bowdoin,	Brunswick,	Me.	Wesleyan Female,	Macon,	Ga
Waterville,	Waterville,	Me.	University of Alabama,	Tuscaloosa,	Ala.
Dartmouth,	Hanover,	N. H.	Florence Wesleyan,	Florence,	Ala.
University of Vermont,	Burlington,	Vt.	Howard,	Marion,	Ala.
Middlebury,	Middlebury,	Vt.	Madison,	Sharon,	Miss.
Norwich University,	Norwich,	Vt.	University of Mississippi,	Oxford,	Miss.
Harvard University,	Cambridge,	Mass.	Mississippi,	Clinton,	Miss.
Williams,	Williamstown,	Mass.	Semple Broaddus,	Centre Hill,	Miss.
Amherst,	Amherst,	Mass.	University of Louisiana,	New Orleans,	La.
Holy Cross,	Worcester,	Mass.	Centenary,	Jackson,	La.
Tufts,	Medford,	Mass.	Washington,	Washington Co.,	La.
Brown University,	Providence,	R. I.	Dolbear's Commercial,	New Orleans,	La.
Yale,	New Haven,	Conn.	Aranama,	Goliad,	Texas.
Trinity,	Hartford,	Conn.	University of Nashville,	Nashville,	Tenn.
Wesleyan University,	Middletown,	Conn.	Franklin,	Near Nashville,	Tenn.
Columbia,	New York,	N. Y.	East Tennessee,	Knoxville,	Tenn.
Union,	Schenectady,	N. Y.	Cumberland University,	Lebanon,	Tenn.
Hamilton,	Clinton,	N. Y.	Jackson,	Columbia,	Tenn.
Madison University,	Hamilton,	N. Y.	Union,	Murfreesboro',	Tenn.
Hobart Free,	Geneva,	N. Y.	Greenville,	Greenville,	Tenn.
University of City of N. York,	New York,	N. Y.	Transylvania,	Lexington,	Ky.
University of Rochester,	Rochester,	N. Y.	St. Joseph's,	Bardstown,	Ky.
St. John's,	Fordham,	N. Y.	Centre,	Danville,	Ky.
College of New Jersey,	Princeton,	N. J.	Georgetown,	Georgetown,	Ky.
Rutgers,	New Brunswick,	N. J.	Kentucky Military Institute,	Franklin Springs,	Ky.
University of Pennsylvania,	Philadelphia,	Penn.	Kentucky,	Harrodsburg,	Ky.
Dickinson,	Carlisle,	Penn.	Ohio University,	Athens,	Ohio.
Jefferson,	Canonsburg,	Penn.	Miami University,	Oxford,	Ohio.
Washington,	Washington,	Penn.	Franklin,	New Athens,	Ohio.
Alleghany,	Meadville,	Penn.	Western Reserve,	Hudson,	Ohio.
Pennsylvania,	Gettysburg,	Penn.	Kenyon,	Gambier,	Ohio.
Lafayette,	Easton,	Penn.	Denison,	Granville,	Ohio.
Franklin and Marshall,	Lancaster,	Penn.	Marietta,	Marietta,	Ohio.
University at Lewisburg,	Lewisburg,	Penn.	Oberlin,	Oberlin,	Ohio.
Polytechnic,	Philadelphia,	Penn.	Ohio Wesleyan University,	Delaware,	Ohio.
Delaware,	Newark,	Del.	Wittenberg,	Springfield,	Ohio.
St. Mary's,	Wilmington,	Del.	Urbana University,	Urbana,	Ohio.
St. John's,	Annapolis,	Md.	Antioch,	Yellow Springs,	Ohio.
St. Charles's,	Ellicott's Mills,	Md.	Indiana State University,	Bloomington,	Ind.
Mount St. Mary's,	Emmetsburg,	Md.	Hanover,	South Hanover,	Ind.
St. James's,	Washington Co.,	Md.	Wabash,	Crawfordsville,	Ind.
Washington,	Chestertown,	Md.	Indiana Asbury University,	Greencastle,	Ind.
Georgetown,	Georgetown,	D. C.	Illinois,	Jacksonville,	Ill.
Columbian,	Washington,	D. C.	Shurtleff,	Upper Alton,	Ill.
William and Mary,	Williamsburg,	Va.	McKendree,	Lebanon,	Ill.
Hampden-Sidney,	Prince Ed. Co.,	Va.	Knox,	Galesburg,	Ill.
Washington,	Lexington,	Va.	University of Chicago,	Chicago,	Ill.
University of Virginia,	Charlottesville,	Va.	St. Louis University,	St. Louis,	Mo.
Randolph-Macon,	Boydon,	Va.	Masonic,	Lexington,	Mo.
Emory and Henry,	Washington Co.,	Va.	University of State of Mo.,	Columbia,	Mo.
Bethany,	Bethany,	Va.	St. Charles,	St. Charles,	Mo.
Richmond,	Richmond,	Va.	University of Michigan,	Ann Arbor,	Mich.
Virginia Military Institute,	Lexington,	Va.	Wisconsin University,	Madison,	Wis.
University of North Carolina,	Chapel Hill,	N. C.	Beloit,	Beloit, Rock Co.,	Wis.
Davidson,	Mecklenburg Co.,	N. C.	Lawrence University,	Appleton,	Wis.
Wake Forest,	Forestville,	N. C.	Milwaukee Female,	Milwaukee,	Wis.
Charleston,	Charleston,	S. C.	Carroll,	Waukesha,	Wis.
South Carolina,	Columbia,	S. C.	Racine,	Racine,	Wis.
Franklin,	Athens,	Ga.	Iowa State University,	Iowa City,	Iowa.
Oglethorpe,	Milledgeville,	Ga.	Iowa Wesleyan University,	Mt. Pleasant,	Iowa
Emory,	Oxford,	Ga.	Santa Clara,	Near San Jose,	Cal.
Mercer University,	Penfield,	Ga.			

STATISTICAL TABLES.

THEOLOGICAL SCHOOLS.

Bangor Theological Seminary,	Bangor,	Me.
Meth. Gen. Bib. Institute,	Concord,	N. H.
Gilmanton Theol. Seminary,	Gilmanton,	N. H.
N. Hampton Theol. Seminary,	New Hampton,	N. H.
Theological Seminary,	Andover,	Mass.
Divinity School, Harv. Univ.,	Cambridge,	Mass.
Theological Institution,	Newton,	Mass.
Theol. Dep., Yale College,	New Haven,	Conn.
Theol. Inst. of Connecticut,	East Windsor,	Conn.
Berkley Divinity School,	Middletown,	Conn.
Theol. Inst., Epis. Church,	New York,	N. Y.
Union Theological Seminary,	New York,	N. Y.
Theol. Seminary of Auburn,	Auburn,	N. Y.
Hamilton Theol. Seminary,	Hamilton,	N. Y.
Rochester Theol. Seminary,	Rochester,	N. Y.
Hartwick Seminary,	Hartwich,	N. Y.
Theol. Sem. Ass. Ref. Church,	Newburg,	N. Y.
Th. Sem. Dutch Ref. Church,	New Brunswick,	N. J.
Th. Sem. Presbyterian Church,	Princeton,	N. J.
Wittemburg Th. Seminary,	Gettysburg,	Penn.
German Reformed,	Mercersburg,	Penn.
Western Theol. Seminary,	Alleghany,	Penn.
Theological School,	Cannonsburg,	Penn.
Theological Seminary,	Pittsburg,	Penn.
Western Theological School,	Meadville,	Penn.
Th. Dep. Lewisburg Univ.,	Lewisburg,	Penn.
St. Mary's Seminary,	Baltimore,	Md.
Epis. Theol. School of Va.,	Fairfax Co.,	Va.
Union Theological Seminary,	Prince Ed. Co.,	Va.
Virginia Baptist Seminary,	Richmond,	Va.
Theological Seminary,	Columbia,	S. C.
Theological Seminary,	Lexington,	S. C.
Furman Theol. Seminary,	Fairfield Dist.,	S. C.
Th. Sem. of Mercer Univ.,	Penfield,	Ga.
Howard Th. Institution,	Marion,	Ala.
Western Bap. Th. Institution,	Georgetown,	Ky.
Danville Theol. Seminary,	Danville,	Ky.
Southwest Theol. Seminary,	Maryville,	Tenn.
Th. School Cumb. Univ.,	Lebanon,	Tenn.
Th. Dep. St. Louis Univ.,	St. Louis,	Mo.
Lane Seminary,	Cincinnati,	Ohio.
Theol. Dep. Kenyon Coll.,	Gambier,	Ohio.
Theol. Dep. West. Res. Coll.,	Hudson,	Ohio.
Granville Theol. Dep't,	Granville,	Ohio.
Oberlin Theol. Dep't,	Oberlin,	Ohio.
Th. Sem. Ass. Ref. Church,	Oxford,	Ohio.
Wittenberg,	Springfield,	Ohio.
Bibl. Dep. Ohio Wesl. Univ.,	Delaware,	Ohio.
New Albany Th. Seminary,	Hanover,	Ind.
Theological Seminary,	Chicago,	Ill.
Alton Theol. Seminary,	Upper Alton,	Ill.
Nashotah Theol. Seminary,	Nashotah,	Wis.

MEDICAL SCHOOLS.

Medical School of Maine,	Brunswick,	Me.
N. H. Medical School,	Hanover,	N. H.
Castleton Medical Coll.,	Castleton,	Vt.
Med. Dep. Univ. Vermont,	Burlington,	Vt.
Vermont Medical Coll.,	Woodstock,	Vt.
Medical School, Harv. Univ.,	Boston,	Mass.
Berkshire Medical School,	Pittsfield,	Mass.
Medical Inst., Yale Coll.,	New Haven,	Conn.
Coll. Phys. and Surg., N. York,	New York,	N. Y.
Geneva Medical Coll.,	Geneva,	N. Y.
Med. Faculty, Univ. N. Y.,	New York,	N. Y.
Albany Medical Coll.,	Albany,	N. Y.
Med. Dep., Univ. Penn.,	Philadelphia,	Penn.
Jefferson Medical Coll.,	Philadelphia,	Penn.
Med. Dep. Penn. Coll.,	Philadelphia,	Penn.
Philadelphia Coll. of Med.,	Philadelphia,	Penn.
Med. School, Univ. Md.,	Baltimore,	Md.
Washington Med. Coll.,	Baltimore,	Md.
Nat. Med. Coll., Columb. Coll.,	Washington,	D. C.
Med. Dep., Georgetown Coll.,	Washington,	D. C.
Med. School, Univ. Va.,	Charlottesville,	Va.
Med. Dep., Hamp.-Sid. Coll.,	Richmond,	Va.
Winchester Med. Coll.,	Winchester,	Va.
Med. Coll. State of S. C.,	Charleston,	S. C.
Med. Coll. of Georgia,	Augusta,	Ga.
Med. Dep., Univ. Louisiana,	New Orleans,	La.
Med. Dep., Univ. Nashville,	Nashville,	Tenn.
Med. Dep., East Tenn. Univ.,	Knoxville,	Tenn.
Med. Dep., Transylvania Univ.,	Lexington,	Ky.
Med. Dep., Univ. Louisville,	Louisville,	Ky.
Med. Dep., West. Reserve Coll.,	Cleveland,	Ohio.
Medical College of Ohio,	Cincinnati,	Ohio.
West. Coll. Homeopathic Med.,	Cleveland,	Ohio.
Starling Medical Coll.,	Columbus,	Ohio.
Rush Medical Coll.,	Chicago,	Ill.
University of Michigan,	Ann Arbor,	Mich.
St. Louis Medical Coll.,	St. Louis,	Mo.
Med. Dep. of Missouri Univ.,	Columbia,	Mo.
Med. Dep. of State Univ.,	Keokuk,	Iowa.
Med. Dep. State Univ.,	Madison,	Wis.

LAW SCHOOLS.

Dane Law School, H. Univ.,	Cambridge,	Mass.
Law School, Yale Coll.,	New Haven,	Conn.
University of Albany,	Albany,	N. Y.
Law School, Columbia Coll.,	New York,	N. Y.
University of Pennsylvania,	Philadelphia,	Penn.
William and Mary College,	Williamsburg,	Va.
Law School, Univ. of Va.,	Charlottesville,	Va.
North Carolina University,	Chapel Hill,	N. C.
University of Louisiana,	New Orleans,	La.
University of Louisville,	Louisville,	Ky.
Kentucky Military Inst.,	Franklin Springs,	Ky.
Cumberland University,	Lebanon,	Tenn.
Law School, Cincin. Coll.,	Cincinnati,	Ohio.
Indiana State University,	Bloomington,	Ind.
Indiana Asbury University,	Greencastle,	Ind.
Maynard L. S., Hamilton Col.,	Clinton,	N. Y.
N. Y. State and National L. S.,	Poughkeepsie,	N. Y.
University of Mississippi,	Oxford,	Miss.
University of Michigan,	Ann Arbor,	Mich.

STATISTICAL TABLES.

NORMAL SCHOOLS.

State Normal School,	Framingham,	Mass.	State Normal School,	Millersville,	Penn.
State Normal School,	Westfield,	Mass.	State Normal School,	Edenboro,	Penn.
State Normal School,	Bridgewater,	Mass.	* Chester County Normal School,	Westchester,	Penn.
State Normal School,	Salem,	Mass.	* McNeely Normal School,	Hopedale,	Ohio.
State Normal School,	Bristol,	R. I.	* S. W. Normal School,	Lebanon,	Ohio.
State Normal School,	New Britain,	Conn.	State Normal School,	Ypsilanti,	Mich.
State Normal School,	Albany,	N. Y.	State Normal University,	Bloomington,	Ill.
State Normal School,	Trenton,	N. J.	State Normal School,	Winona,	Minn.

TELEGRAPH LINES.

LENGTH OF LINES OF LAND TELEGRAPH.

America, (United States,)	35,000	India,	5,000
America, (British Provinces,)	5,000	Italy,	2,500
America, (other parts, and islands,)	5,000	Prussia,	4,000
Australia,	1,200	Russia,	5,000
Austria and Germany,	10,000	Switzerland,	1,500
Bavaria and Saxony,	1,700	Rest of Europe,	1,400
Belgium,	550	Other parts of the World,	500
England,	10,000		
France,	8,000	Total,	96,350

LINES OF SUBMARINE TELEGRAPH.

	Miles.	Wires.	Date.
Dover and Calais,	25	4	1851
Dover and Ostend,	75	6	1852
Holyhead and Howth,	65	1	1852
England and Holland,	115	3	1853
Port Patrick and Donaghadee,	13	6	1853
Port Patrick and Donaghadee, (second cable,)	13	6	1853
Across the Soland, Isle of Wight, (England,)	3	4	1855
Across the Frith of Forth, (Scotland,)	4	4	1854
Denmark, across the Great Belt,	15	3	1854
Denmark, across the Little Belt,	5	3	1854
Denmark, across the Sound,	12	3	1855
Petersburg to Cronstadt,	10	1	1856
Italy and Corsica,	65	6	1854
Corsica and Sardinia,	10	6	1854
Messina to Reggio,	5	1	1856
Across the Danube at Shumla,	1	1	1855
Six cables across the mouth of the Danube at the Isle of Serpents, (each one mile long and having one conductor,)	6	6	1857
Varna and Balaklava, (across the Black Sea,)	340	1	1855
Balaklava and Eupatoria,	60	1	1855
Across the Bosporus at Kandili,	1	1	1856
Across the Hoogly River,	2.51		
Across the St. Lawrence,	74	1	1856
Across the Straits of Northumberland, (Prince Edward's Island,)	10.51	1	1856
Across the Gut of Canso, (Nova Scotia,)	3	3	1856
Across the St. Lawrence at Quebec,	1	1	1855
Across the Mississippi at Paduca,	1	1	1851
Small River Crossings,	20		
Total length of Submarine Cables,	955		

* Private Institutions.

www.ingramcontent.com/pod-product-compliance
Lightning Source LLC
Chambersburg PA
CBHW020924230426
43666CB00008B/1562